Birding Oregon

Help Us Keep This Guide Up to Date

Every effort has been made by the author and editors to make this guide as accurate and useful as possible. However, many things can change after a guide is published—trails are rerouted, regulations change, techniques evolve, facilities come under new management, etc.

We would love to hear from you concerning your experiences with this guide and how you feel it could be improved and kept up to date. While we may not be able to respond to all comments and suggestions, we'll take them to heart, and we'll also make certain to share them with the author. Please send your comments and suggestions to the following address:

The Globe Pequot Press
Reader Response/Editorial Department
P.O. Box 480
Guilford, CT 06437

Or you may e-mail us at:

editorial@GlobePequot.com

Thanks for your input, and happy trails!

Birding Oregon

44 Prime Birding Areas with More Than 200 Specific Sites

John Rakestraw

GUILFORD, CONNECTICUT
HELENA, MONTANA
AN IMPRINT OF THE GLOBE PEQUOT PRESS

A FALCON GUIDE®

Maps created by XNR Productions, Inc. and MaryAnn Dubé © Morris Book Publishing, LLC
All photos by the author, except p. 189 by Marsha Rakestraw

Library of Congress Cataloging-in-Publication Data
Rakestraw, John.
Birding Oregon : 44 prime birding areas with more than 200 specific sites / John Rakestraw.
p. cm. -- (A Falcon guide)
Includes bibliographical references and index.
ISBN-13: 978-0-7627-3913-4
ISBN-10: 0-7627-3913-4
1. Bird watching--Oregon--Guidebooks. 2. Birding sites--Oregon--Guidebooks. 3. Birds--Oregon. 4. Oregon--Guidebooks.
I. Title. II. Series.
QL684.O6R35 2006
598'.07'234795--dc22
2006009209

Manufactured in the United States of America
First Edition/First Printing

Contents

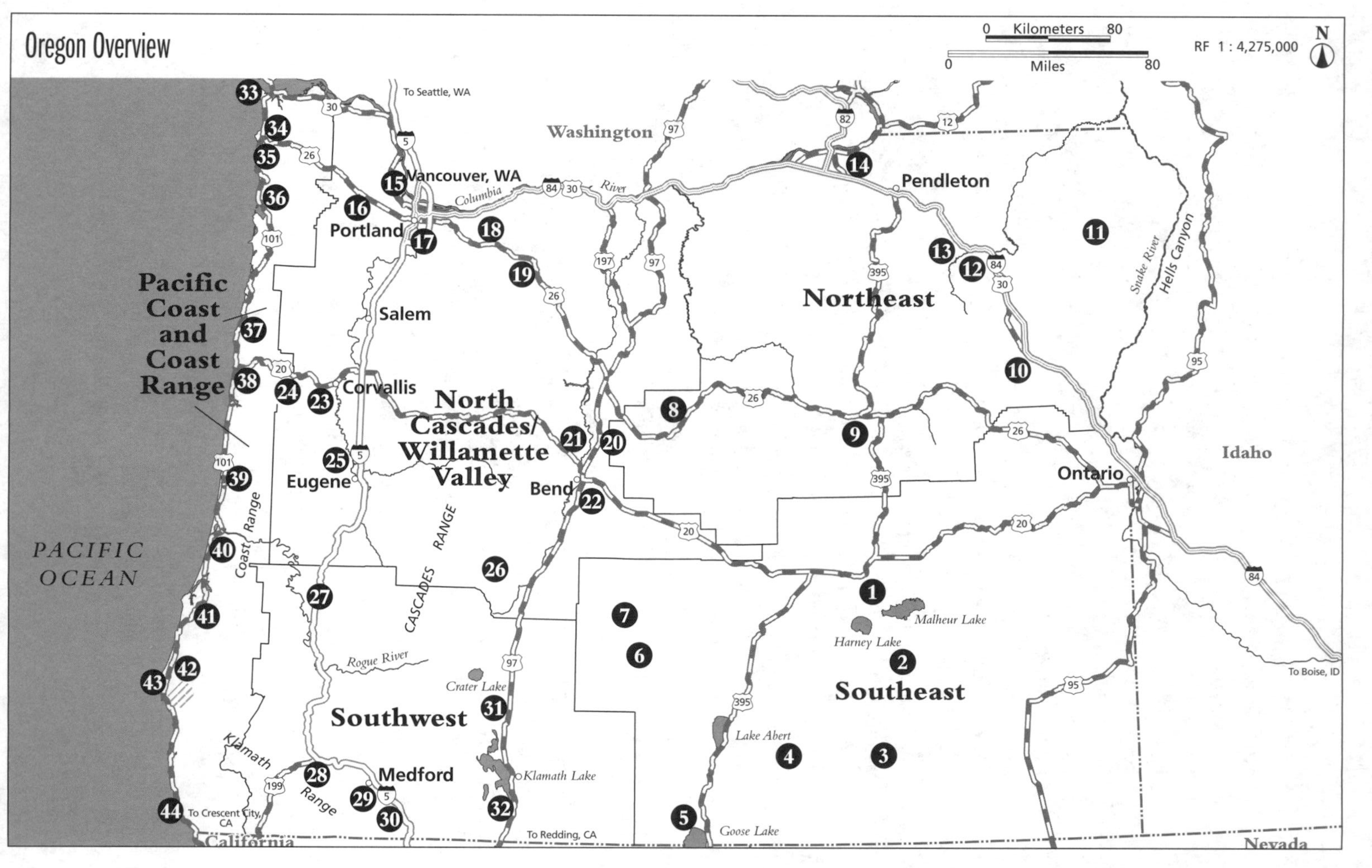
Oregon Overview
0 Kilometers 80
0 Miles 80
RF 1 : 4,275,000
N
Washington
Idaho
Nevada
California
PACIFIC OCEAN
To Seattle, WA
To Boise, ID
To Redding, CA
To Crescent City, CA
Vancouver, WA
Portland
Salem
Corvallis
Eugene
Bend
Medford
Pendleton
Ontario
Columbia River
Snake River
Hells Canyon
Rogue River
Crater Lake
Klamath Lake
Malheur Lake
Harney Lake
Lake Abert
Goose Lake
Coast Range
CASCADES RANGE
Klamath Range
Pacific Coast and Coast Range
North Cascades/ Willamette Valley
Northeast
Southeast
Southwest

Foreword

The book you are holding in your hands is a modern miracle.

When I was an avid young bird-watcher in Ohio in the mid-1970s, the sum total of my birding information was obtained from my well-worn copies of the *Golden Guide to the Birds of North America,* from my *Peterson Field Guide to the Birds,* and from the minds of the people in my local bird club. Birding as a hobby was in its awkward teen years, having emerged from the era of shotgun ornithology over the previous three decades. Optics were basic, field guides were vastly more simplified than they are today, and birders communicated their sightings via mailed letters and the occasional telephone call. There were no specialty bird shops catering to the bird-watching population. And there certainly were few, if any, published bird-finding guides for avid birders.

Today there are more than 400 bird and nature festivals held annually in North America, where birders can gather with other like-minded souls. Want to know what birds have been seen recently? Jump on the Internet and you can access any one of a hundred message boards with up-to-date sightings. And birders today can choose optics from hundreds of excellent options.

Much has changed in the world of birding, but we birders still rely on *books* as the foundation of information and knowledge for our hobby. Today there are bird books galore for the information-hungry birder. But the type of bird book that has evolved most since my early days afield is the bird-finding guide. *Birding Oregon* is a fine example of this evolution.

What is a bird-finding guide? As the name suggests it is a guide to help the reader find birds. Early bird-finding guides were basic, spiral-bound volumes that presented information in a "just the facts, ma'am" style: few graphics, no style, just directions to the birds.

A good bird-finding guide is an invaluable companion in the field. Where a field guide helps you identify the birds you see, it does not tell you specifically where to find the birds. This is where the bird-finding guide takes over.

Whether you are a lifelong Oregon resident or a visitor from afar, *Birding Oregon* is your own personal guide to *forty-four* of the very best birding spots in the Beaver State. Author John Rakestraw is a longtime (and widely respected) birder and frequently published nature writer who has gathered together an incredible volume of information in *Birding Oregon.* I have read, reviewed, and used dozens of bird-finding guides in my thirty-five years of birding. With its breadth and depth of coverage and its easy-to-follow entries for the carefully selected birding locations, *Birding Oregon* stands on the top tier with the very best of our modern-day bird-finding guides.

Oregon is a very "birdy" state, incorporating an enormous diversity of habitat. From the shores of the Pacific Ocean to the high desert of eastern Oregon and the lush forests of the Cascade Range, each of the five ecoregions presented here contains its own blend of birdlife. More than 500 species have been recorded in Oregon, but in order to find these birds, you need to know where to go and, more important, *when* to go. With *Birding Oregon,* your binoculars, and a field guide, you've got everything you need to maximize your Oregon birding experience.

—Bill Thompson, III
Editor, *Bird Watcher's Digest*
March 2006

Acknowledgments

As the old adage goes, the best way to learn something is to teach it. And so I welcomed the opportunity to produce a birding guide for the state of Oregon, for in sharing information about finding birds in the Beaver State, I learned a great deal along the way.

The Oregon birding community, as a whole, is a friendly, sharing group of people, and much of what I know about Oregon birding comes from years of chance encounters in the field with helpful strangers who were happy to answer my questions. Several individuals contributed specifically to this book by providing directions, information about sites or bird distribution, proofreading, birding guidance and companionship, and other means of support. Special thanks go to Joel Greier, Steve Jaggers, Ken Brown, Noah Strycker, Phil Shephard, Harry Nehls, Trent Bray, Laura Whittemore, Alexander Kain, Dennis Vroman, Paul Sullivan, Dan van den Broek, Steve Shunk of Paradise Birding Tours, and Scott Lukens of The Backyard Bird Shops. While the help of others was vital to the creation of this guide, I claim any errors as my own.

It is hard to imagine the amount of stress a project like this puts on a non-birding spouse. So I dedicate this book to Marsha, without whose encouragement and support this project would not have been completed. You are the Eskimo Curlew on the life list of my heart.

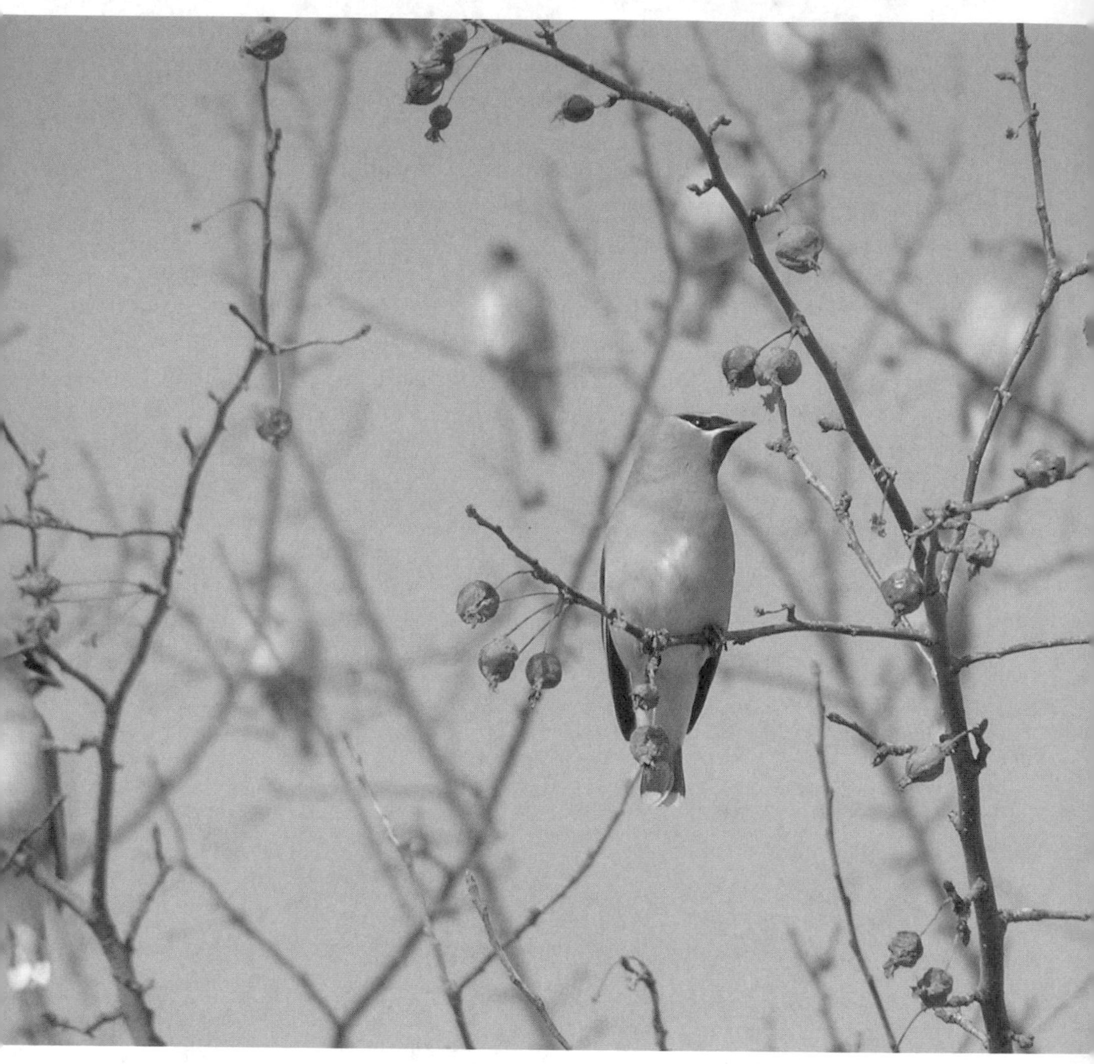

Cedar Waxwings

Introduction

The state of Oregon (pronounced OR-uh-gun) is blessed with an incredible variety of habitats, including the open waters of the Pacific Ocean, temperate rain forests, farmland, alpine tundra, and sage steppe. As you would expect, this diversity of habitats encourages a great diversity of bird species. But the medley of different landscapes also allows a variety of birding styles and experiences. You can blaze across the state in a few days and have Black-footed Albatross and Black-throated Sparrow on the same trip list, or you can spend a week birding in one county and still not see it all. This book serves as a resource for both birding styles and for all in between.

The site guides in this book are divided into five sections, each covering a different part of the state. The introduction to each section describes the habitats, weather, and birding conditions in that part of the state and lists the common species found there.

Following the site guides is a checklist of 505 species of birds known to have occurred in Oregon and a chart of each species' seasonal abundance. Range maps and information about specific habitat preferences are available in a variety of field guides and other sources, so that information is not duplicated here.

The final chapter provides contact information for government agencies, organizations, and outfitters, all of which are valuable resources when planning birding and travel in Oregon.

Potential hazards

As with many outdoor activities, birding brings you into contact with potential hazards. Fortunately, you can minimize most risks with a little common sense and preparation.

Traffic: Statistically, auto travel is the riskiest activity in which most of us engage. Oregon's highway system is quite good. Although traffic in Portland, Oregon's largest city, seems terribly congested at times, the traffic is downright bucolic by most big city standards. Mountainous areas can receive heavy snow in winter, and Oregon law requires tire chains or traction tires in some areas.

Plants: Poison Oak is common in much of Oregon. Poison Ivy is found in the extreme northeast part of the state. Wearing long pants and long sleeves and staying on the trail will usually offer adequate protection from these plants, as well as from blackberries and other thorny growth.

Invertebrate Wildlife: Mosquitoes are most numerous around wetlands in southeastern Oregon and in the lakes in the Cascades. Ticks are most common in southwest Oregon. While these creatures are usually just an annoyance, mosquito-borne West Nile virus was first reported in Oregon in 2004, with five cases reported in 2005. Western Black-legged Ticks can transmit Lyme disease, but only about fifteen cases are reported in Oregon each year, according to the Oregon Department of Human Services.

Vertebrate Wildlife: Oregon has a healthy population of Mountain Lions and Black Bears. There has never been a confirmed Mountain Lion attack on a human in Oregon, and problems with Black Bears usually involve an animal breaking into a cabin or campsite to find food. Encounters are very rare, but common sense is required when birding habitats shared by large predators. Most birders consider themselves lucky to see either of these animals.

The only venomous snake native to Oregon is the Western Rattlesnake. Rattlesnakes inhabit rocky areas in eastern Oregon. They are rare in southwest Oregon and into the southern Willamette Valley. You can usually avoid encounters with rattlesnakes by not stepping or putting your hand into rocky crevasses. The harmless Gopher Snake is very common in eastern Oregon, and it is sometimes mistaken for a rattlesnake. When frightened, Gopher Snakes will imitate rattlesnakes by flattening their heads and vibrating their tails. But Gopher Snakes are much more slender than rattlesnakes and, of course, lack a rattle at the end of their tails.

Jetties and Sneaker Waves: Some of the best birding along the Oregon coast is found on or along the rocky jetties at river mouths, but walking on these rock structures can be extremely dangerous. While the bases of most jetties are fairly smooth, the risk of falling between large boulders increases as you go out farther. This risk is compounded by the occasional sneaker wave, an unusually large wave that appears without warning. As a general rule, avoid having to step from rock to rock, and never turn your back on the ocean.

Fire: The fire season in Oregon lasts from June through September. While fire is an essential part of a healthy forest ecosystem, you do not want to witness this process too closely. Major fires are reported by the news media. For more precise information, consult the Web sites of the various national forests listed in the Resources and Contact Information chapter.

How prevalent are these risks? In the past four years, I have been in one minor traffic accident, been bitten by one tick and several mosquitoes, encountered one Black Bear, found one set of Mountain Lion tracks, and seen smoke from distant fires. I have had no reaction to Poison Oak and have never seen a Western Rattlesnake in Oregon.

Fees

Some sites described in this book require an entrance fee. Fees are charged by Crater Lake National Park and by some state and county parks, Bureau of Land Management sites, and trailheads and parking areas administered by the Forest Service.

Some people resist the concept of paying to enter "our" public lands. But even if you own your own home, you still have to pay to maintain it. Birders should

Mountain Lions range throughout Oregon but are seldom seen by birders.

welcome the opportunity to serve as a major source of income for government agencies charged with the management of public lands. If birders are paying the bills, then habitat protection and restoration will be given more consideration.

Daily passes are available at each site, but you might want to consider buying one of the annual passes described below. Contact the issuing agencies for current costs.

Oregon Pacific Coast Passport: Covers entry, vehicle parking, and day-use fees at all state and federal fee sites along the entire Oregon Coast. You can buy an annual vehicle passport or a five-day vehicle passport.

Northwest Forest Pass: Honored at all Forest Service entrance or day-use fee sites in Oregon and Washington.

Golden Eagle Passport: Covers entrance fees at all National Park Service and U.S. Fish and Wildlife Service sites, in addition to day-use sites managed by the Forest Service and Bureau of Land Management.

Washington and Oregon Recreation Pass: Same benefits as Golden Eagle Passport and is honored at twenty-six Oregon State Parks charging a day-use fee, twenty-two participating Washington State Parks charging a vehicle-parking fee, and six Army Corps of Engineers sites charging facility-use fees.

Oregon State Parks 12- or 24-Month Passes: Good at the twenty-seven Oregon State Parks that charge a day-use fee.

Sno-Park Permits

A valid Sno-Park permit is required if you park in designated winter recreation parking areas (Sno-Parks) between November 15 and April 30. Sno-Parks are located in all mountain passes of the state and in most recognized ski, snowmobile, and snow-play areas. The three types of permits available include an annual permit, a three-day permit, and a daily permit. Permits are sold at all DMV offices and at resorts, sporting-goods stores, and other retail outlets. Sno-Park permits issued by Washington, California, and Idaho are honored in Oregon, and Oregon permits are honored in those states.

Site guides

The site guides are divided into forty-four birding areas, most of which contain several individual sites. These certainly do not include all the places to bird in Oregon. They do, however, include examples from all the major ecoregions and habitats in the state.

The birding sites included in this book meet three criteria. First, all of the sites are accessible to the general public. Most are found in parks, in national wildlife refuges, or on land administered by the USDA Forest Service or U.S. Bureau of Land Management. A few sites are on private land. These sites are identified as such and are, at the time of this writing, open to birders. Birders should always be alert for signs regarding public access. When in doubt, do not trespass.

The second criterion for inclusion is that the site must be accessible in a normal passenger car. There are logging roads running throughout Oregon's state and national forests, and there are dirt tracks through the open rangelands. Many of these roads are impassable without a high-clearance vehicle with four-wheel drive. The roads listed in the site guides are either paved or are well-maintained gravel. The few exceptions are accompanied by appropriate warnings. Be advised that even some of these good roads may be impassable due to winter snow.

You should be able to reach most destinations with the directions and maps in this book. The atlas uses shaded, or shadow, relief. Shadow relief does not represent elevation; it demonstrates slope or relative steepness. This gives an almost 3-D perspective of the physiography of the state and will help you see the location of ranges and valleys.

Close-up maps are supplied for those few sites at which further information will be useful once you reach the location. They use hypsometry (elevation tints) to portray relief and give a clear picture of how to get where you're going.

If you wish to explore the depths of the national forests, be sure to obtain a detailed map from the Forest Service. Commercial road atlases do not always accurately portray Forest Service roads.

Hikers and backpackers who venture into Oregon's wilderness areas can find exceptional birding. While a few site guides mention specific hiking trails, details of long hiking routes are beyond the scope of this book.

Third, and perhaps most important, each area described is a productive birding site. Your birding success, of course, will vary according to the season, the weather, and your own luck. But each site consistently produces good birding year after year.

How to Use the Site Guides

Each site guide begins with an introductory section to give you a quick overview of what the site has to offer. The headings used are: Habitats, Elevation, What to See, Specialty Birds, Best Seasons, Directions, and The Birding.

Habitats: To avoid the need for an advanced degree in botany, I have adopted many of the simplified habitat descriptions used by Evanich (1990). Those wishing for a more detailed description of the plant communities in Oregon should consult the *Oregon Breeding Bird Atlas.* The habitats described in this book include:

Alkali flats: Barren areas of mineral deposits found around seasonal wetlands in the southeastern part of the state.

Alpine: The zone above the treeline.

Brush: Blackberry thickets, fencerows, and shrubby areas.

Chaparral: Limited to the southwest portion of the state, an arid habitat of ceanothus, manzanita, and other shrubs, interspersed with oak and ash.

Dry forest: Found in areas east of the Cascade Crest, this forest is dominated by ponderosa and lodgepole pines. The understory is usually very open and easy to traverse.

Farmland: Crop fields.

Juniper woodland: Located east of the Cascades between the dry forest and the sage steppe, stands of juniper trees are interspersed with sagebrush.

Lake: Open waters of lakes and ponds.

Marsh: Shallow water, either fresh or salt, with emergent vegetation, such as cattails.

Meadow/grassland: Open fields of grasses and forbs.

Mudflats: Exposed mud in coastal estuaries and around inland lakes and wetlands.

Oak savannah: Scattered oaks with a grassy understory.

Ocean: Open waters of the Pacific Ocean, including bays.

Residential: Neighborhoods, often attractive to birds due to bird feeders and to ornamental plantings that provide flowers or fruit.

Rimrock: Cliffs and rocky outcroppings.

Riparian: Areas along streams, usually containing willows, aspen, cottonwoods, and shrubs.

Rocky shores: Includes headlands and jetties along the coast.

Sage steppe: Dry open areas of sagebrush and other desert shrubs.

Sand beach: Coastal sandy beaches and dunes.

Wet forest: Found west of the Cascade Crest and at high elevations in the eastern part of the state. Dominated by Sitka spruce along the coast and by Douglas fir, cedar, and true firs inland. The understory is usually very thick with ferns and shrubs. Deciduous trees include broadleaf maple and alders.

Elevation: The approximate elevation of the area, useful in determining the severity of winter weather, the likelihood of snow accumulation, and relative ease of breathing for flatlanders visiting the mountains. I did not include the elevation of the coastal sites, since it does not generally affect the weather conditions there.

What to see: The types of birds you're likely to see at this spot. Some sites are primarily good for waterfowl, others for migrant songbirds, etc.

Specialty birds: Since each site has a bird list ranging from 50 to 300 species, it would be very tedious to read lists of all the common birds for each location. This heading includes species found at this site that might be difficult to find elsewhere and species that are particularly abundant. It also includes a few common species to give you an idea of the types of bird communities found at this site.

I deliberately did not include lists of vagrant species in the site guides. A vagrant, by definition, can show up anytime, anywhere. It does you no good to hear about the Black Swifts I saw flying between the parked cars at a shopping center in Beaverton. If you go to that shopping center, I can pretty much guarantee that you will not see Black Swifts. And you may be so intent on looking for the Black Swifts that were seen once that you might miss the Thayer's Gull standing in front of you. Go birding when you can, where you can, and enjoy whatever species are there at the time.

Best months: While the best time to bird is whenever you have the chance, this heading lists the time of year when you will find the greatest diversity of species.

Directions: Most of the birding areas surround a particular town or park. This heading provides directions to the area. More detailed directions are provided in descriptions of individual sites.

The Birding: A brief introductory paragraph usually describes the general area, followed by descriptions of individual birding sites.

Map Legend

Transportation

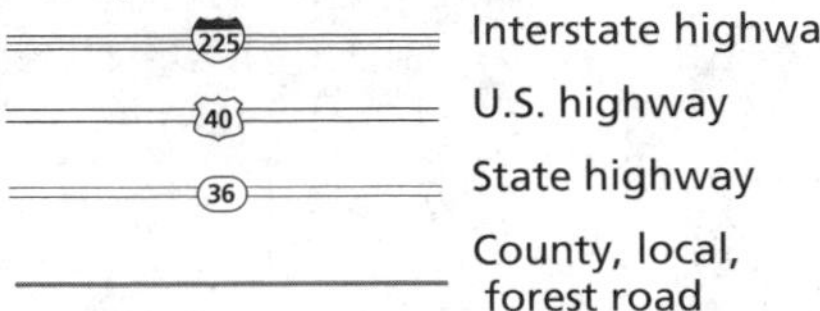

Interstate highway
U.S. highway
State highway
County, local, forest road

Hydrology, Physiography, Boundaries

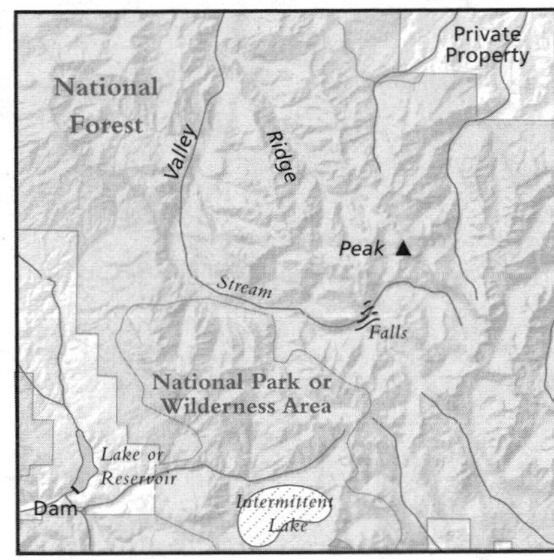

Population

Town City Capital

Symbols

Airport
Rest area
Small national park
State/county park
State/county beach
Campground
Fishing
Lighthouse
Ski area
Mine
Pass
Birding site
Sno-park
Hot spring
Cave
OHV recreation area

Southeast Oregon

The southeast quarter of Oregon contains some of the state's largest expanses of dry sage steppe but also some of its most productive wetlands. These habitats, interspersed with forested mountain slopes and rocky canyons, result in a great diversity of bird species.

Average annual precipitation over most of this area is less than 12 inches. Most of the water in the region's wetlands is supplied by snowmelt from mountain peaks, which can receive up to 60 inches of precipitation. Winter temperatures approach 0 degrees. While summer temperatures can climb to 100 degrees during the day, morning frost is possible all year.

Greater Sage-Grouse, a species experiencing a significant decline over most of its range, can still be found in southeast Oregon. Other species to look for in sage steppe habitat include Swainson's and Ferruginous Hawks, Golden Eagle, Burrowing Owl, Common Nighthawk, Gray Flycatcher, Western Kingbird, Loggerhead Shrike, Black-billed Magpie, and Sage Thrasher. Sparrows include Brewer's, Vesper, Lark, Black-throated, and Sage.

Search rimrock areas for Chukars, Prairie Falcons, Common Poorwills, White-throated Swifts, Rock Wrens, and Canyon Wrens. The top of Steens Mountain (southern Harney County) is the only known Oregon nesting site for Black Rosy-Finches.

Wetlands in southeast Oregon serve as staging areas for large numbers of migrant waterfowl. Waterfowl species that stay to nest include Trumpeter Swan (at Malheur National Wildlife Refuge [NWR]), Gadwall, Blue-winged and Cinnamon Teal, Canvasback, Redhead, Lesser Scaup, and Ruddy Duck. Other breeding birds found in the wetlands and wet meadows of this region include Eared and Western Grebes, American White Pelican, Great and Snowy Egrets, White-faced Ibis, Sandhill Crane, Snowy Plover, Black-necked Stilt, American Avocet, Willet, Long-billed Curlew, Franklin's Gull, Forster's and Black Terns, and Short-eared Owl.

Another main attraction of southeast Oregon is the possibility of finding a vagrant songbird from eastern North America. In late May and early June, and again in September, many Oregon birders descend on Malheur NWR and other sites with little patches of woodland that serve as migrant traps.

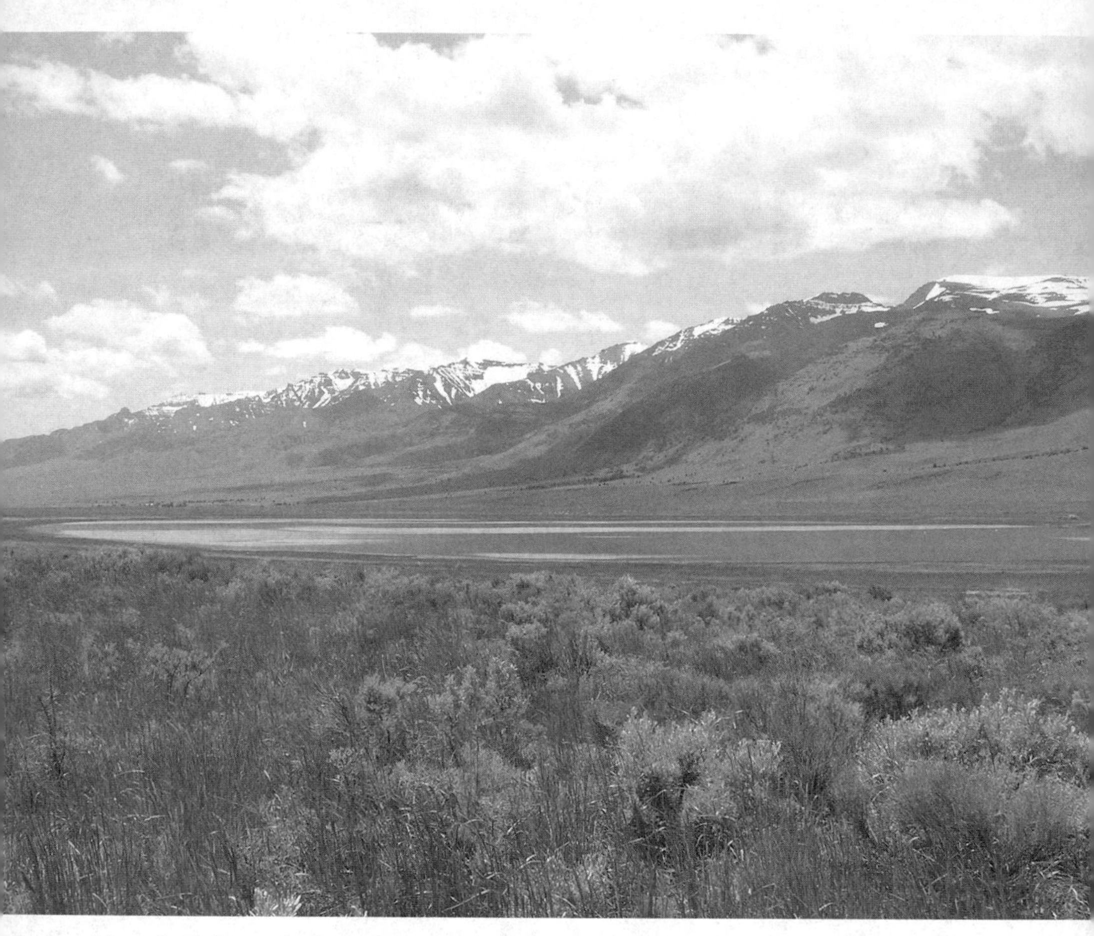

Mann Lake lies at the base of Steens Mountain, surrounded by open sage steppe.

The vastness that makes southeast Oregon such an exciting and productive place to bird also creates potential problems. Towns, especially those with gas stations, are widely scattered in this region of the state. Always start your trip with a full tank of gas and plan ahead for your next fill-up. Cellular phone reception is typically lacking, except in larger towns. Don't venture off the main roads without a sturdy vehicle and a good map, and always carry water and a spare tire. That being said, the southeastern quarter of Oregon contains large areas that receive very little attention from birders. For the birder with the desire to explore, a high-clearance vehicle, and a good map, who knows what avian treasures might be found?

1 Northern Harney County

Habitats: Lake, marsh, meadow, farmland, sage steppe, juniper woodland, dry forest

Elevation: 4,100 feet

What to see: Waterfowl, shorebirds, raptors, high-desert species

Specialty birds: Swainson's, Rough-legged, and Ferruginous Hawks; Black-necked Stilt; American Avocet; Willet; Long-billed Curlew; White-faced Ibis; White-headed Woodpecker; Flammulated Owl

Best months: March–October

Directions: All sites accessed from U.S. Highway 20/U.S. Highway 395 (atlas, p. 202)

The Birding

Harney County covers about 10,000 square miles, much of which is administered by the Bureau of Land Management or the USDA Forest Service. While most birders traveling to Harney County are headed for Malheur National Wildlife Refuge (NWR), several sites close to the city of Burns are well worth exploring.

Chickahominy Reservoir

Located about 30 miles west of Burns on the north side of US 20, Chickahominy Reservoir attracts migrant shorebirds and waterfowl. The lake can be quickly scoped from the upper parking lot. If conditions warrant, you may want to go down to the water's edge for a closer look.

Riley Pond

This small flooded gravel pit sits just west of the US 395 intersection with US 20, about 25 miles west of Burns. A brief stop here often provides close-up views of a few species of waterfowl and shorebirds, and migrant songbirds are possible.

Sage Hen Rest Area

While, despite the name, you are not likely to find Greater Sage-Grouse here, this roadside rest area is good for seeing a few species of songbirds, such as Chipping Sparrows, Cedar Waxwings, and various swallows. The Sage Hen Hill Nature Trail is a 0.5-mile loop, beginning and ending at the south end of the rest area. Follow this trail through sage steppe and juniper woodlands to look for Mountain Bluebirds, Clark's Nutcrackers, and the typical sage species. The rest area is located on the south side of US 20, about 18 miles west of Burns.

Idlewild Campground

Take US 395 north from Burns for about 17 miles to Idlewild Campground. This part of Harney County is dominated by ponderosa pine forest, a cool reprieve from the hot sage steppe and wetlands of Malheur, and an opportunity to add several forest species to your trip list. A trail completely encircles the campground, and the Devine Summit Interpretive Trail forms another 1.5-mile loop. Expect

White-headed Woodpeckers, Mountain Chickadees, Townsend's Solitaires, and Pygmy Nuthatches in the pines. Idlewild has been a consistent site for Flammulated Owls, more often heard than seen. The brushier areas attract the occasional Green-tailed Towhee. Search the rimrock at the west side of the campground for Rock Wrens and Common Poorwills.

Burns

The city of Burns (along with the adjacent town of Hines) is the base of operations for most birders visiting Harney County, offering abundant accommodations, food, and fuel. The area southeast of town offers excellent birding for wetland species. From Burns, travel south on Egan Street past the fairgrounds. When the road comes to a T at Hotchkiss Lane, turn west and continue about 0.5 mile to the sewage ponds on your left. There is a small gravel pullout on the south side of the road. These ponds are great for a wide variety of diving ducks, grebes, gulls, and terns. The wet meadows nearby attract large flocks of White-faced Ibises. Return east on Hotchkiss Lane toward Oregon Route 205. Watch for Wilson's Phalaropes, Wilson's Snipes, Yellow-headed and Red-winged Blackbirds, and Willets.

Turn south onto OR 205. The highway passes through pastures that are home to Long-billed Curlews. Wetter areas produce American Avocets, Black-necked Stilts, and other shorebirds in migration. Three miles south of Hotchkiss Lane, turn west onto Greenhouse Lane. This road leads through more wetland areas and provides a shortcut back to US 20 westbound for those wanting to avoid town on their way back from Malheur. To continue south, turn around and return to OR 205.

As OR 205 continues south toward the refuge, it climbs a line of rocky hills that form the northern rim of the broad Sunset Valley. At the top of these hills is Wright's Point. A gravel parking area on the west side of the road provides a great view of the valley and usually a Rock Wren or two.

Double-O Road

About 28 miles south of Burns, Double-O Road heads west from OR 205, skirting the northern edge of Malheur NWR and Harney Lake. If water levels are high in the lake, Snowy Plovers may be visible along the road. Watch for Burrowing Owls and the regular sage species. Double-O Road leads to the Double-O Station and the wetlands of Malheur's northwest corner. North Double-O Road will lead you to US 20/395 in about 20 miles. Call the refuge headquarters (541–493–2612) for Double-O Road conditions, especially if the area has had much rain.

The Narrows

OR 205 passes over the narrow channel that connects Malheur Lake to Mud and Harney Lakes. In dry years, water does not reach this channel. But in wet years, this site provides good views of waterfowl and shorebirds. There are several very small gravel pullouts along the highway. Just south of the Narrows is a campground/restaurant/convenience store/gas station of the same name. This is the only reliable place to buy gasoline near Malheur NWR.

2 Malheur National Wildlife Refuge

Habitats: Marsh, lake, sage steppe, rimrock, riparian

Elevation: 4,100 feet

What to see: Waterfowl, raptors, shorebirds, high-desert species, migrant songbirds

Specialty birds: White-fronted, Snow, and Ross's Geese; Trumpeter Swan; Sandhill Crane; White-faced Ibis; Black-necked Stilt; Snowy Egret; Greater Sage-Grouse; Short-eared and Burrowing Owls; Swainson's and Ferruginous Hawks; Yellow-breasted Chat; Black-throated Sparrow; eastern vagrants

Best months: March–October; late May/early June and September for migrant songbirds

Directions: From the town of Burns, drive south on Oregon Route 205 for about 30 miles. Turn east at the sign for the refuge headquarters (Narrows-Princeton Road) and continue for another 6 miles. The store/RV park at this intersection is the only reliable source of gasoline in the area. (atlas, p. 208)

The moonlike landscape of Diamond Craters, located just east of Malheur National Wildlife Refuge, is a favorite haunt of Black-throated Sparrows in the summer.

The Birding

Malheur National Wildlife Refuge (NWR) is one of the best-known birding sites in Oregon. The refuge is the scene of spectacular migrations of waterfowl and cranes and home to a long list of nesting species. What draws many Oregon birders to make an annual pilgrimage to Malheur are the eastern species that find their way to the oases of brush and trees scattered throughout the refuge.

Good birding can be found anywhere on the refuge, but a few traditional sites account for most of the rare sightings. The Center Patrol Road (CPR), a rough gravel road running north/south through the heart of the refuge, provides access to most of these sites and lots of birding in between. If you wish to travel more quickly between sites, or if the CPR is closed due to high water, OR 205 runs along the west edge of the refuge.

Refuge Headquarters

One of the most popular and productive sites at Malheur is the refuge headquarters. From OR 205, turn east onto Narrows-Princeton Road and continue for about 6 miles to the headquarters complex. This road passes through wetlands and meadows that are good for waterfowl and shorebirds when water levels are right and for raptors at any time.

The trees and shrubs around the headquarters of the Malheur National Wildlife Refuge create a migrant trap, which attracts large numbers of both birds and birders in late spring and again in September.

The headquarters complex is a collection of small buildings, surrounded by cottonwood trees and lilac bushes and overlooking a small pond. This oasis is very attractive to migrant songbirds in spring and autumn and produces several eastern vagrants each year. Check the feeders for Black-chinned and Rufous Hummingbirds. A pair of Great Horned Owls is usually found in the larger cottonwoods. The numerous ground squirrels that live in the lawn provide food for the owls as well as for the resident Bobcat. The pond at headquarters attracts Franklin's Gulls, Forster's and Black Terns, Double-crested Cormorants, and American White Pelicans. As with many migrant traps, birds come and go throughout the day. So even though the headquarters complex can be birded in less than an hour, it is often profitable to spend several hours there or to make several short visits in the same day.

Stop in at the visitor center for maps, checklists, and information about recent sightings and current road conditions.

Malheur Field Station

From the headquarters, return west on Narrows-Princeton Road. Turn south onto Center Patrol Road at the sign for the Malheur Field Station. The field station is a collection of dormitories, house trailers, and RV campsites used for educational programs and to accommodate visiting birders. In addition to offering convenient (although rather primitive) accommodations right on the refuge, the field station provides good birding for the sage species. Cliff, Barn, Tree, and Violet-green Swallows nest at the compound, and Lark Sparrows, Say's Phoebes, Common Nighthawks, and California Quail can be expected in season. The compound lies between two buttes, North Coyote and South Coyote Butte. The north butte is off-limits, but a trail leads to the top of the larger south butte. Watch for Gray Flycatchers, Loggerhead Shrikes, Western Meadowlarks, Brewer's Sparrows, and the occasional Black-throated Sparrow.

For information about staying at the Field Station, contact: Malheur Field Station, 34848 Sodhouse Lane, Princeton, OR 97721, (541) 493–2629, e-mail mfs@highdesertair.com, www.malheurfieldstation.org. If you wish to stay at the Field Station during late May or early June, reservations may be required a year in advance.

Foster Flat Road

While not part of the refuge, this rough dirt road provides access to a Sage-Grouse lek, active in March and April. From OR 205, about 10 miles south of Narrows-Princeton Road, turn west onto Foster Flat Road and continue about 8 miles to the lek. Birders should remain in their cars to view these birds.

Buena Vista Ponds

Buena Vista Ponds and an overlook are accessed from the CPR or from a well-marked pulloff along OR 205, about 14 miles south of Narrows-Princeton Road. There is a restroom here. The hill above the parking area at OR 205 is a reliable spot for Ash-throated Flycatcher. Follow the gravel road up the hill to the overlook and scan the ponds for Western and Clark's Grebes, waterfowl, gulls, and terns. Common Poorwills call from the rimrock at dusk. Continue east on the gravel road down to the wetlands to search for American Bitterns, Great Egrets, and waterfowl.

Diamond Lane and Diamond Craters

Just south of the turnoff for Buena Vista, turn east onto Diamond Lane, then north at the sign for Diamond Craters Outstanding Natural Area. These roads pass by extensive wetlands and wet meadows. White-faced Ibises, Sandhill Cranes, Black-necked Stilts, Yellow-headed Blackbirds, Franklin's Gulls, and Common Nighthawks use these areas. Watch for Bobolinks and Snowy Egrets in these wet meadows as well.

Diamond Craters Outstanding Natural Area is a site of recent volcanic activity just outside the refuge. This landscape of lava flows, craters, and cinder cones is one of the more reliable sites for Black-throated Sparrows. Rock Wrens are common here, and Chukars sometimes cross the road. Look for Great Horned Owls nesting in the larger craters. Return to OR 205 to continue south.

Krumbo Reservoir

From OR 205 turn east onto Krumbo Lane. This gravel road leads through sage and wetland habitats typical of the refuge. The lake itself offers opportunities to see Western and Clark's Grebes, loons, and diving ducks.

Benson Pond

From Krumbo Lane, just east of OR 205, turn south onto the CPR and continue for about 2 miles to Benson Pond. The cottonwood trees around this pond attract migrant songbirds. The pond itself hosts Forster's and Black Terns, Trumpeter Swans, grebes, and other waterfowl.

P Ranch

At the south end of the CPR lies P Ranch. The many trees at this site attract nesting and migrant songbirds. Turkey Vultures use the old fire tower as an evening roost. The wet meadows just north of the ranch are home to Bobolinks and Wilson's Snipes. A walking trail leads north from the ranch along the main canal. Bank and Northern Rough-winged Swallows nest in the canal's banks. From P Ranch, continue south a short distance to the end of the CPR. From here, you can turn west toward Frenchglen and OR 205, or turn east toward Page Springs Campground and Steens Mountain.

3 Southern Harney County

Habitats: Sage steppe, rimrock, riparian, lake, juniper woodlands

Elevation: 4,100 feet (up to 9,700 feet on Steens Mountain)

What to see: High-desert species, waterfowl, migrant songbirds

Specialty birds: Chukar; Burrowing Owl; American White Pelican; Eared Grebe; Black-throated and Sage Sparrows; various eastern vagrants

Best months: March–October

Directions: Begin at the little town of Frenchglen, on Oregon Route 205 about 62 miles south of Burns. (atlas, p. 208)

The Birding

The southern parts of Harney County contain some excellent birding sites separated by great distances. The towns of Frenchglen and Fields are best known as vagrant traps. Sites to the east of Steens Mountain are more notable for their stunning scenery than for large numbers of birds.

Frenchglen

Situated near the southern tip of Malheur National Wildlife Refuge (NWR), the town of Frenchglen is a popular birding stop. The historic Frenchglen Hotel offers rooms and meals, and gasoline is occasionally available at the general store. The trees around the hotel and the riparian habitat across the street have produced many rare birds over the years. If school is not in session, walk behind the Frenchglen School and scan the tree line beyond the fence. Pine Siskins, Lesser Goldfinches, Bullock's Orioles, and Yellow-headed Blackbirds are common in town.

Page Springs Campground

From Frenchglen follow Steens Mountain Loop Road east to Page Springs Campground. The campground offers riparian habitat along the Donner and Blitzen River and juniper woodland on a rocky bluff. Near the entrance of the campground is the East Canal Road. Walk along this road to find Yellow-breasted Chats. The campground itself is home to Lesser Goldfinches, Black-headed Grosbeaks, Lazuli Buntings, and Bullock's Orioles. Climb the trail up the wooded canyon to find Say's Phoebes, Ash-throated Flycatchers, Rock and Canyon Wrens, Nashville and Black-throated Gray Warblers, and the occasional Long-eared Owl.

Steens Mountain

Just past the entrance to Page Springs Campground, Steens Mountain Loop Road continues on a 68-mile loop to the summit of Steens Mountain, returning to OR 205 about 10 miles south of Frenchglen. This road is only open from July through

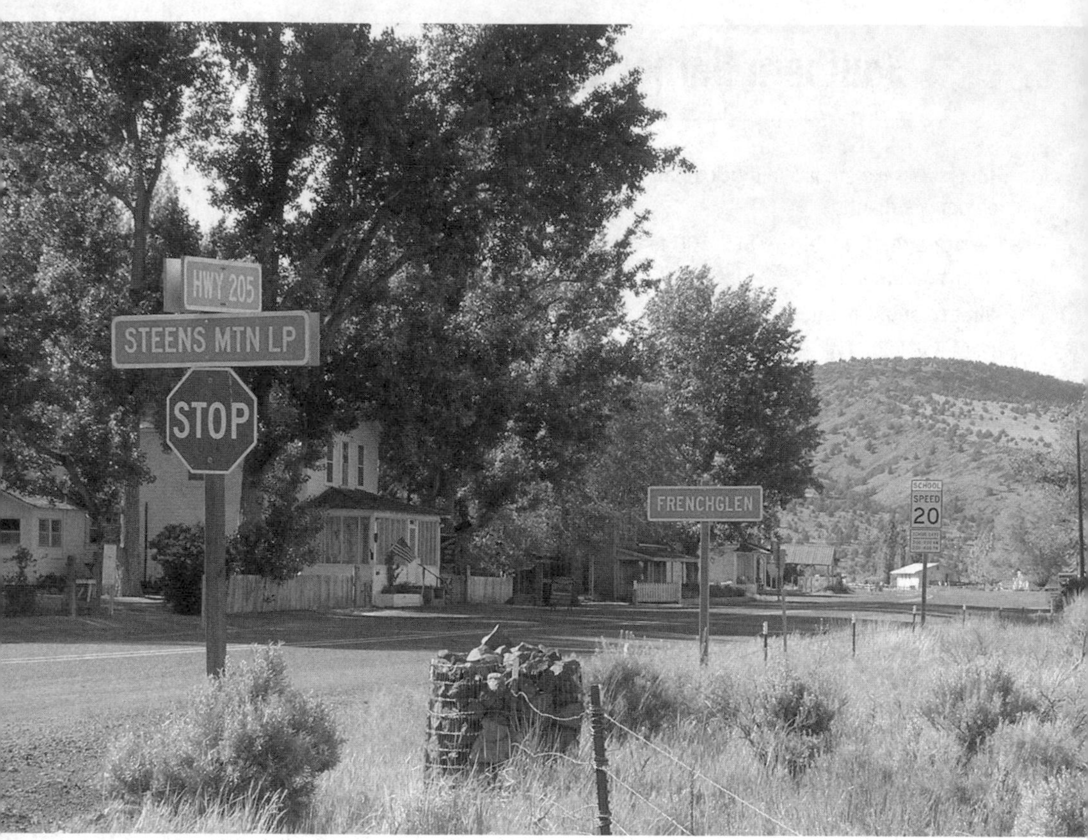

Consisting of just a few buildings and trees, the town of Frenchglen is a productive birding spot at the southern edge of Malheur National Wildlife Refuge.

September. Aside from the beautiful scenery, the main attraction to this arduous drive is the chance to see Black Rosy-Finches. The summit of Steens Mountain is the only reliable site in Oregon to see this species. Do not attempt to drive this road without first checking on the road conditions in Frenchglen or by calling the Bureau of Land Management (BLM) office at (541) 573–4400.

Catlow Valley Road

From Frenchglen continue south on OR 205, which eventually becomes Catlow Valley Road. After about 8 miles you will pass Rock Creek Lane on your right. This road leads to Hart Mountain National Antelope Refuge, a distance of 37 miles. Do not attempt to drive this road without first checking with the refuge headquarters or with the BLM about road conditions.

Catlow Valley Road runs south along the base of Catlow Rim, past wetlands, riparian corridors, and pastures. While there are no public areas along this route, it is often worth stopping along the road to check brushy areas along creeks for migrant passerines and to scan the rimrock for raptors and White-throated Swifts. The road eventually bears southeast and crosses Catlow Rim. Watch for Chukars in this area. Continue on Catlow Valley Road, following the signs to the town of Fields.

Fields

The tiny town of Fields, located 44 miles south of Frenchglen, is an important oasis for both birds and birders. Fields Station is a cafe/convenience store/gas station next to a three-room motel. What draws birders to this remote outpost is the Fields Oasis, located across the road from Fields Station. This little clump of willows surrounding a spring is one of the most productive vagrant traps in Oregon. The Fields Oasis is on private property, but birders are welcome to walk through the area. Check at Fields Station if you have any questions about access. During spring and fall migration, eastern warblers, thrushes, and flycatchers often join the expected Lazuli Buntings, Western Wood-Pewees, and Bullock's Orioles. As with most oases, birds come and go throughout the day. So it is often worthwhile to spend several hours exploring this little site or plan to make several visits.

If you continue south of Fields toward Denio, Nevada, the road crosses several creeks. These riparian areas can be productive. Be sure to check the Fields Oasis again on your return north.

Alvord Basin

From Fields, drive north on the East Steens Highway (Fields-Denio Road on some maps). This road offers dramatic views of Steens Mountain, Alvord Lake, and the Alvord Desert as it passes through extensive areas of sage steppe. There are numerous dirt roads on both sides of East Steens Highway. Many of these provide a place to pull over and explore on foot. Be especially watchful for patches of mature sagebrush, as these areas are most attractive to Black-throated and Sage Sparrows. While much of the Alvord Basin is publicly owned, birders should be alert for NO TRESPASSING signs on the private ranches.

The town of Andrews is just over 14 miles north of Fields. Check the trees here for migrant and nesting songbirds. On the north end of Andrews is Wildhorse Creek, a riparian corridor good for migrants. Pike Creek is another good spot to check, located about 22 miles north of Fields.

Mann Lake

Forty miles north of Fields is the turnoff to Mann Lake Recreation Site. This shallow basin attracts American White Pelicans, Eared and Western Grebes, Caspian Terns, and a variety of waterfowl. Check the sage and grasses around the lake for Brewer's, Red-winged, and Yellow-headed Blackbirds; Western Meadowlarks; and Northern Harriers.

Continue north another 20 miles and turn left onto Oregon Route 78, which will eventually lead you to Burns. If you bear left off of OR 78 onto the Princeton Cutoff, you can then intersect Narrows-Princeton Road to get to the Malheur NWR headquarters. Drive east 6 miles on Narrows-Princeton Road until you reach the refuge headquarters.

Hart Mountain National Antelope Refuge and the Warner Valley

Habitats: Sage steppe, riparian, dry forest, rimrock, grassland, marsh, lake

Elevation: 4,500 feet–8,065 feet

What to see: High-desert species, migrant songbirds, raptors, waterfowl

Specialty birds: Greater Sage-Grouse; Chukar; Brewer's, Vesper, and Sage Sparrows; Flammulated Owl; Green-tailed Towhee; Mountain Bluebird; Sage Thrasher; Western Grebe; American White Pelican; Sandhill Crane

Best months: May–September

Directions: From the town of Lakeview, drive north on U.S. Highway 395 for 5 miles and turn east onto Oregon Route 140. After about 15 miles, bear left onto the Plush Cutoff Road. Follow this road to Plush, turn north onto Hogback Road, then east onto Hart Mountain Road. Follow Hart Mountain Road to the refuge headquarters. *Important:* Fill your gas tank in the town of Lakeview, 65 miles from the refuge. Gas is sometimes available in the town of Plush (25 miles from the refuge headquarters) and in the town of Adel, about 18 miles south of Plush. (atlas, p. 207)

Horned Larks

The Birding

Hart Mountain is a large fault block that rises abruptly almost 3,600 feet above the wetlands of the Warner Valley. From the sharp peaks of the west side, the refuge slopes gently down toward the Catlow Valley to the east. In sharp contrast to the fairly suburban setting of the Willamette Valley Refuges, Hart Mountain National Antelope Refuge is isolated and rugged. But the sheer size and beauty of the place, along with the diversity of habitats, birds, and other wildlife, make this site well worth the effort it takes to get there.

Hogback Road

From the west, Plush Cutoff Road leads you into the little village of Plush. Check the small park at the edge of town for migrant songbirds in June and September. From Plush you can choose to head south on Hogback Road toward Adel or north toward Hart Mountain. Pelican and Crump Lakes lie to the south. These lakes attract large numbers of migrating waterfowl in spring and fall. Nesting species in the area include American White Pelicans, Double-crested Cormorants, Willets, Wilson's Phalaropes, and a variety of ducks and terns.

Hart Mountain Road

Drive north on Hogback Road through Plush and turn right onto Hart Mountain Road. Hart Mountain Road skirts the north edge of Hart Lake. This shallow lake is home to Western and Clark's Grebes, American White Pelicans, Canada Geese, Gadwalls, Northern Shovelers, Redheads, and Black-crowned Night-Herons. Stop at the Warner Wetlands Area of Critical Environmental Concern located on the north side of the road. A primitive toilet and several informational kiosks are found at the parking area. A trail leads through a seasonal wetland to an observation blind. Yellow-headed and Brewer's Blackbirds, Western Meadowlarks, and Cinnamon Teal are among the more common species. Look and listen for Sandhill Cranes in this area. The clouds of insects over these wetlands attract Common Nighthawks and several swallow species.

Past Hart Lake, Hart Mountain Road turns north and runs along the base of Hart Mountain. Scan the ridges for raptors (Golden Eagles, Prairie Falcons, and others in migration) and the occasional White-throated Swift. As the road climbs, you will see several shallow lakes in the valley to your left. Watch for waterfowl or shorebirds, depending on the water levels. The road eventually turns east and climbs Hart Mountain. Be alert for Chukars, Rock Wrens, Canyon Wrens, and other rock-loving species.

Headquarters

Follow Hart Mountain Road to the refuge headquarters. The visitor center here offers a restroom and maps. The center is open all hours, but it is not staffed. Search the trees and shrubs at the headquarters complex for migrant songbirds. Nesting species include House Wrens, Bullock's Orioles, and Cliff and Barn Swallows. Be careful not to intrude on the private residences in the complex.

Most of the refuge consists of sage steppe and short grasslands. Some of the more common summer residents include Horned Larks, Brewer's and Vesper Sparrows, Common Ravens, and Sage Thrashers. Some searching can produce Sage and Black-throated Sparrows. The avian stars of Hart Mountain Refuge are Greater Sage-Grouse. In March and April, check with the refuge office for locations of leks. During the summer months, you will need to hike out into the sagebrush to find individual birds. Females nest under large sage bushes. During the dry season, look for the birds at watering holes at dawn.

Hot Springs Campground

The riparian areas along streams running off Hart Mountain provide a habitat for migrant and nesting songbirds not found in the sage steppe. One of the largest of these areas is at Hot Springs Campground. From the headquarters head south on the main refuge road, known as Blue Sky Road on some maps. In about 2 miles take the right (west) fork in the road to the campgrounds. The patches of willow and alder thickets here and at other riparian areas on the refuge are home to Willow and Dusky Flycatchers, Yellow and Orange-crowned Warblers, House Wrens, and Spotted Towhees. During late May and early June and again in September, the riparian habitats provide the best chance of finding vagrants.

Return to the main refuge road and head south again. The road passes by several jeep trails. Walk these trails to explore the sagebrush, juniper thickets, and rimrock, as well as any additional riparian areas.

Blue Sky

The maintained road ends at the Blue Sky area of the refuge. Blue Sky is an island of ponderosa pine forest, completely different habitat from the rest of the refuge and a magnet for migrants and nesting species not seen elsewhere on Hart Mountain. The large trees provide habitat for Great Horned and Long-eared Owls. Flammulated Owls are common migrants and may nest. Summer residents include Mountain Chickadees, Cassin's Finches, Black-headed Grosbeaks, Green-tailed Towhees, Yellow-rumped and MacGillivray's Warblers, Mountain Bluebirds, and the occasional White-headed Woodpecker. Follow the undeveloped road uphill from the pine forest to find nesting White-crowned Sparrows.

Hart Mountain Refuge covers almost a quarter of a million acres. If you are able, allow plenty of time to hike the jeep trails. In addition to the great birds, the refuge is home to Pronghorn, Mule Deer, Bighorn Sheep, many small mammals, a good variety of lizards and snakes, and even a few species of fish. Ancient native petroglyphs decorate some of the rocky outcrops.

The roads to Blue Sky and to Hot Springs Campground are usually accessible by passenger cars. The more primitive roads are not. Wet conditions in the winter and early spring may make all roads impassible. Contact the refuge office in Lakeview for current conditions.

5 Lakeview

Habitats: Riparian, juniper woodland, lake
Elevation: 5,000 feet
What to see: Migrant and nesting songbirds, migrant shorebirds and waterfowl
Specialty birds: Juniper Titmouse
Best months: May–October
Directions: The town of Lakeview is located along U.S. Highway 395, near the intersection with Oregon Route 140, about 140 miles southwest of Burns or 90 miles east of Klamath Falls. (atlas, p. 207)

The Birding

While Lakeview serves primarily as the base of operations for birders visiting Hart Mountain Refuge and the Warner Valley, the town itself provides some good birding opportunities.

Approaching Lakeview from the north on US 395, you will pass a cemetery on the west side of the road. This is worth a quick stop to check for songbirds or raptors during migration and winter.

From US 395 in Lakeview, turn east onto Center Street and continue to the little city park near the swimming pool. The park and the nearby riparian habitat along Bullard Creek attract songbirds all year. A path behind the restrooms leads uphill into shrubby habitat.

Continue east onto Bullard Canyon Road. Follow this good gravel road for several miles into the Fremont National Forest, taking advantage of pullouts and side roads to stop and look for birds. Watch along the creek for Black-headed Grosbeaks, Yellow Warblers, Yellow-breasted Chats, flycatchers, and various migrants. The juniper woodlands on the uphill side of the road are home to California Quail and Chipping Sparrows. The main target bird of this area is Juniper Titmouse, an uncommon resident of this part of the state.

The Lakeview sewage ponds are located southwest of town. Drive west on South Ninth Street and then take a right onto Roberta Avenue. The ponds are located along Roberta, between South Ninth and South Third Streets. There is no place to park a car on Ninth or Roberta, but a bike path runs along both streets and provides views of the ponds. Turning back east onto Third Street, you will find a softball park, which backs up to the north edge of the pond complex. During migration check the ponds for migrant gulls and shorebirds. Waterfowl, including Barrow's Goldeneyes, may be found in winter.

6 Summer Lake Wildlife Area

Habitats: Marsh, alkali flats, sage steppe, rimrock, dry forest

Elevation: 4,200 feet

What to see: Waterfowl, shorebirds, migrant songbirds

Specialty birds: Tundra Swan; Greater White-fronted, Snow, and Ross's Geese; White-faced Ibis; Bald Eagle; Prairie Falcon; Snowy Plover; Long-billed Curlew; Loggerhead and Northern Shrikes

Best months: February–September

Directions: From Bend, take U.S. Highway 97 south to Oregon Route 31 south to the town of Summer Lake. The wildlife area headquarters are just south of town on this road. (atlas, p. 206)

The Birding

Summer Lake Wildlife Area is located at the north end of Summer Lake, a large basin almost 10 miles long. This is an excellent site for migrant and wintering waterfowl, nesting marsh species, and migrant shorebirds. Summer Lake is a very popular hunting area, so it is best to avoid the area completely from October through January.

Ross's Geese

Snow geese cover the water at Summer Lake Wildlife Area.

Begin your exploration of this site at the headquarters, where you can pick up a map. Directly across the road from the headquarters is a motel and restaurant. The ponds to the south of the motel are good for waterfowl.

The auto tour route begins behind the headquarters and takes you through the various habitats of the wildlife area. Some roads are closed at different seasons, so observe any posted signs or ask at the headquarters. There are plenty of places to park, including three camping areas, so don't hesitate to get out of the car to explore the brushy areas and marsh edges. Great Horned Owls are easily seen in the occasional small trees. Watch for Short-eared Owls at dusk.

During the spring waterfowl migration, February through April, Snow Geese are the most conspicuous species. Canada, Ross's, and Greater White-fronted Geese are present in smaller numbers. Expect all the common dabbling and diving ducks in the wet areas and Sandhill Cranes in the fields. Trumpeter Swans occasionally join the flocks of Tundra Swans.

Nesting wetland species include Cinnamon and Blue-winged Teal, small numbers of Snowy Egrets, Black-necked Stilts, American Avocets, Willets, Forster's and Black Terns, and Yellow-headed Blackbirds. The main lake hosts nesting American White Pelicans and Double-crested Cormorants.

The shallow ponds and alkali flats attract good numbers of migrant shorebirds in April and again in July and August. Summer Lake is one of Oregon's more reliable sites for Snowy Plovers.

The main loop of the auto tour leads through marshy habitat, but the northern part of the wildlife area holds good stands of sagebrush. Sage Thrashers, Brewer's Sparrows, Lark Sparrows, and Sage Sparrows are found here. On the north edge of the wildlife area is Ana Reservoir. Check the brushy areas around the lake for Bullock's Orioles.

The paved road running east-west just north of the wildlife area is Carlon Road. Drive east on this road a short distance to a pullout on the north side at the base of some rimrock. Check here for Canyon and Rock Wrens, Chukars, and various raptors.

The little town of Summer Lake has a rest area about a mile north of the headquarters on OR 31. The large poplars at the rest stop should be checked for migrant and nesting songbirds.

If the roads are dry, you may want to explore the open pine habitat of Winter Ridge in the Fremont National Forest, which overlooks Summer Lake. From the town of Summer Lake, drive south on OR 31 about 15 miles. Turn right at the sign for Harvey Pass onto Forest Service Road 29. Watch for a variety of woodpeckers, Olive-sided Flycatchers, Mountain Chickadees, Mountain Bluebirds, Townsend's Solitaires, Chipping Sparrows, and Cassin's Finches. Since the road is fairly primitive, don't go more than a few miles without an appropriate vehicle and a Forest Service map.

 Fort Rock State Park Area

Habitats: Marsh, meadow, rimrock, sage steppe, dry forest

Elevation: 4,400 feet

What to see: Rimrock and sage species, raptors

Specialty birds: Prairie Falcon; Rough-legged and Ferruginous Hawks; White-throated Swift; Lewis's Woodpecker; Say's Phoebe; Pinyon Jay; Clark's Nutcracker; Violet-green and Cliff Swallows; Rock and Canyon Wrens; Sage Thrasher; Green-tailed Towhee; Brewer's and Sage Sparrows

Best months: March–October; all year for raptors

Directions: From Oregon Route 31 just east of Silver Lake, turn north onto Pitcher Lane. (atlas, p. 206)

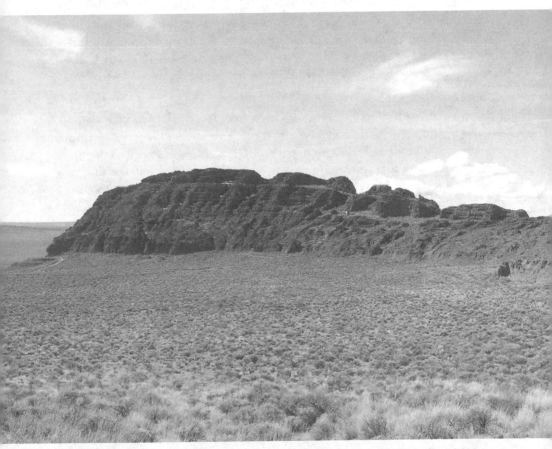

A view from inside horseshoe-shaped Fort Rock. The cliffs attract Prairie Falcons and Canyon Wrens, while the sagebrush is home to Sage Sparrows and Say's Phoebes.

The Birding

Three distinct habitats are found within a span of 25 miles in northwestern Lake County.

Paulina Marsh

Just north of Silver Lake, Pitcher Lane passes through Paulina Marsh. This area is sometimes dry, but if water levels are right, you should expect the typical high desert shorebirds: Black-necked Stilts, American Avocets, Willets, Long-billed Curlews, and Wilson's Phalaropes. Pitcher Lane is also good for raptors, especially in winter. Look for Bald Eagles, Northern Harriers, Golden Eagles, and Red-tailed, Ferruginous, and Rough-legged Hawks. Pitcher Lane passes through private property on both sides, but traffic is light and birding is good from the car.

Fort Rock State Park

When you arrive at the little town of Fort Rock, follow the signs for Fort Rock State Park. In addition to being an interesting geological feature, this U-shaped rock formation is a very reliable site for nesting White-throated Swifts and Prairie Falcons. Trails lead into the formation and up onto the rocky ridges. Sage Sparrows and other typical sage species can be seen along the trails. Both Rock and Canyon Wrens live on the cliffs. Say's Phoebes are regular around the parking lot.

Cabin Lake Campground

From the state park continue north on Cabin Lake Road to Cabin Lake Campground. This site marks the edge between the sage steppe and the open pine forest. The area is home to Lewis's Woodpeckers, Green-tailed Towhees, all three nuthatches, and various sparrows and flycatchers. The main attraction of this site is the two observation blinds, located near the Forest Service buildings just south of the campground. A guzzler at each blind provides water, which in turn attracts most of the area's birds. Pinyon Jays and Clark's Nutcrackers are commonly seen from the blinds.

The well that served this site failed in 2003, causing the Forest Service Station to close and requiring that water be trucked in to supply the guzzlers. Birders might want to contact the Deschutes National Forest office (541–383–5300) to check on the status of the water supply at the two blinds.

Northeast Oregon

Habitats in the northeast quarter of Oregon range from grasslands and sage steppe to forested mountain peaks and alpine lakes. While bird species diversity is great, this part of the state is best known for a few eastern species that are very hard to find elsewhere in Oregon.

Most of this area is very dry, with annual precipitation averaging less than 12 inches. The higher mountain ranges receive up to 40 inches. Temperatures can drop below 0 degrees in winter and climb above 100 degrees in summer.

The forests of this region host many of the same bird species as similar habitats in the western part of the state but with some interesting additions. Great Gray Owls reach their highest density in northeast Oregon. Bohemian Waxwings, Pine Grosbeaks, and White-winged Crossbills are more likely here. Spruce Grouse are found only in higher reaches of the Wallowa Mountains. Boreal Owls are also found at high elevations, usually in autumn.

Check brushy riparian habitats for Long-eared Owls, Red-eyed Vireos, Veeries, Gray Catbirds, and American Redstarts. Grasslands support breeding Grasshopper Sparrows. The extensive Zumwalt Prairie in the northeastern corner of the state is an important nesting area for grassland songbirds and raptors. Sharp-tailed Grouse, extirpated from Oregon by the 1970s, have been reintroduced to this area and may reestablish themselves in the future. A few Upland Sandpipers nest in the grasslands of Grant County. Gray Partridges inhabit brush and farmland along with wintering American Tree Sparrows and Gray-crowned Rosy-Finches.

Marshes around La Grande and reservoirs throughout the region serve as staging areas for migrant waterfowl and shorebirds.

8 Ochoco Mountains

Habitats: Lake, riparian, dry forest, meadow

Elevation: 3,100 feet–5,000 feet

What to see: Waterfowl, migrant songbirds, resident pine forest species

Specialty birds: Western and Clark's Grebes; American White Pelican; Flammulated Owl; White-headed Woodpecker; Willow, Dusky, and Hammond's Flycatchers; Veery; Black-headed Grosbeak

Best months: May–October

Directions: From Prineville, drive east on U.S. Highway 26. (atlas, p. 201)

The Birding

The sites along this stretch of US 26 include a reservoir, a small lake, riparian corridors, and ponderosa pine forest. Most of these sites can either be checked very quickly or serve as starting points for longer explorations of the Ochoco Mountains.

Ochoco Reservoir

Any reservoir in the high desert is worth a look for migrating waterfowl and shorebirds. Ochoco Reservoir is located about 6 miles east of Prineville. The only public access to the lake is at Ochoco County Park, also known as Ochoco Lake State Park on some maps. (The property is owned by the state but leased and operated by Crook County.) The park contains a campground, picnic area, and boat ramp. Look for songbirds in the junipers and scan the lake and shoreline for waterfowl and shorebirds.

Ochoco Ranger Station

About 15 miles east of Prineville, bear right onto Forest Service Road 22 (Ochoco Creek Road on some maps). Follow this road another 9 miles to the Ochoco Ranger Station. Be alert for riparian birds along the way. It's possible to see Lazuli Buntings, House Wrens, flycatchers, and hummingbirds.

Behind the ranger station is a small campground. The riparian habitat between the campground and FS 22 is a reliable site for Veeries. You can park either at the ranger station or at the trailhead along the road. Walk along the road past the ranger station, bearing left at the intersection to remain on FS 22. Just beyond the intersection, turn left onto a gravel path. This will lead you along the creek, through the campground, and back to the ranger station. If you want to explore more heavily wooded habitat, you can take the Lookout Mountain Trail from the trailhead on FS 22.

Wilson Lake Campground

From the Ochoco Ranger Station, continue another 7 miles on FS 22 to Wilson Lake Campground. Park at the day-use area (*fee*) and explore the forest and meadow habitats around the lake. Flammulated Owls have been found here in summer. Retrace your route back to US 26.

Bandit Springs Rest Area

Located on US 26, 29 miles east of Prineville, the Bandit Springs Rest Area serves as a trailhead for a network of ski trails that lead through the pine forest. These make convenient birding trails during the warmer months.

Ochoco Divide Campground

One mile east of Bandit Springs Rest Area, Ochoco Divide Campground provides a quick birding stop along the highway or a convenient campground at which to spend the night. Look for birds in the large pines and along Marks Creek.

9 Southern Grant County

Habitats: Dry forest, grassland, riparian, rimrock, wet forest, sage steppe

Elevation: 3,000 feet–6,000 feet

What to see: Migrant and nesting songbirds, grassland specialties, raptors

Specialty birds: Upland Sandpiper; Sandhill Crane; Williamson's Sapsucker; Flammulated Owl; Chukar; Lincoln's Sparrow

Best months: May–October; late May–June for Upland Sandpiper

Directions: The town of John Day is located on U.S. Highway 26 in east-central Oregon. It provides accommodations, fuel, and the only stoplight in Grant County. (atlas, p. 202)

The Birding

Southern Grant County offers a good variety of habitats within close proximity of each other. For most Oregon birders, the main attraction of this area is the small breeding population of Upland Sandpipers found in Logan and Bear Valleys.

Starr Campground

From John Day drive about 14 miles south on the winding U.S. Highway 395. Starr Campground is a good site for birds of the pine forest. Park at the picnic area and walk around, watching for Hairy and Pileated Woodpeckers, Williamson's Sapsuckers, Hermit Thrushes, Yellow-rumped and Townsend's Warblers, and Mountain Chickadees. Lincoln's and Chipping Sparrows nest in the brushy area around the spring, just south of the picnic area. Flammulated Owls have been found at this site; they are mostly heard after dark.

Logan Valley

Continue south on US 395 to the town of Seneca, located 25 miles south of John Day. Turn east onto Logan Valley Lane, which becomes Forest Service Road 16, and continue about 17 miles to reach Logan Valley. The valley is a broad expanse of grassland, a stark contrast to the pine forests of the surrounding hills. Pull into the wildlife viewing area on the north side of the road and park. The main target species for this site is Upland Sandpiper, most visible in the early morning hours in late May and June. Other grassland birds expected here include Savannah Sparrows, California Quail, Northern Harriers, Western Meadowlarks, Red-winged and Brewer's Blackbirds, American Kestrels, and Sandhill Cranes. Large herds of Elk graze near the tree line and Pronghorns are found throughout the grassland.

Continue east on FS 16 to the turnoff for Big Creek Campground on the left. This campground lies in the transition zone between the grassland and the pine forest. Look for Pygmy Nuthatches, Cassin's Finches, and Hammond's and Dusky Flycatchers. Several mountain-bike trails begin at the campground. These run along the edge of the grassland and into the surrounding forest.

Burned forests are very attractive to woodpeckers, especially Black-backed and American Three-toed. These birds have been known to move into a burned forest while the trees are still smoldering.

Summit Prairie is about 5 miles east of Logan Valley. This is a much smaller pasture area, but it attracts Mountain Bluebirds and other open-country birds.

Return west on FS 16. If you are returning to John Day, take a shortcut by bearing north on FS 15, also known as Canyon Creek Lane. This road intersects US 395 just south of Starr Campground. Along the way, Canyon Creek Campground is worth a quick stop.

Bear Valley

From US 395, 17 miles south of John Day, turn west onto Izee-Paulina Lane, also known as County Road 63. The wet meadows along this road are another nesting site for Upland Sandpipers. If water levels are sufficient, be alert for Wilson's Snipes, Wilson's Phalaropes, Sandhill Cranes, and other grassland species. CR 63 is a narrow two-lane road with no shoulders, but traffic is usually light enough to allow birding from the road. You may have to wait for a herd of cattle to pass as it is being driven across the road from one pasture to another. After about 3 miles you can either turn around and return to US 395 or continue on to FS 21.

Forest Service Road 21

From CR 63, about 4 miles west of US 395, turn north onto FS 21. This road runs 26 miles north to eventually become Fields Creek Road where it intersects US 26. Virtually every habitat in the area is represented along FS 21, and the birding is quite productive at each one. The road is narrow but paved. There are numerous gravel side roads leading off FS 21 that you may want to explore on foot.

At its south end, FS 21 passes through a beautiful area of meadows interspersed with ponderosa pines. The land here is private, but there are many spots along the road where you can pull over and search for birds. As the road enters Malheur National Forest and crosses the Aldrich Mountains, the habitat changes to dense pine forest. As the elevation increases, be alert for Black-backed and American Three-toed Woodpeckers.

When FS 21 makes a sharp right, you can continue straight on Forest Service Road 2170 for 1 mile to reach Oregon Mine Campground. This is a tiny primitive campground, but it lies along a brushy riparian corridor good for migrant and nesting songbirds. Return to FS 21 and continue north.

As FS 21 leaves the national forest, the habitat changes to a rocky mix of juniper, sage, and other shrubs, typical of the John Day River Valley. FS 21 intersects US 26 about 17 miles west of John Day.

Clyde Holliday State Park

Located about 5 miles west of John Day on US 26, Clyde Holliday State Park is an excellent quick stop for riparian species. Park in the day-use area and walk to the John Day River. Follow the trail downstream through the parklike setting of the picnic area to the thick riparian corridor by the campgrounds. Common birds along the river include Lazuli Buntings, Western Wood-Pewees, Willow Flycatchers, swallows, House Wrens, Yellow Warblers, Cedar Waxwings, and Common Nighthawks. Check the river itself for Spotted Sandpipers, Killdeer, and American Dippers (winter). From 1982 to 2002 this riparian habitat hosted small numbers of nesting Least Flycatchers, but this species has not been reported here in recent years.

John Day Fossil Beds (Sheep Rock Unit)

One of three units of the John Day Fossil Beds National Monument, the Sheep Rock Unit provides access to both rock-loving birds of the high desert and riparian species. From US 26, 38 miles west of John Day, take Oregon Route 19 north to the Thomas Condon Paleontology Center on the left side of the road. The center makes a good rest stop and an interesting diversion for those interested in paleontology. The short trail leading uphill from the parking lot may produce a Chukar sighting. The Cant Ranch is just north of the Paleontology Center and across the road; it serves as the headquarters for the monument. The fruit trees and riparian growth here attract Bullock's Orioles, House Wrens, swallows, and other riparian species.

Continue north to the Blue Basin Area. Hiking trails in this upland area are good for Rock and Canyon Wrens, Say's Phoebes, and Western Kingbirds.

Reach Picture Gorge by returning to US 26 and heading east. There are a few places along the John Day River where you can pull off the highway and scan the cliffs for White-throated Swifts, Golden Eagles, and Prairie Falcons.

10 Baker City Area

Habitats: Sage steppe, lake, dry forest, wet forest, riparian

Elevation: 3,300 feet–7,500 feet

What to see: Sage species, migrant shorebirds, waterfowl, forest species

Specialty birds: Tundra Swan; Common and Barrow's Goldeneye; Greater Sage-Grouse; Common Loon; Horned and Western Grebes; Bald and Golden Eagles; Ferruginous Hawk; Baird's and Stilt Sandpipers; Loggerhead Shrike; Gray Jay; Clark's Nutcracker; Sage Thrasher; American Tree, Brewer's, Vesper, Lark, and Sage Sparrows; Gray-crowned Rosy-Finch; Red Crossbill

Best months: April–October; winter is good for raptors and Rosy-Finches

Directions: Baker City is located along Interstate 84, about 45 miles south of La Grande. (atlas, p. 203)

The Birding

The landscape near Baker City is dominated by vast expanses of sage steppe, providing a haven for those species that specialize in this habitat. The reservoirs concentrate large numbers of waterfowl and shorebirds that migrate through this dry area. Just to the west are the Blue and Elkhorn Mountains with their forest and alpine habitats.

Thief Valley Reservoir

From I–84, about 20 miles north of Baker City, take exit 285 to Oregon Route 237 toward Telocaset. Turn onto a gravel road at the sign for Thief Valley Reservoir, and follow this road about 6 miles to the lake.

Surrounded by sage steppe, Thief Valley Reservoir is one of the best sites in northeastern Oregon for migrant shorebirds in summer and autumn, when water levels are low. The site is far enough east to attract species more common to the central flyway, such as Stilt, Baird's, and Semipalmated Sandpipers. The mudflats also attract gulls and terns. California and Ring-billed Gulls are the most common species, but scan the flocks for anything different.

Spring migration brings a good variety of ducks, grebes, and the occasional Common Loon. Check the riparian corridor near the main parking area for warblers, Black-headed Grosbeaks, and Bullock's Orioles.

Bird diversity drops significantly in winter, but look for raptors, Horned Larks, Lapland Longspurs, Snow Buntings, and Gray-crowned Rosy-Finches in the open country around the lake. Check brushy areas for American Tree Sparrows.

National Historic Oregon Trail Interpretive Center *(fee)*

From I–84 near Baker City, take exit 302 to Oregon Route 86 east. Drive about 5 miles, then turn north into the entrance of the National Historic Oregon Trail Interpretive Center. The gate is open from 8:00 A.M. to 6:00 P.M., April 1 through

October 31, and 8:00 A.M. to 4:00 P.M., November 1 through March 31 (closed on New Year's Day, Thanksgiving, and Christmas).

While most people come here to visit the Interpretive Center, this 500-acre site has more than 4 miles of walking trails through sage steppe. Look for the typical sage species anywhere along the trails. Scan the skies for Golden Eagles, Ferruginous Hawks, Swainson's Hawks, and other raptors.

Virtue Flat Off-highway Vehicle Area

From OR 86, just west of the entrance to the Oregon Trail Interpretive Center, bear south onto Ruckles Creek Road. This road angles southeast, then back north to rejoin OR 86 in about 9 miles. The 3,560-acre area framed by Ruckles Creek Road and OR 86 is the Virtue Flat Off-highway Vehicle Area. While, as the name suggests, this area is open to off-highway vehicles, it is still a vast area of sage-steppe habitat open to the public and worth some exploration by birders.

As you travel east on Ruckles Creek Road, you will pass two dirt roads leading off to the right. If road conditions allow, you may want to explore the sage and grassland habitats along these roads. Most of the land south of Ruckles Creek Road is private property, so birders should not leave the roadside.

The third road branching off from Ruckles Creek Road is Love Reservoir Road, which runs through Bureau of Land Management (BLM) land for the first few miles. As with any dirt road in this area, carefully evaluate road conditions before venturing too far.

Phillips Reservoir/Sumpter Valley

From Baker City, head south on Oregon Route 7. Follow this road along the Powder River to Phillips Reservoir at about 16 miles. There are several turnoffs at the dam and along the north shore of the lake, and a hiking trail runs along the entire north shore. During spring and autumn migration, scan the lake for waterfowl. Along with the common ducks and Canada Geese, look for Tundra Swans, Common Loons, and Western Grebes.

In the woods around the lake, watch for Black-capped and Mountain Chickadees, nuthatches, Spotted Towhees, and Rufous and Calliope Hummingbirds. The flats at the west end of the lake can be good for American Pipits and shorebirds.

The area west of Phillips Reservoir was extensively surface-mined for gold in the early twentieth century. The tailings left over from dredging created lots of brushy ponds and sloughs, which can harbor Veeries, Yellow-breasted Chats, and other brush-loving species. Some of this habitat is visible from OR 7, but there are few places to safely pull over. When OR 7 turns southwest, bear right toward the town of Sumpter and Sumpter Valley Dredge State Heritage Area. Hiking trails around the old dredging machine provide access to about eighty acres of tailings.

Anthony Lakes

A paved road leads to this high-elevation area with lakes, meadows, and conifer forest. Heavy snowfall generally restricts birding to June through October. From I–84, 19 miles north of Baker City, take exit 285 and follow the signs to Anthony Lakes on the road that becomes Forest Service Road 73 upon entering the Wallowa-Whitman National Forest. Follow FS 73 for 21 miles to Anthony Lake. You can park at the Elkhorn Crest Trailhead *(fee)* or continue into the campground and park at the picnic area along the lakeshore.

A graveled trail makes an easy 1-mile loop around Anthony Lake. From the southern shore of the lake, take the 0.5-mile spur to Hoffer Lakes and back. For the serious hiker, an 8.2-mile loop around Gunsight Mountain on the Elkhorn Crest and Crawfish Basin Trails will lead you through a nice variety of forest and meadow habitats and some stunning scenery. Consult an official Forest Service map before attempting any major hikes in this area. To reach another easily accessible site, continue west on FS 73 about 1 mile past the ski resort to Grande Ronde Lake.

In addition to the typical forest birds, the high-elevation conifer forest in this area attracts the occasional Pine Grosbeak and White-winged Crossbill. Be alert for Northern Goshawks, American Three-toed and Black-backed Woodpeckers, Dusky Grouse, and Red Crossbills. Great Gray Owls are possible along meadow edges.

11 Enterprise Area

Habitats: Lakes, riparian woods, wet forest, grasslands, farmland, residential

Elevation: 4,000 feet

What to see: Winter finches and sparrows, waterfowl, game birds, raptors

Specialty birds: Gray Partridge; Golden Eagle; Northern Shrike; Townsend's Solitaire; Bohemian Waxwing; American Tree Sparrow; Lapland Longspur; Snow Bunting; Bobolink; Gray-crowned Rosy-Finch; Pine Grosbeak

Best months: All year; December and January for the winter finches

Directions: From Interstate 84 in La Grande, take Oregon Route 82 east approximately 60 miles to Enterprise. (atlas, p. 197)

Wallowa State Park lies at the southern end of Wallowa Lake and at the edge of the Eagle Cap Wilderness.

The Birding

The area around Enterprise is one of the most scenic and productive areas for birding in eastern Oregon. This is a major destination for birders seeking winter finches, but the area offers good birding for migrants and nesting species as well.

OR 82 between La Grande and Enterprise offers many opportunities to pull over and explore the riparian habitats along the Grande Ronde and Wallowa Rivers. (Watch for two more sites along this route: Rhinehart Canyon and Clark Creek Road.) These areas are especially productive for migrants in the spring. Look for Bohemian Waxwings in winter.

Enterprise Wildlife Area

Just west of Enterprise you will see a sign for the Wallowa Fish Hatchery. Turn right onto Fish Hatchery Lane, cross the river, and you will see a small pullout on the left side of the road. Park here for access to the Enterprise Wildlife Area, also known as Wallowa Wildlife Area on some maps. The brushy area here is good for Ring-necked Pheasants, California Quail, sparrows, and Townsend's Solitaires in winter.

Walk south along Fish Hatchery Lane. A path leading east along the main pond is south of the railroad tracks. Watch for sparrow flocks and waterfowl in the winter. In spring and summer, the pond and marsh host rails, Marsh Wrens, and Yellow Warblers. Gray Catbirds and American Redstarts are both possible here. Follow the trail east to the fish hatchery. Another wide trail leads south along the east edge of the pond. Check the nest boxes on the large cottonwoods for Western Screech Owls. The path ends at Fish Hatchery Lane, which has curved to run east-west at this point. Turn right and follow the road a short distance to an opening in the fence, where there is another sign for the Enterprise Wildlife Area. The trail on this side of the pond is on a little bluff overlooking the water. The trail ends at the road close to the parking pullout.

If the pullout is occupied, follow Fish Hatchery Lane to the hatchery, where there is ample public parking and restrooms. Here you can access the wildlife area from the east.

Pete's Pond

From the fish hatchery, continue east on Fish Hatchery Lane to the town of Enterprise. East of the power substation, turn left at the City Center sign. This is Depot Street. Cross the railroad tracks and turn left at the grain elevator. Turn right at your first opportunity onto SW Montclair Avenue (not marked) and you will see the body of water known as Pete's Pond. The pond is on private property, but there is ample room to pull off on the west side of the road. This little pond attracts a good variety of waterfowl in the winter.

From Enterprise you can either follow OR 82 or drive south on Hurricane Creek Road. Both routes lead to the town of Joseph. The Hurricane Creek route

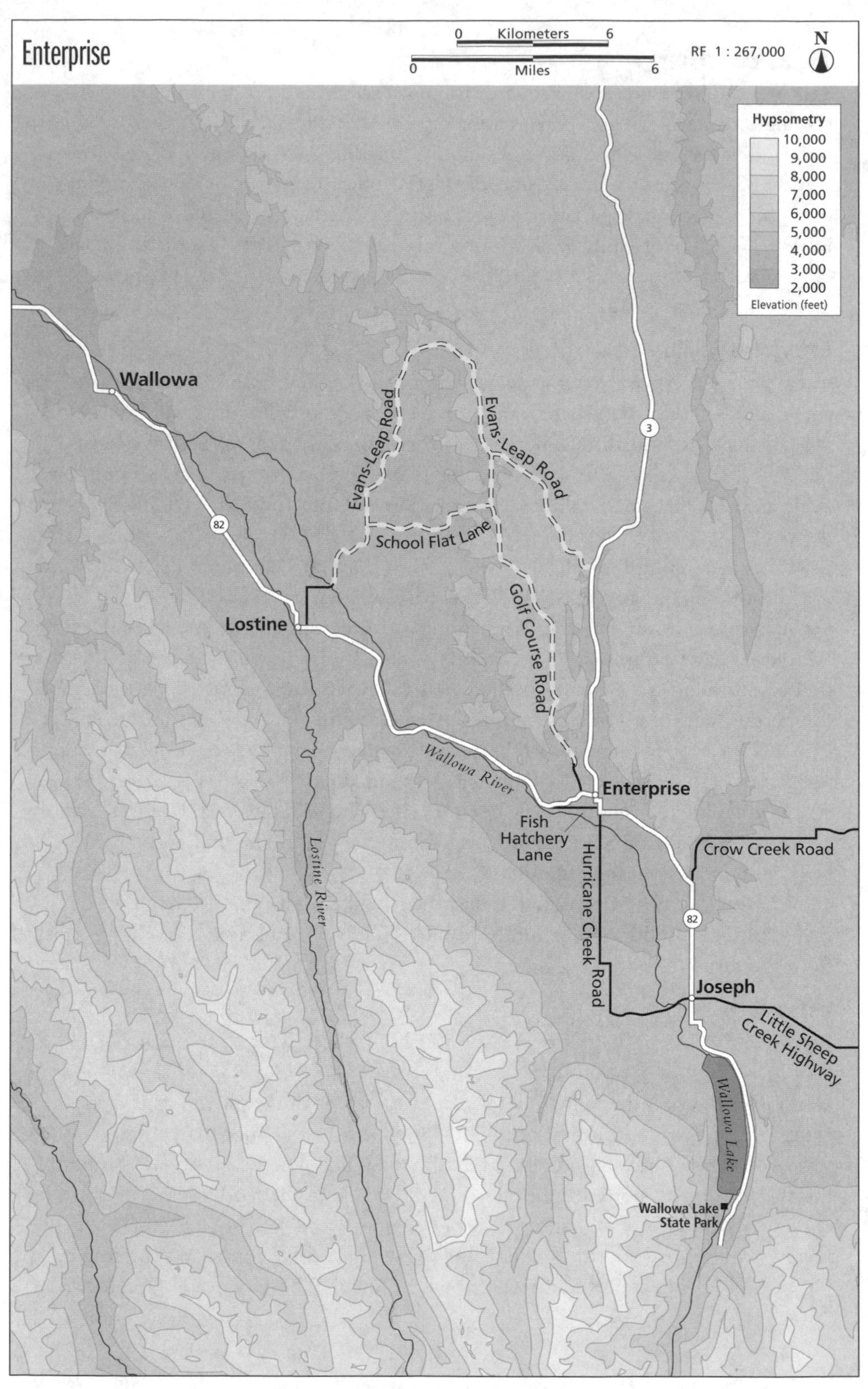

Enterprise
0 Kilometers 6
0 Miles 6
RF 1 : 267,000
N
Hypsometry
10,000
9,000
8,000
7,000
6,000
5,000
4,000
3,000
2,000
Elevation (feet)
Wallowa
82
3
Evans-Leap Road
Evans-Leap Road
School Flat Lane
Golf Course Road
Lostine
Wallowa River
Enterprise
Fish
Hatchery
Lane
Hurricane Creek Road
Crow Creek Road
82
Lostine River
Joseph
Little Sheep
Creek Highway
Wallowa Lake
Wallowa Lake
State Park

passes through pastures that may hold Bobolinks in the summer. Be alert for Gray Partridges in brushy areas anywhere in this region.

Enterprise/Joseph

During the winter months it is worth the time to walk around in the towns of Enterprise and Joseph, looking for feeders and ornamental plantings, especially crabapples. Pine Grosbeaks, White-winged Crossbills, Common Redpolls, and Bohemian Waxwings are more likely to be found in town than out in the countryside.

Wallowa Lake State Park

From Joseph take OR 82 south about 6 miles to Wallowa Lake State Park. The lake itself is nearly 4 miles long, and it harbors good numbers of wintering waterfowl. As you travel south, the woods along the road become thicker, progressing to dense forest at the south end of the lake. Wallowa Lake State Park consists of two units. The north unit is the larger of the two, with a day-use area, campgrounds, and a marina. Check the lake for waterfowl and the riparian area along the Wallowa River for American Dipper and Spotted Sandpiper. Nesting birds include Red-naped Sapsuckers, Mountain and Chestnut-backed Chickadees, Swainson's and Varied Thrushes, and Veeries. Check any feeders for Rufous and Calliope Hummingbirds.

Continuing past the north unit on OR 82, you will pass lodges and cabins on your way to the south unit. This is a day-use area with access to the east and west forks of the Wallowa River and to the Eagle Cap Wilderness area. Spruce Grouse are occasionally found by hiking into the forest from this point.

When you see the stunning scenery at Wallowa Lake, you will understand why this park can be extremely crowded in the summer season. While birding is much slower in the winter, the lack of crowds makes it worth a trip to this lovely park. Mule Deer are common in the area and have lost their fear of people. Be alert for deer that may approach your car for handouts, sometimes sticking their heads into open car windows. I shouldn't have to remind anyone reading this book not to feed the deer, but just in case, "Don't feed the deer!"

Several county roads to the northwest and east of Enterprise offer great birding during the winter. Horned Larks, Snow Buntings, Lapland Longspurs, and Gray-crowned Rosy-Finches form swirling flocks over the pastures and farm fields. Small flocks of American Tree Sparrows forage in the brushy areas. Other birds to watch for include Gray Partridge, Ring-necked Pheasant, and all the winter raptors. Check any groves of trees for Townsend's Solitaires and Bohemian Waxwings, and watch for various blackbirds at cattle feedlots. The nesting season produces open-country birds such as swallows, Western and Eastern Kingbirds, Yellow Warblers, and Savannah Sparrows. *Warning:* These roads are dirt and/or gravel. They may be impassable in wet or snowy weather. Many intersections do not have road signs, so a good map is definitely useful.

Golf Course Road

From OR 82 in northwest Enterprise, drive north on Golf Course Road. Follow Golf Course Road for about 9 miles before turning right onto Evans Leap Road, which runs southeast down to Oregon Route 3. Take OR 3 south back to Enterprise. For a longer loop turn west off Golf Course Road onto School Flat Road. At the end of School Flat Road, turn right onto Evans Leap Road, which makes a long loop north and then south again toward OR 3.

Zumwalt Road/Little Sheep Creek Highway

From Enterprise drive about 2.5 miles east on OR 82 and turn left onto Crow Creek Road. Continue on Crow Creek Road for 5 miles, turn right onto Zumwalt Road, and follow Zumwalt Road for 13 miles before turning right onto Jack Johnson Road (not marked). At this point you enter the Zumwalt Prairie Preserve, a Nature Conservancy site. Continue for 3.7 miles, bearing left at the junction at mile 3.1, and park by the trailhead on the north side of the road. The trail runs approximately 2 miles north into the reserve. In the native prairie habitat, expect Swainson's, Red-tailed, and Ferruginous Hawks, which feed on the numerous ground squirrels. Songbirds here include Vesper and Savannah Sparrows, Horned Larks, and Western Meadowlarks. In rocky canyon areas watch for Golden Eagle and Prairie Falcons.

If you continue to follow the road through the preserve, you will reach the Little Sheep Creek Highway near the little town of Imnaha, 12 miles from where you turned off Zumwalt Road. The last few miles of this road may not be suitable for some passenger cars. If you do continue to Imnaha, the Little Sheep Creek Highway (paved) will lead you back southwest toward the town of Joseph.

12 La Grande Area

Habitats: Farmland, lake, marsh, riparian, sage steppe, residential, dry forest, wet forest

Elevation: 2,700 feet–6,000 feet

What to see: Waterfowl, shorebirds, grassland species, raptors, forest species

Specialty birds: Blue-winged and Cinnamon Teal; Gray Partridge; Spruce Grouse; Long-billed Curlew; Wilson's Phalarope; Short-eared Owl; Bank Swallow; Bohemian Waxwing; American Tree Sparrow; Pine Grosbeak

Best months: All year

Directions: La Grande is located along Interstate 84, 44 miles north of Baker City, and about 258 miles east of Portland. (atlas, p. 196)

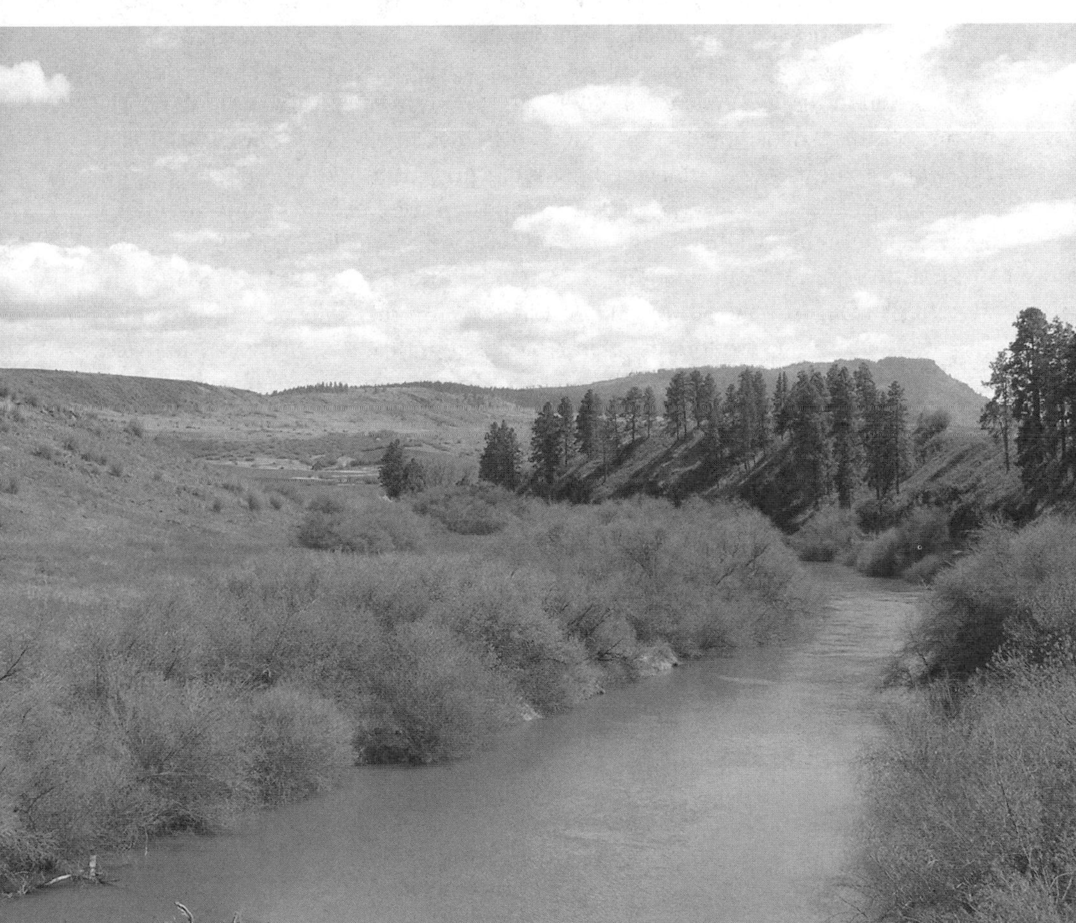

The Grande Ronde River flows through Rhinehart Canyon, north of La Grande.

The Birding

Located in the broad Grande Ronde Valley between the Blue and Wallowa Mountains, the area around La Grande offers excellent birding for wetland and grassland species. Access the Wallowa Mountains and their forest birds at the eastern edge of the valley. Opportunities to see winter finches during invasion years are similar to those in the Enterprise area.

Ladd Marsh Wildlife Management Area (West Unit)

From La Grande take U.S. Highway 30 south toward the southeast corner of town, where you will see signs for the state forestry and wildlife offices. Bear right here onto 20th Street (not well marked). After crossing Gekeler Lane, bear left onto Foothill Road. The Ladd Marsh Overlook is about 4 miles south of Gekeler Lane, on your left. Only a small yellow sign is visible from the road, but once you turn onto the drive and climb the hill to the parking area, there is a large sign for Ladd Marsh. The overlook is a good distance from the water, so a scope is useful here.

From the overlook watch and listen for American Bitterns, Black-crowned Night-Herons, Soras, Virginia Rails, Marsh Wrens, and Yellow-headed Blackbirds during the nesting season. A small population of Sandhill Cranes breeds here, as well. Watch for Bobolinks in the wet fields along Foothill Road just north of the overlook.

In winter, as long as the water remains unfrozen, a good variety of waterfowl and raptors use the marsh. Check the brushy areas for American Tree Sparrows.

From the overlook continue south on Foothill Road for just over 0.5 mile to the Oregon Department of Fish and Wildlife barn on the right side of the road. Park by the barn and explore the old orchard and grassland to the south and west.

Wild Turkeys

This area is good for migrant songbirds in the spring. Look for nesting Lazuli Buntings and various sparrows in the summer. Long-eared Owls have been found in the locust trees in this area.

La Grande Wastewater Treatment Plant

From La Grande take Oregon Route 203 southeast toward Union. Just after the road passes under I–84, you will see the La Grande sewage ponds on the right side of the highway. Continue past the main ponds to the facility entrance on your right. The driveway passes by the police firing range training area on the way to the wastewater treatment plant. Be alert for sparrows and other brush-loving species here, assuming the area is not being used by law enforcement at the time. You will also pass two shallow ponds along this driveway. If water levels are sufficient (they are dry some years), these ponds host nesting American Avocets and Wilson's Phalaropes. The main treatment ponds are located within the fenced area by the plant building. These ponds are large enough to support good numbers of migrant and wintering waterfowl, migrant shorebirds, and nesting marsh species. *Birders must have special permission to enter the fenced area around the main ponds.* The ponds are usually not accessible during weekends. Check with personnel at the plant or contact the La Grande Department of Public Works at (541) 962–1325.

Ladd Marsh Wildlife Management Area (East Unit)

From the wastewater treatment plant, continue southeast on OR 203 about 1 mile to Pierce Lane. Turn left onto Pierce, cross the railroad track, and immediately turn right onto Airport Road. This paved road soon becomes gravel and passes through grassland and irrigated farmland. Watch for Long-billed Curlews, Savannah Sparrows, Red-tailed and Swainson's Hawks, Northern Harriers, and California Quail. Short-eared Owls are found here late in the day.

After a couple of miles, turn north onto Peach Lane. The field north and west of this intersection once hosted the only colony of Burrowing Owls in the Grande Ronde Valley. The colony declined due to cattle grazing and was wiped out completely during construction at the airport. After an absence of several years, at least two birds were found in the area in the spring of 2005.

Return to Airport Road and continue east until the road turns south and becomes Peach Lane. At this corner check the small sand pit for nesting Bank Swallows. As the road continues south, you will pass by marshy areas, willow thickets, and patches of larger trees. Watch for migrant shorebirds in the wet areas and for raptors perched in the trees. Turn east onto the driving loop of the Tule Lake Wetland. From the parking lot you can access a hiking trail that leads through wetlands and past rows of trees. This area may be closed to entry during waterfowl hunting seasons, so watch for signs.

Follow Peach Lane south until the road ends at OR 203. Turn right toward La Grande, then left onto Hot Lake Lane. Hot Lake is fed by hot springs, so it remains unfrozen during the winter. If surrounding wetlands have frozen over, Hot

Lake can be productive for waterfowl. Check the wet areas on either side of the road for rails and waterfowl.

Rhinehart Canyon

From La Grande drive north on Oregon Route 82. North of the town of Imbler, just past mile marker 18, the highway crosses the Grande Ronde River. Take an immediate right onto Philberg Road. This road follows the river south through riparian thickets and thin stands of ponderosa pines. The road gradually degrades until it ends at a big rock pile. From here you can walk to the old bridge. The approach to the bridge has been blasted away to prevent vehicles from driving on it, but with proper care, you can climb onto the structure to look down onto the thickets along the river.

Rhinehart Canyon is a good site for migrant songbirds in both spring and fall. Nesting species include Canyon and Rock Wrens, Lazuli Buntings, Black-headed Grosbeaks, Yellow and MacGillivray's Warblers, Willow Flycatchers, Veeries, Gray Catbirds, and Yellow-breasted Chats. The pines occasionally host Pygmy Nuthatches and Green-tailed Towhees.

Clark Creek Road

Additional good riparian habitat can be found by continuing north on OR 82 to the town of Elgin. Turn right onto Cedar, which becomes Clark Creek Road. Follow this good gravel road for about 6 miles past farms and thickets. Check any hummingbird feeders for Calliope and Rufous Hummingbirds. American Dippers can be found in the creek. As you get closer to the forest, watch for nesting Golden Eagles. Ruffed Grouse can be heard booming in the spring.

After 6 miles Clark Creek Road becomes rather steep and rough before leveling off again in high mountain-meadow habitat. Great Gray Owls are a remote possibility here. You will eventually need to retrace your route back to OR 82.

Cove/Moss Springs Guard Station

The tiny town of Cove lies about 15 miles east of La Grande. The windbreaks and brushy fencerows in this area are good for Gray Partridges and other open-country birds. From La Grande take OR 82 to the edge of town, and then turn east onto Oregon Route 237 to Cove. For a more winding route, or to make a loop, take Geckler Lane east from the south side of La Grande. Geckler intersects OR 237 near Cove.

From the southeast corner of Cove, take Mill Creek Road east toward the Moss Springs Guard Station. This road, which becomes Forest Service Road 6220 in the national forest, is only open from June through October. Drive about 7 miles to the guard station, where there is a campground and an entrance to the Eagle Cap Wilderness Area. It is best to explore the side roads and trails in this area on foot. Watch for all the typical forest species (Gray Jays, thrushes, flycatchers, Townsend's Solitaires, finches), but be especially alert for Spruce Grouse. In Oregon this species is only found in the Wallowa Mountains; the Moss Springs Guard Station is one of the more easily accessible sites for this species.

13 Old Emigrant Hill/Spring Creek Roads

Habitats: Wet forest, dry forest

Elevation: 3,500 feet

What to see: Forest species, owls, woodpeckers

Specialty birds: Ruffed Grouse; Northern Goshawk; Northern Pygmy-Owl; Great Gray Owl; American Three-toed and Black-backed Woodpeckers

Best months: February–May for owls; May–June for nesting songbirds; December–January for winter finches

Directions: These roads are accessible from Interstate 84, starting about 30 miles east of Pendleton. (atlas, p. 196)

The open pine forest along Spring Creek Road is a favorite haunt of Great Gray Owls.

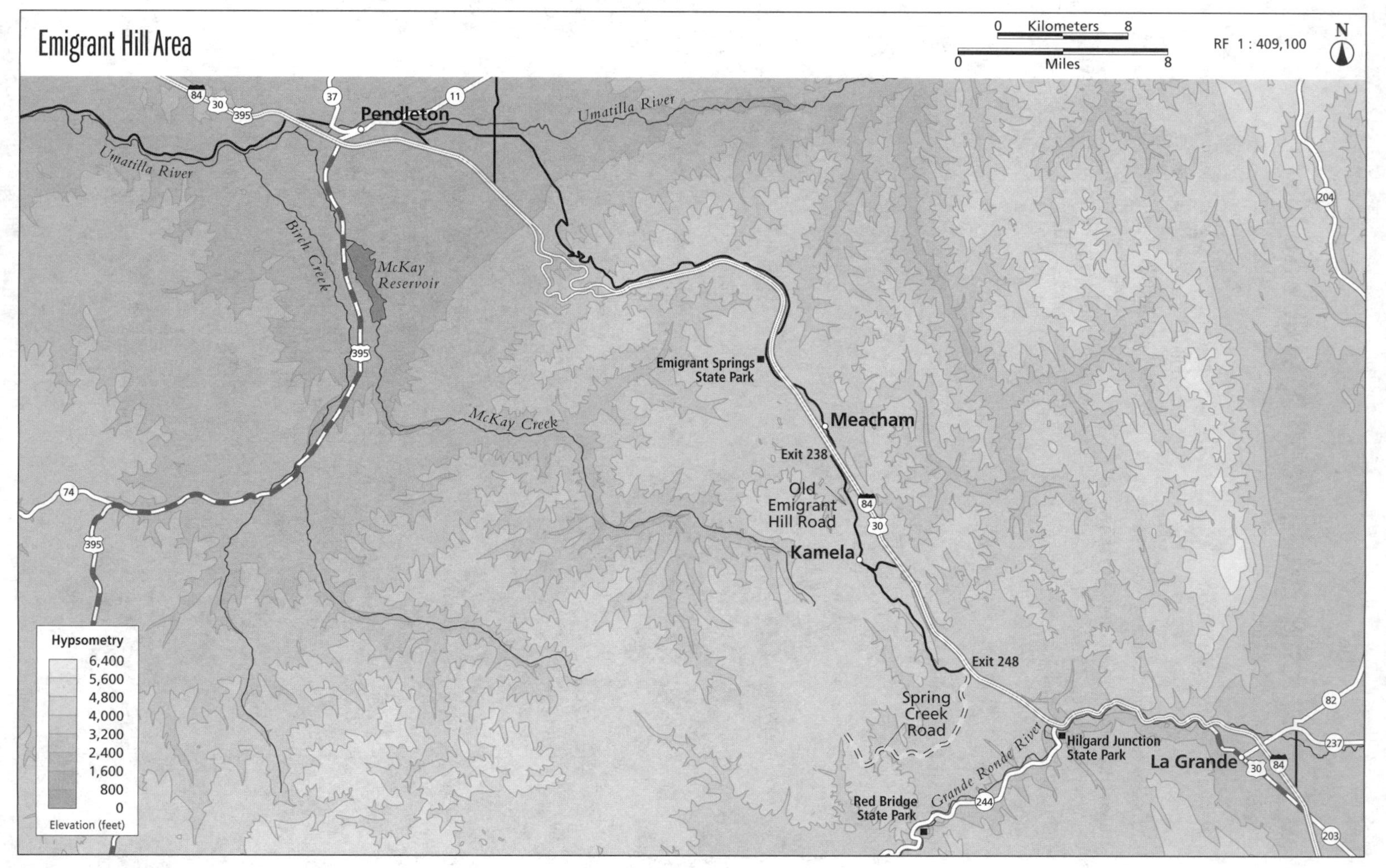
Emigrant Hill Area
0 Kilometers 8
0 Miles 8
RF 1 : 409,100
N
Pendleton
Umatilla River
Umatilla River
Birch Creek
McKay Reservoir
McKay Creek
Emigrant Springs State Park
Meacham
Exit 238
Old Emigrant Hill Road
Kamela
Exit 248
Spring Creek Road
Hilgard Junction State Park
La Grande
Grande Ronde River
Red Bridge State Park
84
30
395
37
11
204
74
82
237
244
203
Hypsometry
6,400
5,600
4,800
4,000
3,200
2,400
1,600
800
0
Elevation (feet)

The Birding

From eastbound I–84, take exit 238 to continue east on Old Emigrant Hill Road. This two-lane paved road parallels I–84, but provides a much more scenic drive through pine forest, with far less traffic and several places to pull off to look for birds. Watch and listen for Ruffed Grouse, Brown Creepers, Pine Siskins, and Pileated Woodpeckers. In winter, this stretch of road can be quite good for Northern Pygmy-Owls.

Emigrant Hill Road ends at I–84, exit 249. Instead of reentering the highway, follow the road under the interstate to the beginning of Spring Creek Road (Forest Service Road 21). Follow Spring Creek Road into the forest for about 3 miles and park. This good gravel road is open from late March through November. There are other roads branching off from FS 21, but these are best explored on foot.

This area of the Wallowa-Whitman National Forest is known as the Spring Creek Great Gray Owl Management Area. It contains the highest density of nesting Great Grays in the country. These birds are not common, but you have a good chance of finding one here. The birds nest on artificial platforms, old Goshawk nests, and broken snags. The easiest time to locate a Great Gray Owl is in May and early June, when the young birds are about to fledge and are very vocal. Great Gray Owls nest in dense stands of Douglas firs and hunt in the open stands of ponderosa pines. To make your search easier, every spring the Forest Service produces a map that shows the location of active nests. Contact the La Grande Ranger District, 3502 Highway 30, La Grande, OR 97850; (541) 963–7186.

While Great Gray Owls are an obvious attraction at Spring Creek, don't neglect the more common forest birds. Both American Three-toed and Black-backed Woodpeckers can be found here, along with Western Bluebirds, Purple Finches, various warblers, and Wild Turkeys, to name a few. You can follow FS 21 for several miles, but will eventually want to retrace your path back to I–84.

Once you return to I–84, headed east toward La Grande, it is worth a quick stop at Hilgard Junction State Park, near the intersection of I–84 and Oregon Route 244. The riparian habitat here is good for migrant and nesting songbirds.

14 Cold Springs/Umatilla National Wildlife Refuges

Habitats: Lake, mudflat, marsh, sage steppe, brush, riparian woods, farmland

Elevation: 300 feet–600 feet

What to see: Migrant and wintering waterfowl, migrant and nesting songbirds, shorebirds, winter raptors and sparrows

Specialty birds: Tundra Swan; Horned and Eared Grebes; Black-crowned Night-Heron; Black-bellied Plover; American Avocet; Long-billed Curlew; Western and Least Sandpipers; Long-eared and Short-eared Owls; Western Kingbird; Bewick's and House Wrens; American Tree and Grasshopper Sparrows; Yellow-headed Blackbird; Bullock's Oriole

Best months: All year

Directions: Both of these refuges are close to the Columbia River and are easily accessed from Interstate 84, near the towns of Hermiston and Boardman. (atlas, p. 195)

The Birding

Both these sites lie in the Columbia Plateau, a region that has been largely converted from grassland to agriculture. Small patches of grassland still attract Grasshopper Sparrows, Long-billed Curlews, and other grassland species. Cold Springs Reservoir and the impounded Columbia River attract large numbers of wintering and migrant waterfowl.

Cold Springs National Wildlife Refuge

Cold Springs National Wildlife Refuge lies around an irrigation reservoir. The open water attracts large numbers of waterfowl, and the surrounding sage steppe, brush, and riparian woods provide critical habitat in an area dominated by agriculture. The northern section of the refuge is closed to public entry, but the south end provides year-round access. Hunting is allowed on Tuesday, Thursday, and Saturday during pheasant and waterfowl seasons. There are no restroom facilities at this refuge. The refuge is open from 5:00 A.M. until one-and-a-half hours after sunset, at which time the gate automatically closes.

From I–84 take exit 182 to Oregon Route 207 north. Just north of the interstate, turn east onto Umatilla Meadows Road and follow this road through marshes and wet meadows. This area is good for shorebirds, herons, and waterfowl. Red-winged and Yellow-headed Blackbirds are occasionally joined by Tricolored Blackbirds. You can continue east on Umatilla Meadows Road to the little town of Stanfield, where you will hit Stanfield Loop Road. This road zigzags northeast, then heads north to the gravel refuge entrance road.

If you are starting from the town of Hermiston, drive east on East Highland Avenue. After 1.5 miles, bear left onto Stanfield Loop Road. Continue for another 5 miles to the gravel road that leads north to the refuge entrance.

The refuge access road runs east-west along the southern shore of the reservoir. Park at any of the five parking lots and explore the upland habitats. Ring-necked Pheasants and California Quail are present all year. Breeding songbirds include Western Wood-Pewees, Western and Eastern Kingbirds, Bewick's Wrens, and Lazuli Buntings. It's possible to sight Burrowing Owls. Check sparrow flocks in winter for the occasional American Tree and Harris's Sparrows.

In the winter months, explore any dense stands of willows and Russian Olives for roosting Long-eared, Great Horned, and Barn Owls. Western Screech Owls may be found in the cottonwoods. Bald Eagles are expected in the cottonwoods in winter, along with Red-tailed and Cooper's Hawks.

When full in the spring, Cold Springs Reservoir has 1,550 acres of open water. By late summer, this area is reduced to about 200 acres. The resulting mudflats provide feeding and resting areas for migrant shorebirds. The common species include Black-bellied and Semipalmated Plovers, Killdeer, American Avocets, both yellowlegs, Western and Least Sandpipers, and Long-billed Dowitchers, but anything could appear in July and August. The resident Ring-billed and California Gulls are occasionally joined by other gulls and terns on these mudflats.

In addition to the typical migrating and wintering waterfowl, the lake itself attracts American White Pelicans, Double-crested Cormorants, five species of grebes, and Common Loons.

Umatilla National Wildlife Refuge

Umatilla National Wildlife Refuge consists of 20 miles of the Columbia River and upland units in both Oregon and Washington. The McCormack Unit offers the best public access for birding. Waterfowl and upland game-bird hunting are allowed on Wednesday, Saturday, and Sunday during the hunting season, so you might want to time your visit accordingly. From I–84, east of Boardman, exit the interstate onto U.S. Highway 730 toward Irrigon. About 4 miles northeast of the interstate, turn north onto Paterson Ferry Road and continue another 2 miles to the McCormack Unit of the refuge.

As you enter the refuge on Paterson Ferry Road, you will come to the hunter check station on your left. Here you will find restrooms and an information kiosk. The parking lot at Kathy's Pond is a little farther north on your right. A walkway leads to an observation platform overlooking this seasonal pond. This area is closed to hunting year-round. If water levels are sufficient, look for shorebirds and waterfowl. Black-billed Magpies and Western Meadowlarks inhabit the grass/sage areas.

The gravel Auto Tour Road is across the road from the lot at Kathy's Pond. This loop leads through farm fields, sage steppe, and wetland areas. Watch for Bald

Eagles, Red-tailed Hawks, and other raptors in the larger cottonwood trees. At parking lot D, walk along the closed section of paved road along McCormack Slough. Look for all the common waterfowl, rails, and herons, as well as Red-winged and Yellow-headed Blackbirds.

In the winter search groves of willows and Russian Olives for roosting Barn and Long-eared Owls. Some of the less common sparrows that have nested in this area include Black-throated, Sage, and Grasshopper.

North Cascades and Willamette Valley

This section of Oregon includes the northwest quarter of the state, minus the coast and Coast Range. This includes the long, flat Willamette Valley, the wet western slopes of the Cascades, and the drier eastern slopes of that range.

Precipitation ranges from around 40 inches annually in the Willamette Valley to half that on the eastern side of the mountains. October through May is the wet season, with very little precipitation falling the rest of the year. Temperatures in the valley rarely fall below freezing in winter, but higher elevations in the Cascades receive considerable snowfall. Summer temperatures average between 80 and 90 degrees.

The scenery in the Willamette Valley is the type that Midwesterners come to Oregon to escape; flat farmland interspersed with sprawling urban areas. But tucked into this region are remnants of prairie, oak savannah, conifer forest, and wetlands.

The valley is a major wintering area for waterfowl and raptors. Cackling, Canada, and Snow Geese; Tundra Swans; a wide variety of ducks; and Sandhill Cranes all use the wetlands and farm fields during migration and winter. Bald Eagles; Northern Harriers; Sharp-shinned, Cooper's, Red-shouldered, Red-tailed, and Rough-legged Hawks; Peregrine Falcons; and the occasional Gyrfalcon all pass through here. Glaucous-winged Gulls are the most common wintering gulls. They are joined by Mew, Ring-billed, California, Herring, and Thayer's.

Wetlands serve as nesting sites for herons, rails, dabbling ducks, and swallows. When water levels drop in the summer, southbound shorebird numbers can be impressive.

In open areas watch for California Quail, Western and Eastern Kingbirds, Western Scrub-Jays, Horned Larks, Western Bluebirds, Yellow-breasted Chats, Lazuli Buntings, and Western Meadowlarks. Winter sparrow flocks often include Savannah, Fox, Song, Lincoln's, White-throated (rare), White-crowned, Golden-crowned, and Dark-eyed Junco.

In forested or urban park settings, typical species include Band-tailed Pigeon; Barn, Western Screech, and Great Horned Owls; Vaux's Swifts; Anna's Hummingbird; Red-breasted Sapsucker; Downy, Hairy, and Pileated Woodpeckers; Hutton's and Warbling Vireos; Steller's Jay; Western Scrub-Jay; Black-capped and Chestnut-backed Chickadees; Bushtits, Bewick's, and House Wrens; Varied Thrush; Black-throated Gray Warbler; Spotted Towhee; Black-headed Grosbeaks; and House Finches.

As you travel up into the Cascades, the avifauna changes accordingly. The forests are home to Ruffed and Sooty Grouse; Vaux's Swifts; Hairy, American Three-toed, Black-backed, and Pileated Woodpeckers; Olive-sided, Hammond's, and Pacific-slope Flycatchers; Cassin's Vireos; Gray and Steller's Jays; Common Ravens; Winter Wrens; Swainson's, Hermit, and Varied Thrushes; Hermit Warblers; and Red Crossbills. Lincoln's Sparrows nest in wet meadows in the Cascades. A few Spotted Owls still reside in patches of mature forest, although their numbers continue to decline. Boreal Owls occur at several high-elevation sites.

Mountain streams host American Dippers, Harlequin Ducks, and Common Mergansers, while lakes in the region attract Barrow's Goldeneyes and various migrant waterfowl.

The east side of the Cascades is considerably drier than the west. The forest changes from lush Douglas fir/hemlock/spruce communities to more open ponderosa pine forest and then to juniper woodland. Green-tailed Towhees and Fox Sparrows nest in shrubby habitats here, along with Dusky and Gray Flycatchers. Eleven species of woodpeckers can be found on the east slopes of the Cascades, particularly in burned areas.

15 Sauvie Island

Habitats: Wetlands, farmland, riparian woods, oak savannah

Elevation: 15 feet

What to see: Waterfowl, raptors, winter sparrow flocks, migrating songbirds and shorebirds

Specialty birds: Snow and Cackling Geese; Tundra Swan; Sandhill Crane; Bald Eagle; Rough-legged Hawk; Merlin; Peregrine Falcon; Red-breasted Sapsucker; Purple Martin; White-breasted Nuthatch; White-throated Sparrow

Best months: October-March for waterfowl, raptors, and wintering sparrows; July–September for shorebirds; April–June for songbirds

Directions: From Portland take U.S. Highway 30 west about 10 miles to the Sauvie Island Bridge. Turn right to cross the bridge. *A parking permit is needed for many sites on the island.* Daily or annual permits can be purchased at the convenience store just north of the east end of the bridge and at several campgrounds and marinas on the island. (atlas, p. 193)

The Birding

Sauvie Island is one of the best sites in the state for wintering waterfowl and raptors. Most of the southern half of the island is privately owned farmland. While driving along the main roads in winter, be alert for large flocks of waterfowl, gulls, or blackbirds in the farm fields and raptors on the utility poles. There are few places to safely pull over, so be careful not to block traffic.

Much of the northern half of the island is included in the Sauvie Island Wildlife Area, administered by the Oregon Department of Fish and Wildlife. The wildlife area is made up of wetlands, grasslands, lakes, and sand beach. Most of the wildlife area is closed to public access, except for hunters, from October 1 through April 15. But even during the closed season, there are several productive sites accessible to birders.

Wapato Access Greenway State Park (aka Virginia Lake)

From the Sauvie Island Bridge, drive north on Sauvie Island Road for 2.4 miles to the gravel parking lot on the left. Wapato Access is an excellent site for songbirds and marsh species. The body of water in this park (Virginia Lake) is seasonal, flooding in the winter and drying up completely by midsummer. From the parking lot follow the gravel path past the woodlot to a grassy area with a picnic shelter. A trail leads all the way around the lake, approximately 2 miles. Left of the picnic shelter, a spur trail on the right leads to a viewing platform on the lake. Other lake viewpoints can be found on the boardwalk at the north end of the lake and at the viewing blind at the south end. The west side of the loop trail provides access to Multnomah Channel, where you can find Double-crested Cormorants, gulls, Bald Eagles, and diving ducks.

American Goldfinch

The woods at Wapato Access are reliable for Red-breasted Sapsuckers year-round. Other common species in season include Ruby-crowned and Golden-crowned Kinglets, Winter Wrens, Cassin's Vireos, Bushtits, and Willow Flycatchers. During the spring check the lake for Blue-winged and Cinnamon Teal, Soras, and Virginia Rails. The more open brushy areas attract Western Meadowlarks and mixed flocks of sparrows.

Return south on Sauvie Island Road. Just north of the intersection with Reeder Road is the headquarters of the Oregon Department of Fish and Wildlife. Stop here for maps and information. Across the street from the nearby fire station is a house with an active Purple Martin colony. Martins can also be seen on pilings in Multnomah Channel along Sauvie Island Road.

Oak Island *(permit required)*

From Sauvie Island Road, turn north onto Reeder Road, then left onto Oak Island Road. During the closed season, most of Oak Island is inaccessible, but drive to the end of the pavement and park at the locked gate.

Where the pavement ends, you will find The William L. Finley and Edgar F. Averill Memorial. This brushy area is good for sparrows in winter. Along with the common Golden-crowned Sparrows, look for Fox, Song, and White-throated sparrows and Spotted Towhees. The trees nearby provide perches for Merlins and Peregrine Falcons.

During the open season, continue past the memorial on the gravel road for 1 mile (bearing left at the fork in the road in 0.5 mile) to a parking lot. A hiking path from this lot leads you on a 2.5-mile loop through mature oaks and grasslands. Watch for Bullock's Orioles, White-breasted Nuthatches, and House Wrens along this trail. These oaks used to house Lewis's and Acorn Woodpeckers, but these species are no longer expected here. The trail also provides access to Sturgeon Lake, where you can see waterfowl, Bald Eagles, and occasionally, American White Pelicans. Return to Reeder Road.

Coon Point *(permit required)*

Continue north on Reeder Road about 2 miles to the gravel parking area at Coon Point on your left. Walk up the paved ramp to the top of the dike where you can see Sturgeon Lake.

During the closed season you cannot go beyond a short section of this dike, but you still have good views of the lake, home to waterfowl and Bald Eagles. Scope the flocks of Cackling and Canada Geese for Tundra Swans, Snow Geese, Ross's Geese and the rare Emperor Goose. The field to the left may harbor Sandhill Cranes in addition to waterfowl.

From July through September, the mudflats on Sturgeon Lake attract migrant shorebirds. From the top of the dike above the parking lot, turn left and walk to the gate and then down off the dike to the edge of the lake. Water levels vary with tides and with the flow from dams upstream.

Rentenaar Road *(permit required)*

Continue north on Reeder Road, past its intersection with Gillihan Road to Rentenaar Road on your left. There is a gravel parking lot on both ends of this 1-mile stretch of road, but the birding is much better if you park at the east end and walk to the end of Rentenaar and back.

Rentenaar Road often offers the best birding on Sauvie Island. The brambles on either side of the road are home to large winter sparrow flocks. Expect Savannah, Fox, Song, Lincoln's, White-crowned, and Golden-crowned Sparrows. Less common species include Swamp and White-throated Sparrows. Also watch for California Quail and Ring-necked Pheasant along the road.

The fields and sloughs along Rentenaar Road provide feeding and resting areas for waterfowl, Sandhill Cranes, and shorebirds. Snow Geese and Greater White-fronted Geese are more common here than at other sites on the island. Frequently seen raptors include Red-tailed Hawks, Northern Harriers, American Kestrels, Ospreys, and Bald Eagles.

During the waterfowl-hunting season, hunting is usually allowed along Rentenaar Road every other day. It is imperative that you plan your visit on days that hunting is not taking place if you wish to get decent views of any ducks and geese. Check the current hunting regulations for dates or call the Oregon Department of Fish and Wildlife (ODFW) headquarters on Sauvie Island at (503) 621–3488. The hunting season usually ends after January, so a walk along Rentenaar Road in February or March can be especially productive.

Reeder Road *(permit required)*

If you continue north on Reeder Road past Rentenaar Road, you will find several parking areas where you can stop to explore the Columbia River to the east. The northern tip of Sauvie Island has extensive sand beaches along the river. The beaches may be crowded in summer, but a quick search in the cooler months could produce gulls and waterfowl on the river and Snow Buntings and American Pipits on the beach.

An observation platform overlooking a small body of water is located about 1.5 miles south of Rentenaar Road, on the west side of Reeder Road. This is a good site for spotting waterfowl and raptors during the winter. Check for marsh and grassland species in the summer.

16 Washington County Wetlands

Habitats: Marsh, lake, riparian

Elevation: 200 feet

What to see: Wintering waterfowl, raptors, herons, rails, songbirds

Specialty birds: Cackling Goose; Tundra Swan; Eurasian Wigeon; Common Teal (Eurasian Green-winged Teal); California Quail; American Bittern; Bald Eagle; Baird's Sandpiper; Mew Gull; Virginia Rail; Sora; Acorn Woodpecker (in Forest Grove)

Best months: All year; October–April for waterfowl; July–October for shorebirds

Directions: Washington County is the county immediately west of the Portland metropolitan area. From Portland take U.S. Highway 26 west to Oregon Route 8 (Canyon Road). Continue west on OR 8 to the towns of Hillsboro and Forest Grove. For an alternate route, you can stay on US 26 west to the exits for Hillsboro and Forest Grove, but traffic on this highway is extremely heavy at times. (atlas, p. 193)

Fernhill Wetlands is a productive site for both shorebirds and waterfowl.

The Birding

All three of the wetlands described below can be birded in one day, and each offers unique habitat and bird species. If your time is limited, Fernhill Wetlands should be your first priority.

Jackson Bottom Wetland Preserve

From OR 8 in the town of Hillsboro, drive south on Oregon Route 219 (First Street). In 0.5 mile you will see an observation platform on the left. This provides good views of the north end of the marsh. In another 0.5 mile you will come to the visitor center on the left. Park here to access the trails through the site.

Although invasive Reed Canary Grass and Poison Hemlock cover much of Jackson Bottom, the wetland is still an important wintering site for waterfowl. Tundra Swans can be quite common here, along with Cackling and Canada Geese, American Wigeons, Northern Shovelers, Northern Pintails, and the raptors that feed on them. From the visitor center several trails wind through the property. The woods and brush along the Tualatin River host Black-headed Grosbeaks, Western Wood-Pewees, and Willow Flycatchers in summer, and sparrow flocks in winter. Both American and Lesser Goldfinches and Cedar Waxwings are year-round residents. California Quail are common near the visitor center.

Cackling Geese

The trail leading east from the parking lot eventually leads you to a bridge over a creek. Cross the bridge and follow the path to the gravel road. From here you can see a lake to your right and marsh to your left. Scan the lake for Common and Hooded Mergansers and other diving ducks. The marsh is good for shorebirds in migration and American Wigeons in winter (check for Eurasians). Follow the gravel road north and then west back to the visitor center. In summer check the many Tree, Violet-green, and Barn Swallows for the less common Northern Rough-winged and Cliff Swallows.

Fernhill Wetlands

From OR 8 (Pacific Avenue) in Forest Grove, turn south on the Oregon Route 47 Bypass toward McMinnville. After 0.5 mile turn left onto Fernhill Road, then left into the gravel parking lot in 0.2 mile. This site is not terribly scenic, but it is one of the most productive birding sites in the state. Fernhill Wetlands consists of a series of lakes and wetlands separated by dikes. The elevated gravel roads on the dikes make for easy walking and excellent viewing of the many shorebirds and waterfowl that use this site throughout the year. The brushy areas host sparrow flocks in winter and in migration. Look for Savannah, Fox, Song, Lincoln's, Golden-crowned, and White-crowned Sparrows, along with American and Lesser Goldfinches.

Fernhill Lake is the body of water closest to the parking lot. Scan the lake for Western, Horned, Eared, and Pied-billed Grebes. Mew and Glaucous-winged Gulls are common in winter, and are joined by smaller numbers of California, Ring-billed, Herring, and Bonaparte's Gulls. This lake is the most likely to host diving ducks, such as Lesser Scaups, Canvasbacks, Common Goldeneyes, and Ruddy Ducks. Watch for Ospreys in the summer and Bald Eagles all year.

Follow the path east along Fernhill Lake. The grassy field is a favorite hangout for Common Yellowthroats and Savannah Sparrows. Numerous nest boxes host Tree and Violet-green Swallows. Just before the path turns south, you will find Dabbler's Marsh on your left. This wooded wetland is a favorite hangout for Wood Ducks, Mallards, Buffleheads, American Coots, and Wilson's Snipes. In the spring and summer, check the trees in this area for Yellow Warblers and Warbling Vireos.

Mitigation Marsh is at the east end of Fernhill Lake. From autumn through spring this shallow wetland hosts huge flocks of Cackling and Canada Geese, American Wigeons, Northern Pintails, Northern Shovelers, and Green-winged Teal. Great Egrets join the resident Great Blue Herons at this time of year. Marsh Wrens are common in the tall grasses all year, joined by Common Yellowthroats in the warmer months. Follow the path around the east end of Fernhill Lake and continue south.

Cattail Marsh is the pond south of Fernhill Lake. This shallow body of water is a favorite of the dabbling ducks and Hooded Mergansers. Green Herons hunt along the shorelines. The trees along the east edge of Cattail Marsh provide habitat for Black-headed Grosbeaks and Western Tanagers in spring and summer. Listen for Willow Flycatchers in this area as well. The trees provide perches for a variety of raptors, including Bald Eagles, Red-tailed and Red-shouldered Hawks, Peregrine Falcons, and Merlins. Note that the trail on the east edge of Cattail Marsh may flood in late winter or early spring.

As water levels drop in late summer, the western corners of Cattail Marsh provide excellent mudflat habitat for migrating shorebirds. Least and Western Sandpipers are most common, but you can expect Semipalmated Plovers, both yellowlegs, Long-billed Dowitchers, Dunlins, and Pectoral Sandpipers in good numbers. Less common migrants include Red-necked and Wilson's Phalaropes, Baird's Sandpipers, American and Pacific Golden Plovers, and Sharp-tailed Sandpipers.

Eagle's Perch Pond is the southernmost body of water at Fernhill. In the spring this pond holds dabbling ducks, including Blue-winged, Green-winged, and Cinnamon Teal, and the occasional American Bittern. As the summer progresses, this pond is the first to dry up, providing shorebird habitat in July. Geiger Road runs along the south edge of Eagle's Perch Pond, separating Fernhill Wetlands from the riparian woods along the Tualatin River. The brushy woods along this stretch of road hold sparrow flocks in the winter and a variety of songbirds in migration.

As you walk back north toward the parking lot, check the fields and wetlands across the road. Depending on water conditions, these fields may hold geese, gulls, shorebirds, or dabbling ducks. The marsh across the street from the parking lot is good for dabbling ducks and Black-crowned Night-Herons.

The town of Forest Grove is home to one of the northernmost colonies of Acorn Woodpeckers. From the Fernhill Wetlands parking lot, drive north on Fernhill Road (which becomes Maple Street after crossing the highway) and turn west onto 18th Avenue. Continue to Rogers Park, at the intersection of Elm and 18th. There is a parking lot on the south end of the park along 17th Avenue. If you miss the woodpeckers here, drive north on Elm, then turn left onto Pacific Avenue (OR 8). In 3 blocks you will reach the campus of Pacific University on your right. The campus has a grove of oaks, which attract Acorn Woodpeckers and White-breasted Nuthatches.

Killin Wetlands

From Forest Grove drive north on OR 47 to Oregon Route 6, then travel west on OR 6 for 3.3 miles. Turn north on Cedar Canyon Road, bearing right at the Y intersection to stay on Cedar Canyon, and continue for 1 mile to Killin Road. There is a small parking area on the side of Killin Road just west of Killin Wetlands. Walk along Cedar Canyon Road to view the marsh.

This is a small site, but a very reliable one for American Bitterns, Virginia Rails, and Soras in the spring. The common marsh species, Red-winged Blackbird, Marsh Wren, several swallow species, dabbling ducks, and more can be expected throughout the summer. As water levels drop, the site occasionally attracts a few shorebirds.

17 Portland Metro Area

Habitats: Riparian, grassland, lake, marsh, wet forest, brush

Elevation: 200 feet

What to see: Migrant and nesting songbirds, wintering waterfowl and gulls, migrant shorebirds, raptors

Specialty birds: Wood Duck; Eurasian Wigeon; American White Pelican; Great Egret; Green Heron; Osprey; Bald Eagle; Northern Harrier; Peregrine Falcon; Thayer's and Glaucous-winged Gulls; Band-tailed Pigeon; Barred Owl; Vaux's Swifts; Anna's and Rufous Hummingbirds; Pileated Woodpecker; Olive-sided, Hammond's and Pacific-slope Flycatchers; Western and Eastern Kingbirds; Cassin's, Hutton's and Red-eyed Vireos; Winter Wren; Varied Thrush; warblers; Savannah, Fox, and Golden-crowned Sparrows; Lazuli Bunting; Lesser Goldfinch

Best months: All year

Directions: The Portland area is located at the intersection of Interstates 5 and 84. (atlas, p. 193)

The Birding

Despite being the largest urban area in Oregon, Portland offers a good variety of habitats and bird species throughout the year. The sites described below are just a few of the most productive and easily accessible in the metro area.

Sandy River Delta

From Portland drive east on I 84. Take exit 18 to the large dirt parking area north of the highway. The Sandy River marks the eastern edge of the Portland metropolitan area. The extensive grasslands and groves of cottonwoods here provide habitat for several species of birds that are hard to find anywhere else in the region. There are several main trails through the site and many little footpaths, so a birder can hit the main habitats quickly or spend hours exploring.

From the parking lot the main path that leads north will take you through a grove of large cottonwoods. Look and listen for Red-eyed Vireos, Black-headed Grosbeaks, and Bullock's Orioles. In about 2.5 miles, the trail ends at the Columbia River, where you can look for loons, grebes, and gulls. This area near the river has hosted Yellow-breasted Chats, but it is occasionally inaccessible due to spring flooding.

The main path that leads east from the parking lot takes you through a large area of grass and patches of brush. In this habitat look for Western and Eastern Kingbirds, Willow Flycatchers, and sparrow flocks. Follow the dirt road that runs along the interstate to several intermittent ponds. These ponds attract migrant shorebirds in spring and early fall and dabbling ducks and herons in the spring.

The Columbia River/Marine Drive

The northern edge of the Portland metropolitan area is bordered by the Columbia River. The river itself can be accessed from Marine Drive, which runs along the

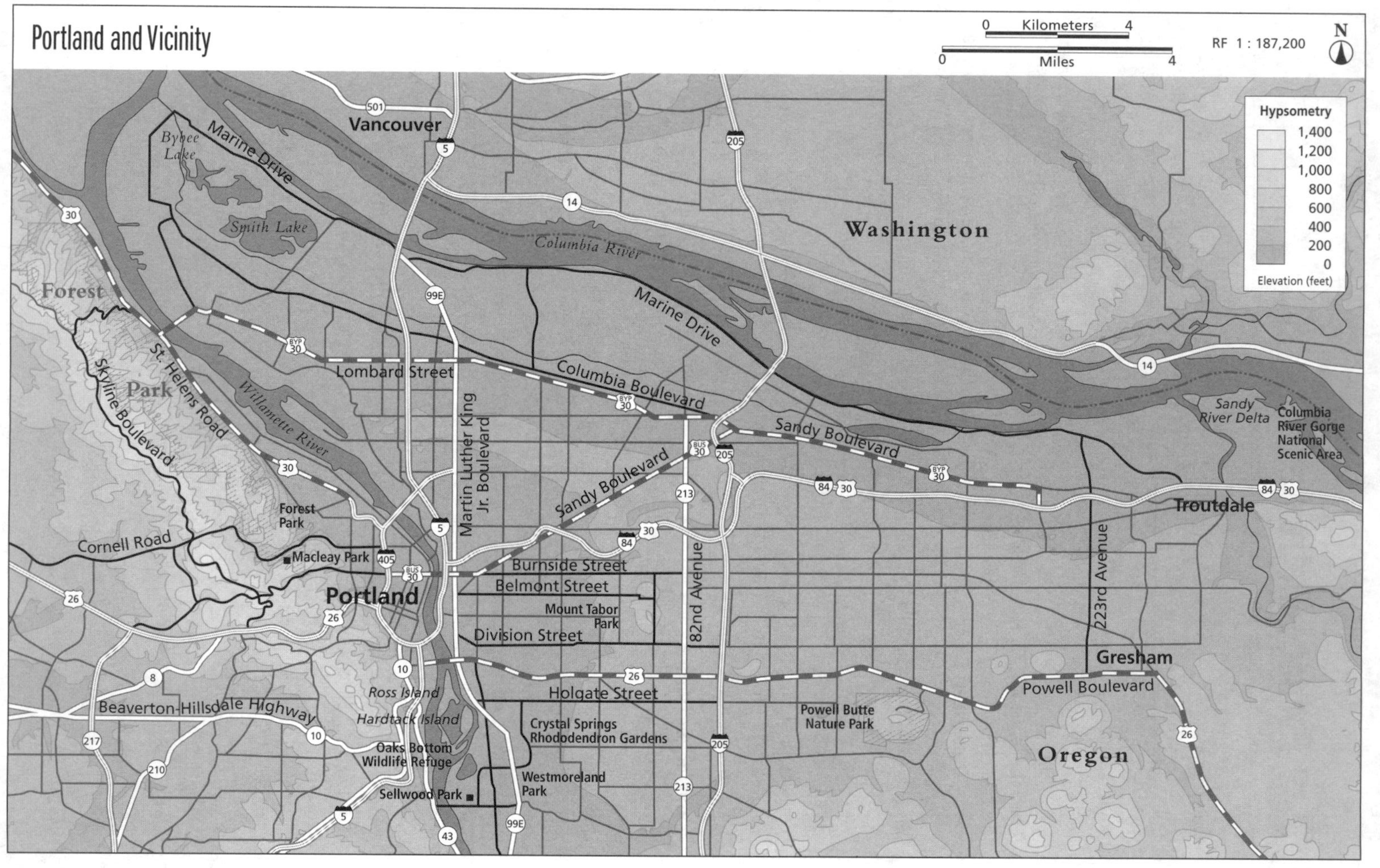
Portland and Vicinity
0 Kilometers 4
0 Miles 4
RF 1 : 187,200
N
Hypsometry
1,400
1,200
1,000
800
600
400
200
0
Elevation (feet)
Vancouver
Washington
Oregon
Portland
Troutdale
Gresham
Bybee Lake
Smith Lake
Marine Drive
Columbia River
Willamette River
Forest Park
St. Helens Road
Skyline Boulevard
Cornell Road
Forest Park
Macleay Park
Lombard Street
Columbia Boulevard
Sandy Boulevard
Martin Luther King Jr. Boulevard
Burnside Street
Belmont Street
Mount Tabor Park
Division Street
Holgate Street
Powell Boulevard
82nd Avenue
223rd Avenue
Ross Island
Hardtack Island
Oaks Bottom Wildlife Refuge
Sellwood Park
Crystal Springs Rhododendron Gardens
Westmoreland Park
Powell Butte Nature Park
Beaverton-Hillsdale Highway
Sandy River Delta
Columbia River Gorge National Scenic Area

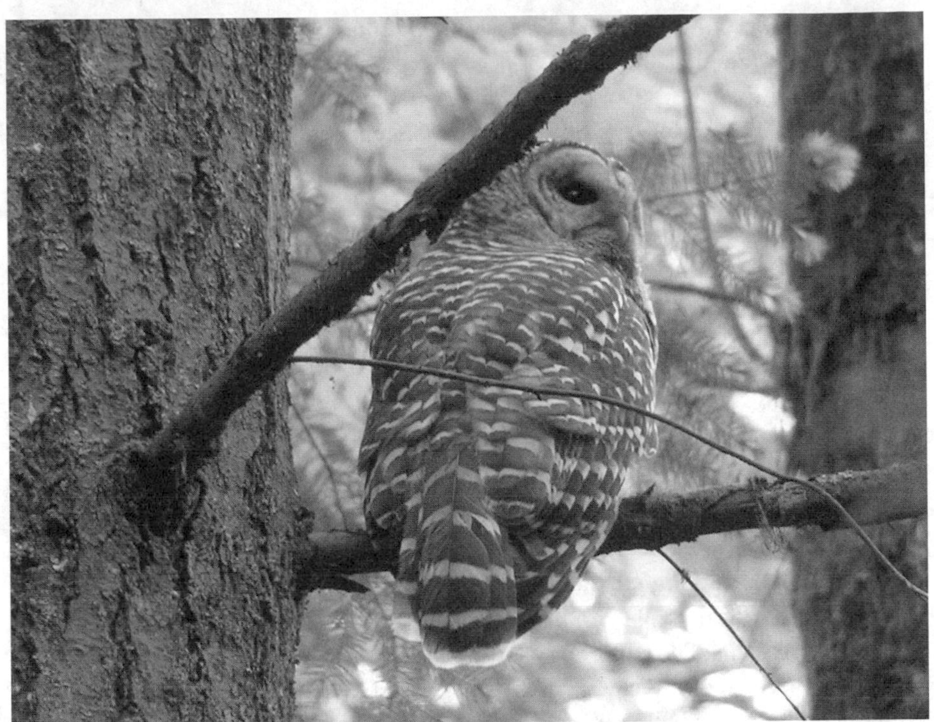

First discovered in Oregon in 1974, Barred Owls are now established in the Blue Mountains of northeast Oregon and the forests of western Oregon.

river just north of Portland International Airport. There are several places to park along Marine Drive. Walk along the bike path between Marine Drive and the river to view birds on the water and in the grassy areas around the airport. During migration and winter, watch for Common, Red-throated, and Pacific Loons; Western and Horned Grebes; and a variety of gulls on the river. The grassy areas host raptors, Western Meadowlarks, and Brewer's Blackbirds.

Smith and Bybee Lakes Wildlife Area

From I–5 take exit 307 and follow signs for Marine Drive west. Follow Marine Drive west for just over 2 miles to the parking lot on your left. Smith and Bybee Lakes Wildlife Area is a 2,000-acre oasis in the middle of a vast industrial area. From the parking lot follow the paved path through a stand of cottonwoods. This little grove is home to Red-eyed Vireos in the spring and Varied Thrushes in winter. Virtually anything could turn up in migration.

If you bear right at trail intersections, the paved path will lead you out of the woods and through a grassy area to an observation blind overlooking Bybee Lake. Check the open habitat for wintering sparrows, raptors, and the occasional Northern Shrike. The lake is good for dabbling ducks and herons. When water levels are low (these lakes are tidal), this is an excellent site for migrant shorebirds. Bald

Eagles nest on the utility towers. The pavement ends at the observation blind, but the path continues into the marsh.

Return on the paved path through the cottonwoods, bearing right to take the loop to the blind overlooking Smith Lake. In recent summers, Smith Lake has hosted a nonbreeding flock of American White Pelicans.

Kelley Point Park

From the Smith and Bybee parking lot, if you continue west on Marine Drive, you will come to Kelley Point Park. Drive through the park to the last parking lot and walk to the point at the confluence of the Willamette and Columbia Rivers. In winter check for waterfowl and gulls. In spring and summer look for songbirds in the brush and cottonwoods and Caspian Terns on the rivers.

Mount Tabor Park

From SE Belmont Street turn south on SE 69th, then west on SE Taylor to the large parking lot at the entrance of Mount Tabor Park. Mount Tabor, an extinct volcano, is one of the best sites in the Portland area for migrant songbirds in the spring. From the parking lot walk uphill past the playground to the mountain's summit. The big-leaf maples are a favorite of migrating warblers, but don't neglect the tall Douglas firs. The shrubby woods south of the summit are good for flycatchers. Check any flowering shrubs for Rufus Hummingbirds in migration and Anna's Hummingbirds all year. The area around the South Reservoir is the most reliable for Lesser Goldfinches.

Resident Red-breasted Nuthatches and Chestnut-backed Chickadees are joined by Varied Thrushes and Fox Sparrows in the winter.

Powell Butte Nature Park

From SE Powell Boulevard (U.S. Highway 26), turn south on SE 162nd Avenue. Continue up the hill to the parking area, where you will find maps and restrooms. Another volcano within the Portland city limits, Powell Butte is notable for its open grassland habitat interspersed with brush. This is the best site in the Portland area for nesting Lazuli Buntings and Savannah Sparrows. Ring-necked Pheasants are often heard crowing from the brushy patches.

From the parking area walk the paved trail to the summit. The small trees and brush along this trail hold migrant warblers and sparrows, including Lincoln's and Fox Sparrows. At the summit of the butte is an old orchard with a great view of Mount Hood and other peaks. Check this area for House Wrens, Lazuli Buntings, Red-tailed Hawks, Western Meadowlarks, and Common Yellowthroats. In the winter, watch for Golden-crowned and White-crowned Sparrows and Northern Shrikes.

The western and southern slopes of Powell Butte are forested, with pockets of large western red cedar and Douglas fir. While generally not as productive as the more open habitats, these woods are home to Great Horned Owls; Swainson's, Varied, and Hermit Thrushes; Winter Wrens; and Steller's Jays.

Oaks Bottom Wildlife Refuge

From the east end of the Sellwood Bridge (SE Tacoma Street), turn north on SE Sixth Avenue. After 1 block turn west on SE Spokane Street, cross the railroad tracks, and turn north on SE Oaks Park Way. Follow this road to the Oaks Amusement Park and park in the lot. From here you can walk up to the paved bike path or walk under the bike path to the south end of the lake. The south end of the park can also be accessed from Sellwood Park. From SE Tacoma turn north on SE Seventh Avenue. Sellwood Park will appear on the left. Park in the lot at the north end of Sellwood Park and take the steep trail down into Oaks Bottom. The north

Oaks Bottom Wildlife Refuge offers a view of the Portland skyline in the distance.

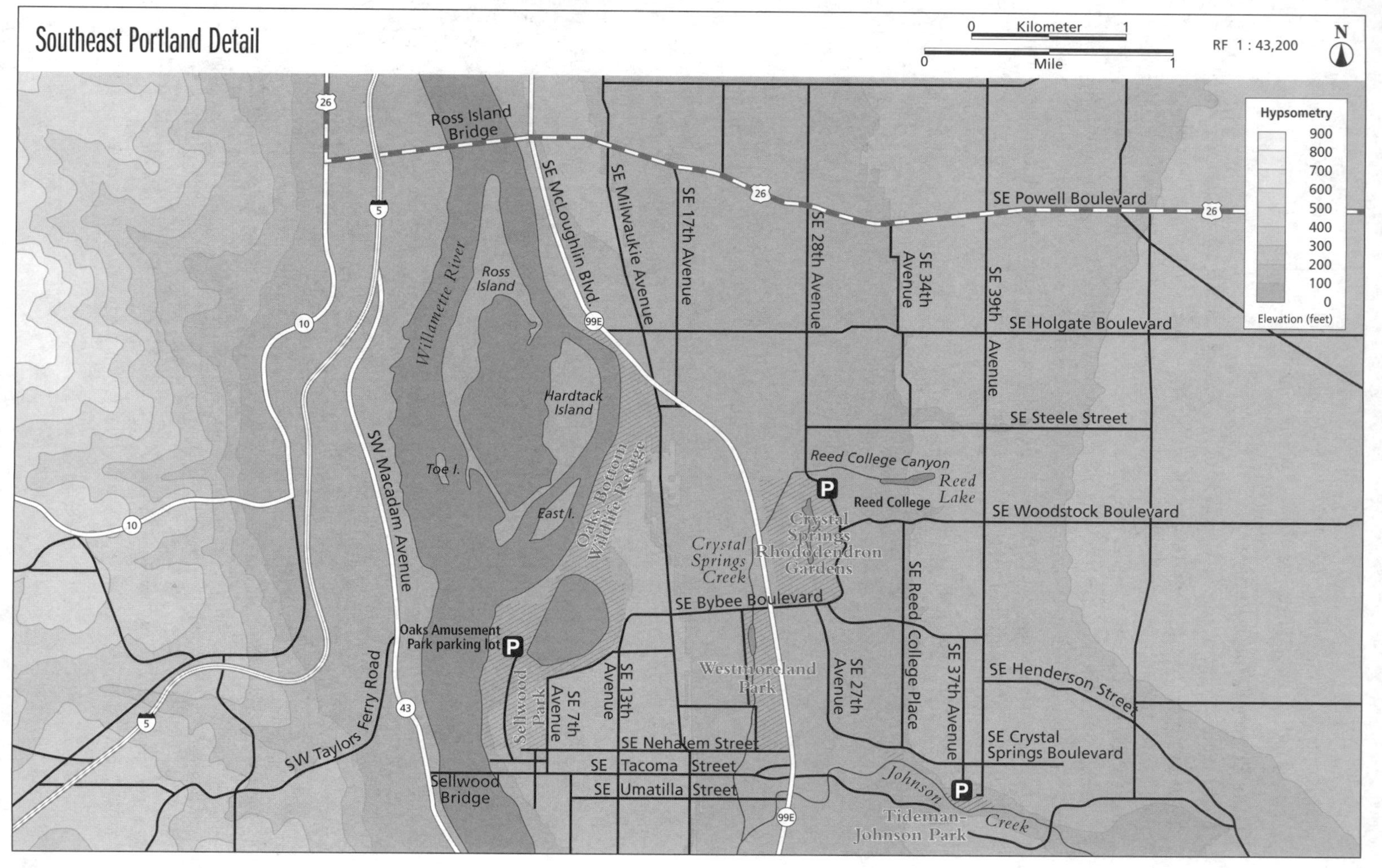
Southeast Portland Detail
0 Kilometer 1
0 Mile 1
RF 1 : 43,200
N
Hypsometry
900
800
700
600
500
400
300
200
100
0
Elevation (feet)
Ross Island Bridge
SE McLoughlin Blvd.
SE Milwaukie Avenue
SE 17th Avenue
SE 28th Avenue
SE 34th Avenue
SE 39th Avenue
SE Powell Boulevard
SE Holgate Boulevard
SE Steele Street
Reed College Canyon
Reed Lake
Reed College
SE Woodstock Boulevard
Crystal Springs Rhododendron Gardens
Crystal Springs Creek
SE Bybee Boulevard
Westmoreland Park
SE 27th Avenue
SE Reed College Place
SE 37th Avenue
SE Henderson Street
SE Crystal Springs Boulevard
Johnson Creek
Tideman-Johnson Park
SE 13th Avenue
SE 7th Avenue
Sellwood Park
SE Nehalem Street
SE Tacoma Street
SE Umatilla Street
Sellwood Bridge
Oaks Amusement Park parking lot
Oaks Bottom Wildlife Refuge
Willamette River
Ross Island
Hardtack Island
Toe I.
East I.
SW Macadam Avenue
SW Taylors Ferry Road
26
5
10
43
99E
P

end of Oaks Bottom is accessed from a parking lot off SE Milwaukie Avenue (just over 1 mile south of Powell Blvd, or 1.5 miles north of Tacoma Street).

The paved bike path that runs along the west edge of Oaks Bottom provides a good vantage point for watching birds on the lake. Large numbers of Cackling and Canada Geese, along with American Wigeons, Green-winged Teal, Northern Shovelers, Buffleheads, and Lesser Scaups use this site during the winter. In late summer and early autumn, water levels drop to create mudflats for migrant shorebirds. Western, Least, and Spotted Sandpipers; both yellowlegs; and Long-billed Dowitchers can be expected. Check the small trees and brush for songbirds and Anna's Hummingbirds. Nesting platforms for Ospreys have been placed on utility poles along this path. It's possible to sight Bald Eagles and Peregrine Falcons all year.

As you continue north on the bike path, you will be able to see the Willamette River and East and Hardtack Islands on your left. Check the river for Common Mergansers and gulls. The islands are home to a Great Blue Heron rookery.

Leave the bike path when you come to the trail on your right. This trail leads you through the wooded areas on the north and east sides of the park. The woods are home to Western Screech Owls, Bewick's Wrens, Black-capped Chickadees, Bushtits, Downy Woodpeckers, and Song Sparrows, which are joined by Hermit and Varied Thrushes and Winter Wrens in the winter and by a host of migrants in spring and autumn.

Westmoreland Park

From the south end of Oaks Bottom, drive east on SE Tacoma Street, north on SE Milwaukie Avenue, and east on SE Bybee Boulevard. Turn south on SE 23rd Avenue and immediately left into a parking lot by the tennis courts. Walk across the street to the north end of Westmoreland Park.

At first glance the little lake at the north end of Westmoreland Park appears like any other urban duck pond, complete with its contingent of mongrel domestic ducks and geese. But in the winter this lake attracts rafts of wild waterfowl and gulls that can be easily studied at close range. Eurasian Wigeons are to be expected here. Canvasbacks, Lesser Scaups, and Buffleheads float on the water, while large flocks of American Wigeons, Cackling Geese, and Canada Geese graze the lawns.

Wintering gulls at this site include Glaucous-winged, Glaucous-winged X Western hybrids, Ring-billed, Mew, Thayer's, Herring, and California.

Crystal Springs Rhododendron Gardens

From Westmoreland Park continue east on SE Bybee Boulevard. Turn north on SE 28th Avenue and follow this very winding road to the parking lot for Crystal Springs Rhododendron Gardens *(fee charged March–August)*. Crystal Springs is another urban park that attracts a surprising number of wintering waterfowl. When you first enter the park, you will notice the heavily manicured grounds and the fat Eastern Fox Squirrels that approach you for a handout. But when you walk down toward the water, you will see colorful Wood Ducks, Lesser Scaups, Buffleheads, and Ruddy Ducks floating within arm's reach of the boardwalk. Flocks of American Wigeons (check for Eurasians) and geese graze the golf course across the lake. Varied and Hermit Thrushes feed around the shrubs. If you visit the park in May, you should see good numbers of warblers and other migrant songbirds.

Audubon Society of Portland/Forest Park

From downtown Portland drive west on Lovejoy, which becomes Cornell Road. Follow Cornell through two tunnels to Macleay Park on your right. The headquarters of Portland Audubon is 100 yards farther on Cornell, but parking is limited.

Lying at the edge of 5,000-acre Forest Park, the headquarters of the Audubon Society of Portland provides an easily accessible sample of this large forest ecosystem. From the parking lot at Macleay Park, walk west on the path along Cornell Road to the visitor center. Feeders at the windows provide visitors with close looks at Rufous and Anna's Hummingbirds, Band-tailed Pigeons, Black-headed Grosbeaks, Black-capped and Chestnut-backed Chickadees, and Steller's Jays. The bookstore has trail maps for the Audubon Sanctuary and the largest selection of birding references in the Portland area. The trails around the sanctuary are home to Winter Wrens, Dark-eyed Juncos, and a very dusky northwest race of Song Sparrow. Barred Owls have established themselves in the sanctuary in recent years.

During spring migration it is worth the 1-mile hike (uphill) to Pittock Mansion. From the Macleay Park parking lot, cross Cornell Road and take the Upper Macleay Trail, then the Wildwood Trail to Pittock Mansion Acres Park. This park consists of a hilltop mansion and the forty-six acres surrounding it. The elevation of the site makes it a prime spot for viewing migrating songbirds in the spring. Along with a good variety of spring warblers, watch for Hutton's Vireos, Red Crossbills, Pine Siskins, Winter Wrens, and Band-tailed Pigeons any time of year. To reach Pittock Mansion by car from downtown Portland, drive west on West Burnside, turn right onto NW Barnes Road, and follow the signs through the neighborhood to the park.

18 Larch Mountain

Habitats: Wet forest, riparian, brush, rimrock

Elevation: 800 feet–4,056 feet

What to see: Forest species

Specialty birds: Sooty Grouse; Northern Pygmy-Owl; Pileated Woodpecker; Olive-sided and Pacific-slope Flycatchers; Gray Jay; Band-tailed Pigeon; Varied Thrush; Hermit and MacGillivray's Warblers; Chipping Sparrow; Red Crossbill

Best months: May–October

Directions: From Portland take Interstate 84 east to exit 22. From the exit ramp, turn right (south) onto Corbett Hill Road. At the top of the hill (in 1.3 miles), turn left onto Crown Point Highway. In another 1.8 miles bear right onto Larch Mountain Road. From this point it is 14 miles to the summit of Larch Mountain. (atlas, p. 193)

The Birding

Larch Mountain provides easy access to birds of the coniferous forest. The birder can choose to drive all the way to the summit, walk short distances into several clear-cuts, or hike for several miles through forest and meadow habitats. Birding is easiest in late May and June, when breeding species are in full song. Larch Mountain Road is closed past milepost 10 from late autumn until the snow melts sometime in May. Birders can walk past the gate if they wish to explore the mountain in early spring.

On your way up Larch Mountain Road, there are two good places within the Mount Hood National Forest where you can walk down logging roads to explore clear-cuts. These brushy areas attract Willow Flycatchers, House Wrens, MacGillivray's Warblers, Band-tailed Pigeons, woodpeckers, Swainson's Thrushes, and Northern Pygmy-Owls. You can scan the clear-cuts from their edges or walk into them. Thick brush and stumps make walking difficult, but birding can be more productive farther off the path.

The first clear-cut is just past milepost 9. Park by the sign for Mount Hood National Forest on your right. Walk past the gate about 300 yards to a large clear-cut on your right (partially obscured by a row of trees). You may wish to continue on this road, as it provides easy walking into the forest.

The other good clear-cut is just past milepost 12, where you will see another gate on your right. Walk past this gate about 0.25 mile to the clear-cut. Watch the trees along the way for Hermit Warblers, Dark-eyed Juncos, and Ruby-crowned Kinglets.

Between mileposts 12 and 14, be especially alert for Sooty Grouse along the road. Male grouse can be heard calling in May. At the summit park in the large lot *(fee)* and walk the 0.25-mile trail up to Sherrard Point. The view of several Cascade peaks is worth the walk, but some good birds are occasionally visible from the point as well. Scan for Clark's Nutcrackers, Vaux's Swifts, and raptors. The scree below the point has produced Rock Wrens and Gray-crowned Rosy-Finches a few times. Check the parking lot and picnic area for Gray Jays and Chipping Sparrows.

If you want to avoid the crowds at the summit and spend a few hours hiking, a series of trails provides a 6-mile loop through the Larch Mountain crater and around the west rim. You can start the loop at the summit, but then the latter half of your hike will be uphill. Another option is to start at the lower trailhead located at mile 11.6 on Larch Mountain Road. Park your car along the road near the end of the guardrail, and walk past the gate on a rough gravel road for about 0.25 mile. The Larch Mountain Trail (Trail 441) intersects this road. Turn left to follow the trail for just under 0.5 mile and then turn right onto Multnomah Creek Way Trail. (If you continue on Trail 441, it will lead you through some patches of mature forest, along brushy riparian corridors, and eventually to Multnomah Falls in about 5 miles.) Follow Multnomah Creek Way Trail along the creek through a meadow and patches of mature hemlocks and up the ridge. Turn right onto Oneonta Trail and follow it to Larch Mountain Road. Turn right onto the road and follow it another 0.3 mile to the summit. Coming down from Sherrard Point, turn right past the picnic area to find Trail 441 (Larch Mountain Trail), which will lead you back down the ridge to your car.

19 Mount Hood National Forest

Habitats: Alpine, wet forest, riparian, lake, marsh

Elevation: 500 feet–6,000 feet

What to see: Migrant and nesting songbirds, migrating raptors

Specialty birds: Prairie Falcon; Black-backed Woodpecker; Pacific-slope Flycatcher; Gray and Steller's Jays; Clark's Nutcracker; Chestnut-backed Chickadee; American Dipper; Varied Thrush; Hermit, Townsend's, and Black-throated Gray Warblers; Gray-crowned Rosy-Finch

Best months: May–October

Directions: From Portland travel east on U.S. Highway 26. (atlas, p. 194)

The Salmon River flows through the Wildwood Recreation Site.

The Birding

Located about an hour's drive east of Portland, Mount Hood National Forest provides a variety of habitats ranging from mature wet forest to brushy riparian corridors to alpine tundra. The sites described below are some of the most easily accessible. Birders wishing to explore some of the many back roads and hiking trails should obtain a good map from the Forest Service.

Wildwood Recreation Site

Wildwood Recreation Site *(fee)* is located on US 26, 15 miles east of Sandy, just east of milepost 39. (If the entrance gate is closed, there is a small parking lot by the highway from which you can walk onto the site.) Drive south to the trailhead parking lot. Wildwood is a developed recreation site with picnic areas and paved interpretive trails. Despite the developed parklike setting, birding here can be quite productive, especially during spring migration. A kiosk near the parking area provides maps to the various trails.

From the east end of the parking lot, walk south toward the Wetland Boardwalk Trail. While crossing the bridge over the Salmon River, watch for American Dippers, Common Mergansers, Spotted Sandpipers, and Harlequin Ducks. A gravel trail follows the river and then connects to a boardwalk through the wetland. Pacific-slope and Hammond's Flycatchers, Winter Wrens, Hairy and Downy Woodpeckers, and Wilson's Warblers are found along this trail.

Back on the north shore of the river is the Cascade Streamwatch Trail. The noise from the river makes it hard to hear birds along this trail, but the underwater viewing window is a fun little diversion.

Walking north from the parking lot, you will intercept the Old Mill Trail, which leads to the group picnic area. The trail is good for upland forest birds, such as Hermit and Townsend's Warblers, Evening Grosbeaks, and Ruffed Grouse. Don't neglect the forest edges around the group picnic area.

Timberline Lodge

From US 26, just east of the town of Government Camp, turn north onto Timberline Road and continue for 6 miles to the large parking area at Timberline Lodge. This historic lodge is the only site in the Cascade Range where you can drive to the tree line on a paved road. As a result, the lodge is very popular with skiers year-round and with tourists in the summer. Despite the crowds, Timberline is still worth a trip for the chance to see alpine birds, most notable being Gray-crowned Rosy-Finches. If you don't mind a little hiking, you can leave most of the tourists behind at the parking lot.

There are several paths that lead uphill from the lodge area. Mountain Bluebirds, Common Ravens, Clark's Nutcrackers, Yellow-rumped Warblers, Mountain Chickadees, White-crowned Sparrows, and Prairie Falcons are some of the more frequently encountered species near the lodge. If you are up for a strenuous climb, make the 2.2-mile loop up to Silcox Hut and back. If you wish to keep your hike a little more level (remember, you start at 6,000 feet here), walk a short distance uphill to intersect the Pacific Crest Trail, which runs east-west above the lodge. If you follow the trail to the west, you will pass through a mix of woods and tundra. A scenic viewpoint overlooks Zigzag Canyon in 2.2 miles. Following the Pacific Crest Trail to the east of the lodge takes you through more open habitat. Gray-crowned Rosy-Finches form flocks of up to 200 birds in the autumn and can be seen foraging on the barren slopes.

During September and October, migrating raptors take advantage of the updrafts coming off the ridges on Mount Hood. Red-tailed, Cooper's, and Sharp-shinned Hawks are common. Ospreys sometimes carry a fish with them on migration. Golden Eagles and Northern Goshawks are an occasional treat.

Little Crater Lake

From Government Camp continue east on US 26 for about 12 miles. Turn right onto Forest Service Road 42 (Skyline Road) for 5 miles, then right onto Forest Service Road 58 (Abbott Road) for 2 miles to Little Crater Lake Campground. Drive through the campground to the parking area at the trailhead. Little Crater Lake is an artesian spring, which glows an eerie turquoise blue. The wet meadows here are nesting habitat for Lincoln's and White-crowned Sparrows, Nashville Warblers, Common Yellowthroats, Sandhill Cranes, and Wilson's Snipes. Walk the trail past the spring and into the woods to intersect the Pacific Crest Trail. Typical woodland species here include Pileated and Hairy Woodpeckers, Hammond's Flycatchers, Varied and Hermit Thrushes, Chestnut-backed Chickadees, and Western Tanagers. The Pacific Crest Trail continues along the eastern shore of Timothy Lake (see below).

High Rock Campground

From Little Crater Lake Campground, turn left back onto FS 58 (Abbott Road) and continue another 13 miles. There are several signs pointing the way to High Rock, but none once you actually get there. Look for a wide, gravel parking area on the right side of the road with a nice view of Mount Hood. (If the pavement runs out, you have gone too far.) Park here and walk uphill on a gravel road to an overlook, looking for forest birds along the way. On the way to High Rock, stop anywhere along FS 58 that looks birdy. Any clear-cuts or burned areas should be checked for woodpeckers and Mountain Bluebirds. Return to FS 42.

Timothy Lake

From FS 58 (Abbott Road), turn right onto FS 42 (Skyline Road) for 4 miles, then right onto Forest Service Road 57 for 2 miles. Surrounded by coniferous forest and meadow, Timothy Lake is an excellent site for migrant water birds in autumn. A variety of loons, grebes, ducks, terns, and gulls can be expected here. Four campgrounds line the south shore of Timothy Lake, providing easy access for scoping the water. Various trails completely encircle the lake, forming a 12-mile loop for more ambitious hikers.

20 Smith Rock State Park

Habitats: Rimrock, juniper woodlands, riparian

Elevation: 3,000 feet

What to see: Rimrock and riparian species, beautiful rock formations above the Crooked River

Specialty birds: Prairie Falcon; White-throated Swift; Ash-throated Flycatcher; Mountain Bluebird; Gray-crowned Rosy-Finch

Best months: All year

Directions: From the town of Terrebonne, on Oregon Route 97 (halfway between Bend and Madras), turn east onto B Avenue and follow the signs to Smith Rock State Park *(fee)*. (atlas, p. 200)

The Birding

For many birders the main attraction of Smith Rock State Park is the nesting colony of White-throated Swifts. If you just want to see this species, you can simply pull into the first day-use parking lot, pay your day-use fee, and spend five or ten minutes watching the swifts. But the park has miles of hiking trails along the river and over the rock formations, so you could easily spend all day birding here.

From the first day-use parking lot, walk the trail through the juniper/sage habitat along the top of the gorge. Ash-throated Flycatchers, Lark Sparrows, and various migrants are found here in season. This upper trail provides eye-level views of White-throated Swifts, Turkey Vultures, and raptors in flight.

Drive a little farther north to the main day-use parking area. This lot is usually more crowded, but provides access to restrooms, picnic areas, a pay phone, and the trail leading down to the river. Pick up a trail map at the information kiosk.

The trail along the river is good for waterfowl and riparian species, such as Yellow-breasted Chat and Lazuli Bunting. Any riparian habitat in the dry eastern two-thirds of Oregon can attract interesting birds during migration.

Walk up into the juniper/sage habitat to look for various wrens, sparrows, and flycatchers. In the winter, watch for Mountain Bluebirds, Townsend's Solitaires, and Black-billed Magpies. Large flocks of Gray-crowned Rosy-Finches have been found in winter as well.

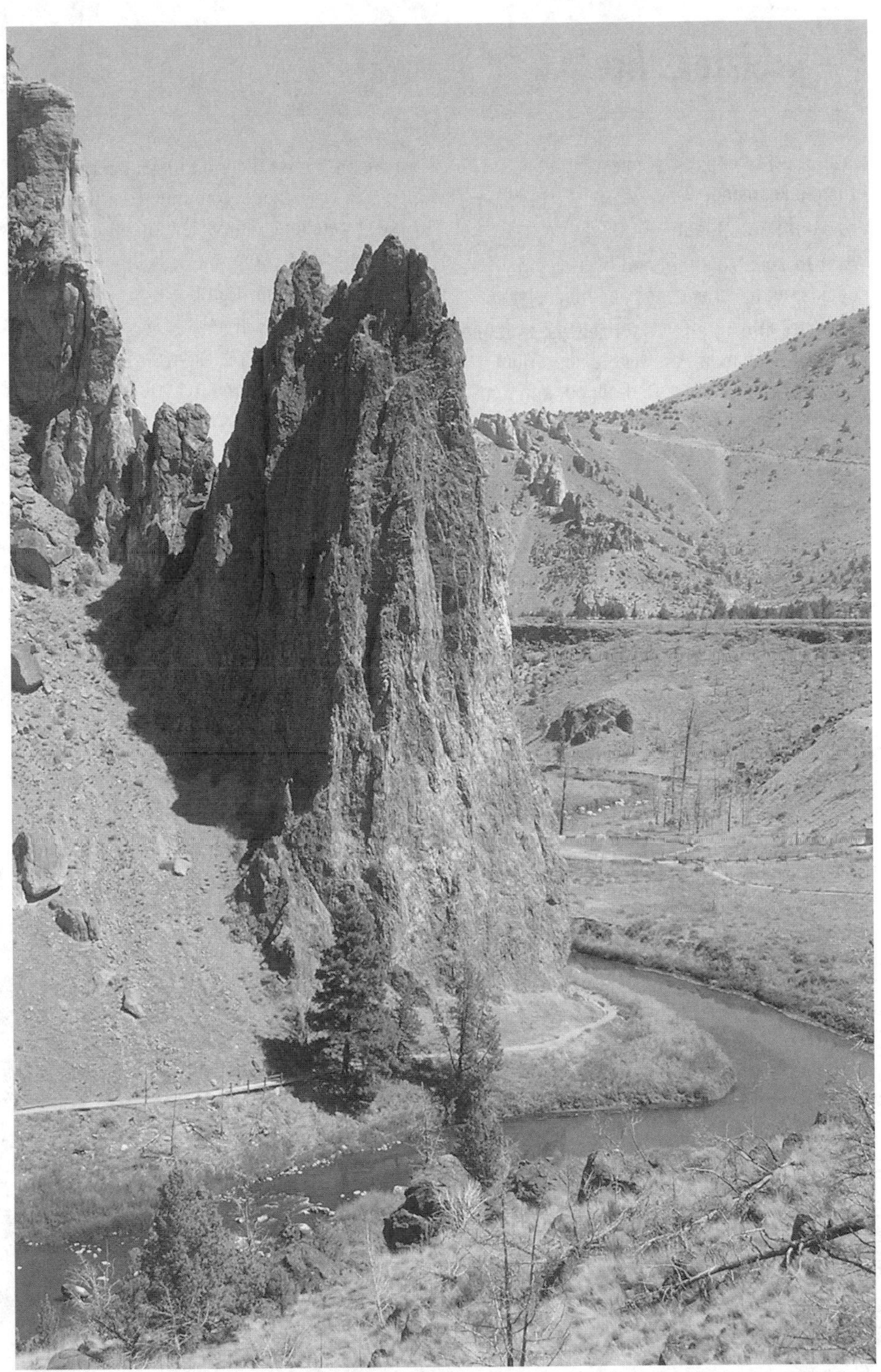

Smith Rock is a reliable site for White-throated Swifts.

21 Sisters Area

Habitats: Dry forest, wet forest, riparian, brush, lake, meadow

Elevation: 3,200 feet–4,000 feet

What to see: Mountain and high-desert species, eleven species of woodpeckers

Specialty birds: Barrow's Goldeneye; Northern Goshawk; Common Poorwill; Calliope Hummingbird; Williamson's, Red-naped, and Red-breasted Sapsuckers; Lewis's, White-headed, American Three-toed, and Black-backed Woodpeckers; Olive-sided, Hammond's, Dusky, and Gray Flycatchers; Pinyon Jay; Green-tailed Towhee; Fox Sparrow

Best months: April–October

Directions: The town of Sisters is located at the intersection of U.S. Highway 20 and Oregon Route 242, about 110 miles southeast of Salem. (atlas, p. 200)

The peaks known as The Three Sisters dominate the view in Deschutes County.

The Birding

Sisters makes a good base of operations when exploring the eastern slope of the Cascades. Numerous campgrounds and resort areas provide birders easy access to pine forests, riparian habitats, and juniper/sage steppe. These habitats, combined with large areas of burned forest, make this area particularly appealing to a wide variety of woodpeckers.

Sisters

Sisters is a quaint little town that is very popular with tourists. As a result summer weekends can be very crowded. Even so, keep your eyes open for birds while in town. Western Scrub-Jays are recent arrivals to this part of Oregon, as are Anna's Hummingbirds. The western part of town is home to a large flock of Pinyon Jays. From downtown head west on OR 242 (McKenzie Highway) and turn north onto Trinity Way. There are several churches on this road. Pull into the large parking areas to check for the jays.

Cold Springs Campground

Cold Springs Campground is 4 miles west of Sisters on OR 242. Park in the day-use area and explore the pine/aspen forest for White-headed Woodpeckers, among others. As you work your way uphill, the habitat changes to a brushy mix of pine/manzanita/juniper. Watch for Fox Sparrows, Green-tailed Towhees, and Cassin's Finches in this habitat. Flycatchers include Olive-sided, Dusky, Hammond's, Gray, and Western Wood-Pewees.

Whispering Pines Campground/Trout Creek Swamp

From Cold Springs Campground continue west on OR 242 for another 1.7 miles, then turn left onto Forest Service Road 1018. The clear-cuts along FS 1018 are home to many Fox Sparrows and Green-tailed Towhees and the occasional Mountain Quail. After 4.3 miles turn left onto Forest Service Road 1520. The campground is just down this road on the north side. A trail that leads into Trout Creek Swamp, a wet meadow surrounded by pine forest, is on the south side of the road. The forest is home to Pileated Woodpeckers, Townsend's and Hermit Warblers, and Pacific Slope Flycatchers. Watch for Lincoln's Sparrows closer to the meadow. If you continue for 1 mile on FS 1520, the habitat changes to manzanita scrub on the hillside.

Calliope Crossing

From Sisters drive north on Locust Street/Camp Polk Road for 2.8 miles. Turn left (north) onto Indian Ford Road and continue another 2.1 miles. Turn left onto Pine Street, cross the creek, and park along the road. Calliope Crossing gets its name from the Calliope Hummingbirds that regularly sit on willow snags in the creek bed, but this site is good for a wide variety of migrant and nesting birds. American Redstarts are rare but regular here. The pine forest along the riparian corridor is home to Northern Goshawks, Cassin's Vireos, Williamson Sapsuckers, and Gray Flycatchers. Trails follow the creek for 1 mile upstream and 0.5 mile downstream.

Indian Ford Campground

From Sisters drive 5.5 mile northwest on US 20. Turn right onto Indian Ford Road, then turn immediately right into the campground. Indian Ford is another good area of ponderosa pine forest with a riparian corridor, which attracts the area's typical nesting species and a good selection of migrant songbirds. The brushy habitat along the creek is good for Northern Pygmy-Owls.

Just north of the campground, bear left onto Forest Service Road 11, also known as Green Ridge Road. After dark the paved portion of this road is a good place to find Common Poorwills. Drive slowly, watching for the pink reflection of the birds' eyes in your headlights.

Gobbler's Knob/Glaze Meadow

Forest Service Road 300 (dirt) is across US 20 from Indian Ford Road. Follow this track northwest for 0.6 mile and park near the gate. The brushy hillside attracts Green-tailed Towhees and Fox Sparrows. Explore the wet meadow to the southwest for waterfowl, rails, Wilson's Snipes, bluebirds, and various swallows.

Metolius Preserve

Owned by the Deschutes Basin Land Trust, the Metolius Preserve provides access to open pine forest and riparian habitats. From Sisters drive 10.6 miles northwest on US 20. Turn right onto Forest Service Road 2064 and continue for 2.6 miles. Turn right onto Forest Service Road 800, then turn right again onto Forest Service Road 810 to a parking area and information kiosk. Follow the trail to the north section of the preserve and along the creek.

Listen for singing Veeries in the brushy thickets along the creeks. This is the westernmost breeding location for this species in Oregon. White-headed Woodpeckers and Williamson's Sapsuckers are common in the pines.

Suttle Lake

Located along US 20 about 13 miles northwest of Sisters, Suttle Lake is a large reservoir that attracts good numbers of migrant and wintering waterfowl. Nesting birds at the lake include Barrow's Goldeneye, Bald Eagle, and Osprey. Take Forest Service Road 2070 along the south shore of the lake. Stop at the Cinder Beach and Link Creek Mouth *(fee)* day-use areas to scan the lake and bird the brushy areas. Check any burned areas for Black-backed Woodpeckers.

Round Lake Road

The area around Round Lake was involved in the massive B&B Burn in the summer of 2003. The resulting charred lodgepole pine forest is particularly attractive to American Three-toed Woodpeckers. About 12 miles northwest of Sisters on US 20, turn onto Forest Service Road 12. Turn left onto Forest Service Road 1210,

Cavities made by Black-backed Woodpeckers typically show a beveled lower edge.

which makes a loop of approximately 10 miles to Round Lake and back. Parts of this road may be quite rough. It is a good idea to check with the Sisters Ranger District Office (541–549–7700) about road conditions and to obtain a detailed map.

Lost Lake/Big Lake

Lost Lake, a shallow body of water surrounded by willow thickets and pine forest, lies about 20 miles west of Sisters, just a couple of miles east of the junction of US 20 and Oregon Route 22. Pull into the campground and scan the water for nesting Barrow's Goldeneyes. The pines are home to Hermit Warblers, the occasional Northern Goshawk, and a variety of woodpeckers, including Black-backed and American Three-toed. Check the willow thickets for migrant songbirds. Northern Waterthrushes are occasionally found along the stream inlet southeast of the lake.

From Lost Lake drive east on US 20 about 2 miles, then turn south onto Forest Service Road 2690 at the sign for Hoodoo Ski Bowl. Big Lake is located 3 miles down this road. Check the lake for waterfowl and the campgrounds for high-elevation species such as Gray Jays, Clark's Nutcrackers, Hermit Thrushes, Western Tanagers, and Pine Siskins.

22 Bend

Habitats: Dry forest, juniper woodland, riparian

Elevation: 3,600 feet

What to see: Migrant and resident songbirds

Specialty birds: Anna's Hummingbird; Lewis's Woodpecker; Williamson's Sapsucker; *Empidonax* flycatchers; Mountain Chickadee; Pygmy Nuthatch; American Dipper; Green-tailed Towhee; Fox Sparrow

Best months: Spring–fall

Directions: The city of Bend is located at the intersection of U.S. Highway 97 and U.S. Highway 20. (atlas, p. 200)

The Birding

This sprawling city on the western edge of the High Desert has several parks that attract good numbers of both migrant and resident species. Tumalo State Park and Sawyer Park offer extensive riparian habitat. Shevlin Park and Pilot Butte State Scenic Viewpoint contain drier ponderosa pine and juniper woodland habitats, respectively.

Tumalo State Park *(fee)*

Tumalo State Park is located 3.5 miles north of Bend along US 20. Follow the signs into the park and to the day-use area along the Deschutes River. Trails lead both upstream and down from the parking area. Watch for American Dippers and Ospreys along the river.

Sawyer Park

From North Third Street (US 20) in Bend, travel northwest on O. B. Riley Road for 0.5 mile to the park entrance. A footbridge over the Deschutes River leads to a trail that runs 2 miles in either direction. Wood Ducks and Hooded Mergansers winter by the bridge.

Shevlin Park

From Third Street in central Bend, travel west on Greenwood Avenue, which becomes Newport Avenue and finally Shevlin Road. The park entrance is 4.5 miles from Third Street. The bottom of the canyon along Tumalo Creek contains willows, aspens, and mixed conifers, while trails along the canyon walls lead through drier ponderosa pine forest. There are 8.5 miles of trails in this 652-acre park. Consider taking the 4.5-mile loop trail around the canyon rim.

Pilot Butte State Scenic Viewpoint

Pilot Butte is a small cinder cone located along US 20 on the eastern edge of Bend. From the parking lot at the base of the butte, take one of several trails, all of which lead to the top. The habitat here is juniper/sage steppe. Cultivated trees at the summit are attractive to migrants.

23 Willamette Valley National Wildlife Refuge Complex

Habitats: Marsh, farmland, grassland, oak savannah, wet forest, brush

Elevation: 400 feet

What to see: Wintering waterfowl, marsh species, raptors, shorebirds, upland songbirds

Specialty birds: Cackling and Canada Geese; Peregrine and Prairie Falcons; Ruffed Grouse; Least and Western Sandpipers; Band-tailed Pigeon; Burrowing Owl; Acorn Woodpecker; Olive-sided Flycatcher; Horned Lark; Wrentit; Black-throated Gray and MacGillivray's Warblers

Best months: All year, winter for waterfowl and raptors

Directions: These three refuges are all close to the Interstate 5 corridor, near Salem and Corvallis. See individual accounts for specific directions to each site. (atlas, p. 199)

The Birding

Established in the 1960s to preserve the wintering habitat of the rare Dusky Canada Goose, the three refuges of the Western Oregon Complex provide protection for a variety of habitats in the heavily farmed Willamette Valley. Since the primary goal of the refuges is to provide safe haven for wintering waterfowl, most areas are closed to public access from October through March. But even during the winter closures, the perimeter roads, parking areas, and some hiking trails remain open and provide excellent birding.

Canada and Cackling Geese cover the ground at Finley National Wildlife Refuge.

William L. Finley National Wildlife Refuge

The largest of the three Willamette Valley refuges, Finley covers 5,325 acres. Since the refuge lies along the edge of the Coast Range, Finley has the greatest diversity of habitats as well. Reach the refuge by taking Oregon Route 99W south from Corvallis for 11 miles or north from Eugene about 27 miles.

From OR 99W turn west onto Bruce Road. The first parking area upon entering the refuge is at McFadden's Marsh. A short gravel trail leads to an observation blind overlooking the water. If water levels are high, check the field to the east of the trail for shorebirds and dabbling ducks.

Continue west on Bruce Road past wet areas, pastures, and farm fields. Large flocks of geese feed in these fields. Look through the many Cackling and Canada Geese for Snow, Ross's, and Greater White-fronted Geese. Brant and Emperor Geese are possible. The next two parking areas along Bruce Road serve as trailheads during the open season. Trails lead to ponds and marshy areas in the heart of the refuge. The trail to Pigeon Butte provides access to oak savannah and young oak forest. Mineral springs near the quarry at the end of the trail attract Band-tailed Pigeons and migrant songbirds.

Bruce Road continues west out of the refuge, then turns to the south. After about 1 mile turn right onto Bellfountain Road, which curves back north toward the west entrance of the refuge. The west side of Finley is open all year and provides access to upland habitats. The Woodpecker Loop and Mill Hill Loop Trails take you through pockets of oak, mature maple, and Douglas fir forests. Look for upland species such as Acorn Woodpeckers, Red-breasted Sapsuckers, Ruffed Grouse, Chestnut-backed Chickadees, and Western Scrub-Jays. Mountain Quail are occasionally found on this side of the refuge.

Follow the refuge road to the headquarters, where you will find maps and other information. The feeders at the headquarters attract Fox Sparrows, Dark-eyed Juncos, Spotted Towhees, Western Scrub-Jays, and Rufous Hummingbirds. The trail to Cabell Marsh begins at the headquarters parking lot. Cabell Marsh is a good spot for Ospreys, Bald Eagles, Great Egrets, and American Bitterns.

Continue on the refuge road, past oak savannah and wetlands to an information kiosk overlooking the largest remaining remnant of native wet prairie in the Willamette Valley. Watch for Western Meadowlarks, Short-eared Owls, and other grassland species. Follow the road out of the refuge and back to OR 99W.

Baskett Slough National Wildlife Refuge

Baskett Slough covers 2,492 acres of wetlands, farm fields, and oak savannah. The refuge is located west of Salem along Oregon Route 22. A wildlife viewing area with restrooms and an information kiosk overlooking South Slough Pond is 2 miles west of the intersection of OR 22 and OR 99W. This is a good spot to scope the flocks of geese, swans, and ducks. Scan the farm field surrounding the pond for Brewer's Blackbirds, Horned Larks, and American Pipits.

Continue west on OR 22 to the next intersection, turn north onto Smithfield Road, and then turn immediately east onto Coville Road. This road takes you east past South Slough Pond for a closer, ground-level look at the waterfowl. Coville Road jogs north, then east again. At the second jog you will find a parking area and the trailhead for the Baskett Butte Trail. The trail is open all year and leads up through oak savannah and mixed woods for a great view of the surrounding wetlands.

Follow Coville Road east to the intersection of OR 99W. Turn north, and after a little over 1 mile, turn west onto Smithfield Road. Smithfield Road leads you back onto refuge property. Watch for waterfowl on the small ponds. The north part of the refuge is especially good for raptors. Gyrfalcons are occasionally found in this area in winter. When a Gyr is present, it is possible to find all five species of falcons in a single day. Another rare winter raptor species to watch for is the Burrowing Owl. Check culverts along Smithfield and Livermore Roads.

A parking lot and the trailhead for the Morgan Lake Trail are near the intersection of Smithfield Road and Livermore Road. The trail is open from April 1 to September 30 and loops through the northern part of the refuge. Watch for the typical marsh species in spring and for shorebirds as water levels drop in the summer.

During the winter months it is worth a drive north on Livermore Road. This rough gravel road leads through pastures, farm fields, and wetlands, which attract

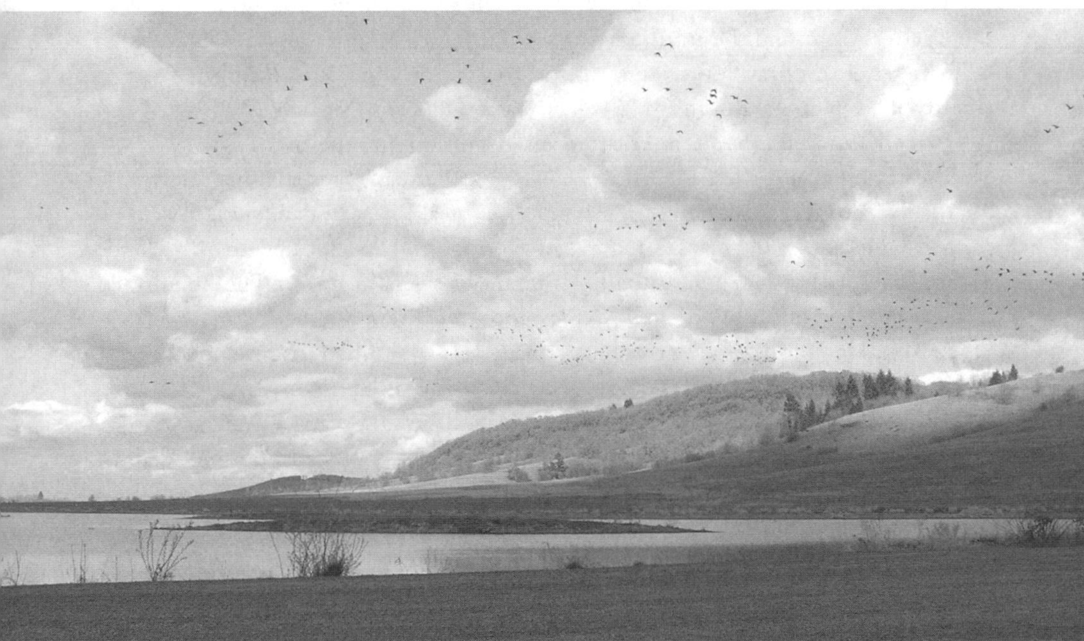

Baskett Slough National Wildlife Refuge, along with Ankeny and Finley NWRs, are major wintering sites for waterfowl.

shorebirds, waterfowl, and raptors. Watch for Northern Shrikes, mixed sparrow flocks, and Western Bluebirds. Please note that the land on either side of the road is private property, but traffic is very light and good birding can be had along the road. Livermore Road ends at Bethel Road, which will take you east to OR 99W.

Ankeny National Wildlife Refuge

Ankeny National Wildlife Refuge covers 2,796 acres of farmland, marshes, and riparian woods. From I–5, about 12 miles south of Salem, take exit 243 and drive west about 0.25 mile. At the intersection turn right onto Ankeny Hill Road and continue 1.5 miles to the Ankeny Overlook, where you will find restrooms and an observation deck. Scan the farm fields and tree lines for waterfowl and raptors in the winter.

Continue on Ankeny Hill Road to Buena Vista Road and turn left. There are several pullouts along this road before you reach the kiosk at Eagle Marsh. This is one of the larger bodies of water on the refuge, so it attracts diving ducks as well as dabblers.

Continue on Buena Vista to Wintel Road and turn left. After about 1 mile you will cross a set of railroad tracks. A gravel parking lot overlooking Pintail Marsh is just past the tracks, on the north side of the road. This is an excellent site for waterfowl. During the open season walk east to Frog Pond. When water levels are low, this little pond attracts migrant shorebirds, such as Long-billed Dowitchers, both yellowlegs, and Wilson's Snipes. Watch for Green Herons and other waders. Check the large snags around the north end of the pond for woodpeckers and raptors.

Just east of this gravel lot is the parking area for the Pintail and Egret Marsh Boardwalk. Open all year, this 0.25-mile boardwalk leads through a brushy riparian corridor and ends at an observation blind overlooking the marshes.

The parking lot for the Rail Trail is a little farther east. This trail includes a boardwalk through a wetland of Oregon ash. Typical forest birds include Black-capped Chickadees, Bewick's Wrens, Downy Woodpeckers, Spotted Towhees, and White-breasted Nuthatches. Watch for migrant warblers in spring. The boardwalk ends at an observation blind overlooking Wood Duck Pond. Check for Wood Ducks and Hooded Mergansers when water levels are high and shorebirds when levels are low. The boardwalk section of the Rail Trail is open all year.

During the open season you can continue past the observation blind to two other trails. If you continue straight across the dike, the trail leads into woodland habitat. Follow the trail through the woods to another dike, turn right and follow the dike trail back to the observation blind. If you turn left after the observation blind, the trail loops around Dunlin Pond and overlooks farm fields. This area can be very good for shorebirds in the summer, depending on water levels. The trail rejoins the Rail Trail near the beginning of the boardwalk.

Continue east on Wintel Road, taking advantage of two additional pullouts. Just past the refuge boundary, Wintel Road turns north and returns you to your starting point near I–5.

24 Marys Peak

Habitats: Wet forest, meadow

Elevation: 4,000 feet

What to see: Songbirds, raptors, grouse

Specialty birds: Ruffed and Sooty Grouse; Northern Pygmy-Owl; Hairy and Pileated Woodpeckers; Hutton's Vireo; Gray and Steller's Jays; Western Bluebird; Snow Bunting; Gray-crowned Rosy-Finch

Best months: October-December for Snow Buntings and Gray-crowned Rosy-Finches; May–July for nesting forest species

Directions: From the town of Corvallis, take U.S. Highway 20/Oregon Route 34 west to the town of Philomath. Where the two highways diverge, turn left to stay on OR 34. Follow this road about 10 miles, and then turn right onto Forest Service Road 30 (Marys Peak Road) and right again onto Forest Service Road 3010. (atlas, p. 198)

The Birding

Although included in this section of the book because of its close proximity to Corvallis in the Willamette Valley, Marys Peak *(fee)* is actually the highest point in the Coast Range and part of the Siuslaw National Forest. A mature forest of noble fir covers most of the mountain. The summit is covered by an open meadow, which attracts edge and grassland species.

Shortly after the turnoff from FS 30 onto FS 3010, a short spur on the right leads to Conner's Camp Picnic area. From here you can access the East Ridge Trail, which leads to the summit in 2.6 miles. If you continue past the turnoff for Conner's Camp, you will soon come to another parking area at milepost 5.5. The gate at this point is locked from December 1 to April 1 (sometimes later due to heavy snow). If the gate is closed, you can park your car and walk up the road toward the peak, a distance of about 4 miles.

Follow FS 3010 up the mountain, stopping at turnouts along the way to watch and listen for forest birds. Sooty Grouse can be common along this road. A small day-use area and a trailhead for the Meadowedge Trail are at Mary's Peak Campground, but parking and facilities are better at Observation Point, just a little farther up the road.

Observation Point has a large parking lot, picnic tables, restrooms, and lovely views of the Cascades and Coast Range. From here you can access the North Ridge Trail, which leads north down the mountain; the East Ridge Trail, which leads to Conner's Camp; and the short Summit Trail, which leads rather indirectly to the peak. For an easier, and perhaps more productive, route to the summit, walk past the gate and up the gravel road to the top of the mountain. It is along this road where Gray-crowned Rosy-Finches and Snow Buntings are most often

The grassy meadows at the top of Marys Peak attract snow buntings and Gray-crowned Rosy-Finches in autumn and winter.

reported. Check the grassy areas for sparrow flocks. Savannah, Song, White-crowned, and Golden-crowned Sparrows can be expected.

From the Summit Trail, you can access the Meadowedge Trail (also accessible from the campground). This loop trail circles a grove of mature noble firs and crosses a small stream. Watch for owls and woodpeckers in the larger trees. Winter Wrens and various thrushes use the brushy habitat along the stream.

25 Fern Ridge Reservoir and Wildlife Area

Habitats: Lake, marsh, grassland, riparian, farmland, brush, wet forest

Elevation: 400 feet

What to see: Wintering and nesting waterfowl, marsh species, shorebirds, raptors, migrant and nesting songbirds

Specialty birds: American Bittern; White-tailed Kite; Red-shouldered Hawk; Wilson's Phalarope; Black Tern; Acorn Woodpecker; Marsh Wren; Swainson's Thrush; Grasshopper Sparrow; Yellow-headed Blackbird

Best months: All year

Directions: Fern Ridge Reservoir lies about 10 miles west of Eugene. From the city you can access the area by driving west on Oregon Route 126, Royal Avenue, or Clear Lake Road. (atlas, p. 199)

The Birding

Marshes and grasslands cover the east side of the Fern Ridge Reservoir area, while the west side provides more wooded and brushy habitats. The open water of the lake itself is best viewed from the dam at the north side. Water levels vary greatly throughout the year, with the highest levels in April and the lowest in November. As the water recedes throughout summer and autumn, extensive mudflats provide habitat for migrant shorebirds. Much of the area to the south and east of the reservoir is included in the Fern Ridge Wildlife Area. Parts of the wildlife area may be closed during various seasons to protect wintering and nesting waterfowl. Look for signs listing closures at any of the parking areas or check at the area headquarters.

Fern Ridge Wildlife Area (South Units)

From Eugene drive west on OR 126 (11th Avenue). Bear left on Neilson Road, which curves south to intersect Cantrell Road. Turn west onto Cantrell, stopping at the wildlife area headquarters if you need maps and other information, and continue west to Central Road. Driving north on Central will lead you back to OR 126. This loop takes you around the East Coyote and West Coyote Units of Fern Ridge Wildlife Area. The habitats here are mostly farm fields, brush, and riparian woods. In winter watch for large numbers of Cackling and Canada Geese feeding in the fields. Check brushy areas for sparrow flocks. White-tailed Kites and Red-shouldered Hawks are two of the more interesting raptors that hunt in this area. During summer look for Vesper and Savannah Sparrows, Lazuli Buntings, Bullock's Orioles, and Lesser and American Goldfinches.

Fern Ridge Wildlife Area (East Units)

Take OR 126 west from Eugene. The parking area for the Fisher Butte Unit is on the north side of the highway, about 0.5 mile west of the intersection with Fisher Road. Check the farm fields for grazing waterfowl and the brushy areas for sparrows.

The grassland research area to the east hosts Western Meadowlarks and other grassland species.

One of the better birding sites at Fern Ridge is the west end of Royal Avenue. You can follow Royal Avenue west out of Eugene, or from OR 126 drive north on Fisher Road to its intersection with Royal Avenue. There is a grove of oaks at this intersection. Pull over here and look for the resident Acorn Woodpeckers. Continue west on Royal Avenue to the parking area at the end of the road.

Royal Avenue divides the Fisher Butte Unit from the Royal Amazon Unit. Walk along the dikes of the Fisher Butte Unit to look for breeding marsh species. Grasshopper Sparrows are rare breeders in the fields near the parking lot. In the winter watch for White-tailed Kites (which sometimes roost in good numbers), winter sparrow flocks, and Short-eared Owls.

South-side Parks

Two sites at the southern end of the reservoir provide good birding for passerines in wooded habitats and access to mudflats, which attract migrant shorebirds.

Perkins Peninsula Park is a favorite among local birders. A trail and boardwalk run along the west side of the park, providing easy birding. From OR 126, across

Black-bellied Plover

from Central Road, turn north into the park. Restrooms are available here. An entrance fee is charged from May through September.

Return to the highway and continue west to Ellmaker Road. Drive north on Ellmaker and turn right onto Jeans Road. Follow Jeans to the entrance of Zumwalt Park. Park near the entrance gate and explore the various wooded and open habitats. In addition to the typical songbirds, watch for the introduced Wild Turkeys in this area.

Fern Ridge Wildlife Area (Applegate Unit)

Drive west on either Jeans Road or OR 126 to Territorial Road and turn north. On the east side of Territorial Road, you will pass two parking areas that provide access to the Applegate Unit of the wildlife area. The first lot is the Long Tom River Access. Trails follow the river through riparian woods and meadows. The second access point is just north of the little town of Elmira. This area's brushy and wooded habitats are good for upland species.

Kirk Park and Fern Ridge Dam

Continue north on Territorial Road and turn east onto Clear Lake Road. Just north of Fern Ridge Dam is Kirk Park. Park in the lot and explore the brushy habitats around Kirk Pond. Wrentits are among the many resident and migrant songbirds to be found here. From Kirk Park, you can walk under Clear Lake Road to the dam to scope for gulls and waterfowl in winter.

Continue east on Clear Lake Road to Green Hill Road. Turn south to return to Royal Avenue or OR 126.

26 Salt Creek/Waldo Lake Area

Habitats: Wet forest, lake, riparian, meadow

Elevation: 4,000 feet–5,400 feet

What to see: Forest species, waterfowl

Specialty birds: Sooty Grouse; Bald Eagle; Boreal Owl; Black Swift; American Three-toed and Black-backed Woodpeckers; Townsend's Solitaire; Townsend's and Hermit Warblers

Best months: May–October

Directions: From Eugene drive about 64 miles southeast on Oregon Route 58. (atlas, p. 200)

The Birding

Large water features surrounded by high-elevation forest create several excellent birding sites in this area. The scenery attracts more than birds and birders, however, so summer weekends are often very crowded with campers and boaters. Mosquitoes are also quite numerous from June to August. Winter snows prevent access to some of these sites, so most birding is limited to summer and autumn.

Salt Creek Falls *(fee)*

From OR 58, 23 miles east of Oakridge, turn at the sign for Salt Creek Falls Observation Site. From the large parking area, walk to the falls overlook. Salt Creek Falls is a reliable site for Black Swifts in summer. Look for the swifts early in the morning or in the evening. A hiking trail leads down through mature forest to the base of the falls. Watch for both forest and riparian species along this trail. The brushy riparian zone upstream of the falls can be very productive as well.

Waldo Lake *(fee)*

About 2 miles east of Salt Creek Falls on OR 58, turn north onto Forest Service Road 5897 toward Waldo Lake. Waldo Lake is a large natural lake with three campgrounds on its eastern shore (Shadow Bay, Islet, and North Waldo from south to north).

The campgrounds are best avoided on busy summer weekends (Shadow Bay and Islet are not quite as busy as North Waldo), but there are numerous hiking trails in the area that provide birding opportunities. South of the campgrounds, trailheads on FS 5897 lead to Bobby Lake to the east and Betty Lake to the west. Other trails lead all the way around Waldo Lake (20 miles) and into the Waldo Lake Wilderness. Look for Gray Jays, Mountain and Chestnut-backed Chickadees, and Western Tanagers among the typical forest species.

FS 5897 forks as it approaches the north end of Waldo Lake. The left fork leads to Islet and North Waldo Campgrounds. The right fork is Taylor Burn Road, a rough track unsuitable for most cars. North on this track is one of the more reliable sites for Boreal Owls. The owls are most frequently heard calling in September and October.

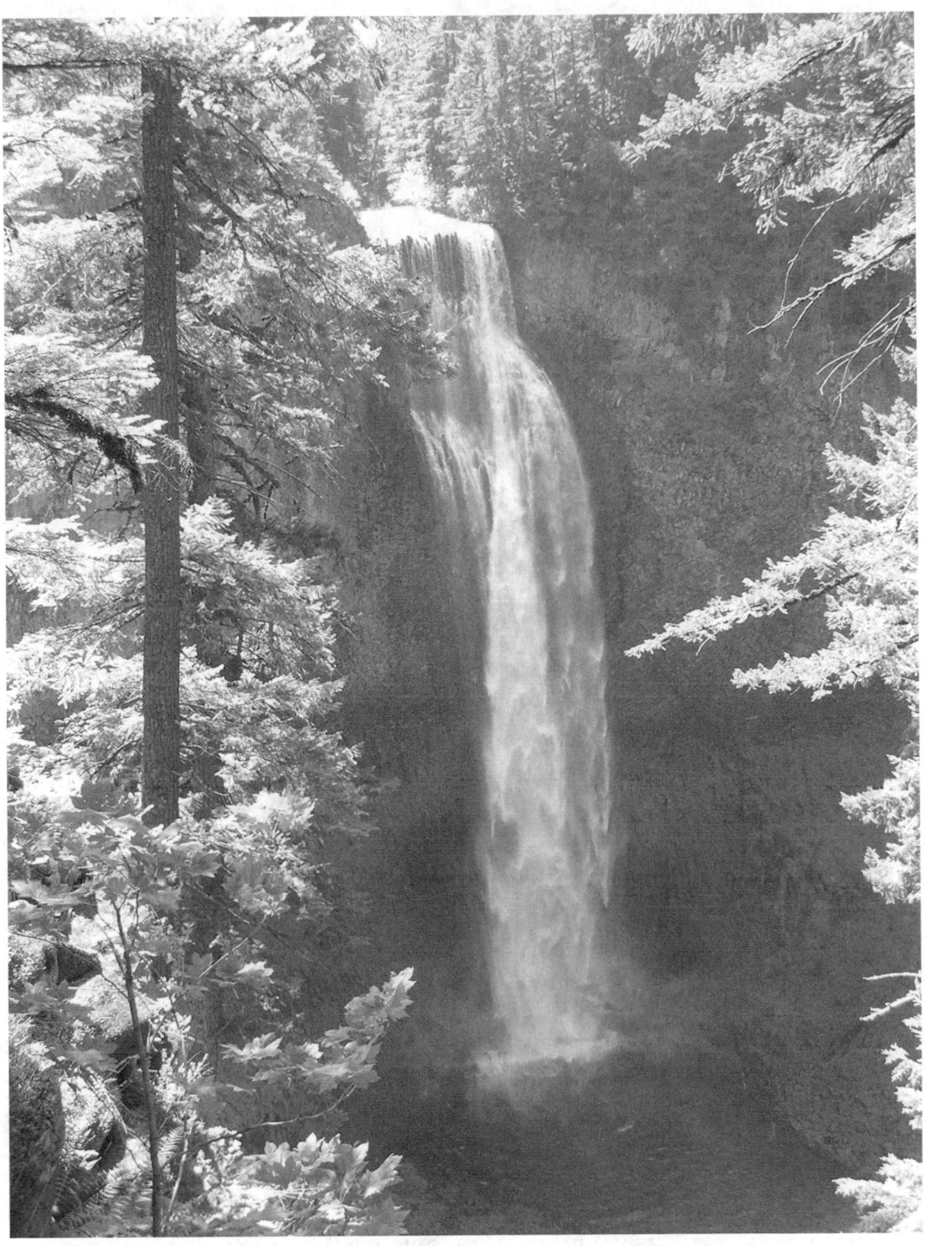

Salt Creek Falls, the second highest in the state, is a reliable site for Black Swifts.

Gold Lake

Return to OR 58 and continue east for another 2 miles. Turn north onto Gold Lake Road (Forest Service Road 500) and drive 2 miles to the campground and day-use area. Follow the trail along the west shore of the lake to the Gold Lake Bog. Watch for Spotted Sandpipers, Virginia Rails, and Soras in the wet areas.

Odell Lake

From OR 58, about 1 mile east of Gold Lake Road, turn south onto Forest Service Road 5810 and drive 2 miles to Trapper Creek Campground. Here you will find a nice combination of conifer forest, open water, and riparian habitat. Two trails at this end of Odell Lake lead into the Diamond Peak Wilderness. The Yoran Lake Trail (Trail 49) runs 5.3 miles through forest and wet meadows to Yoran Lake. The Whitefish Creek Trail (Trail 42) runs along Trapper Creek.

Davis Lake

Return to OR 58 and continue east for about 9 miles. Bear left onto the Crescent Cutoff Road (Forest Service Road 61) and, after 4 miles, turn left onto the Cascade Lakes Highway (Forest Service Road 46) toward Davis Lake. (If you continue east on FS 61, past the turnoff for FS 46, you will soon come to Crescent Creek Campground. The riparian habitat here has hosted nesting Northern Waterthrushes, a difficult species to find in Oregon.)

The Davis Lake area contains meadows, burned and unburned forests, and riparian corridors. Sandhill Cranes nest in the meadows, while Western Grebes, American White Pelicans, and various waterfowl can be seen on the lake. Black-backed Woodpeckers are common in the large areas of forest burned by The Davis Fire of 2003. Typical forest species include Olive-sided Flycatcher, Western Wood-Pewee, Steller's Jay, Mountain Chickadee, Yellow-rumped Warbler, and Pine Siskin.

FS 46 runs north, skirting the eastern shore of Davis Lake. Near the south end of the lake, turn into the East Davis Lake Campground to access the lake and the riparian corridor along Odell Creek. The entrance to Lava Flow Campground is farther north on FS 46. The rocky habitat near this part of the lake attracts open-country birds, such as Mountain Bluebirds, Green-tailed Towhees, and Rock Wrens.

Forest Service Road 4660 intersects FS 46 both north and south of Davis Lake, forming a loop around the west side. The birding along this road is often more productive than along the highway, but this road may not be suitable for all cars.

Wickiup Reservoir

Wickiup Reservoir is a large impoundment just northeast of Davis Lake. The best time to bird Wickiup is in autumn, when boaters and campers are fewer, migrant waterfowl are plentiful, and water levels drop to form extensive mudflats. Waterfowl and gulls are best viewed from the dam. Mudflats at the upper reaches of the lake attract shorebirds, American Pipits, and occasional longspurs. The southern shore is part of the Davis Burn, while the northern shore is adjacent to unburned forest.

From FS 46 turn east onto Forest Service Road 44 to access the south shore of Wickiup Reservoir. This gravel road leads to Reservoir and Round Swamp Campgrounds.

To access the north shore from FS 46, turn east onto Forest Service Road 42 (paved) and then south onto Twin Lakes Road to Gull Point Campground. A gravel road continues around the north shore of the lake to the dam.

Southwest Oregon

Habitats in southwest Oregon range from the wet conifer forests of the Siskiyou and Cascade Mountains to dry chaparral on the valley floors to the expansive wetlands of the Klamath Basin.

The weather in this region of the state varies with elevation. Higher sites near the coast receive more than 100 inches of precipitation each year, while some valleys receive only 20 inches. Summer temperatures frequently climb above 90 degrees, while winter temperatures are often well below freezing.

The avian specialties of southwest Oregon's drier habitats include California Quail, Common Poorwill, Acorn Woodpecker, Oak Titmouse, Blue-gray Gnatcatcher, California Towhee, and Lesser Goldfinch.

In the higher elevation forests, the bird life is similar to that of other forests in western Oregon. Gray-crowned Rosy-Finches, Clark's Nutcrackers, and Gray Jays live in the higher reaches of Crater Lake National Park. A few Spotted Owls remain in the Siskiyou National Forest and Great Gray Owls are occasionally found in the Cascades and in the northern Klamath Basin.

The Klamath Basin is famous as a staging area for migrant and wintering waterfowl. These birds, in turn, attract large concentrations of wintering Bald Eagles. Nesting species of special interest to birders in the Klamath Basin include Red-necked, Western, and Clark's Grebes; American and Least Bitterns; White-faced Ibis; Yellow Rail; and Tricolored Blackbird.

27 Sutherlin Area

Habitats: Lake, marsh, wet forest
Elevation: 500 feet
What to see: Migrant waterfowl, wetland species, raptors
Specialty birds: Osprey; Bald Eagle; Virginia Rail; Sora; Purple Martin; Tricolored Blackbird
Best months: April for wetland birds: October–April for waterfowl
Directions: Sutherlin is located along Interstate 5 about 12 miles north of Roseburg. (atlas, p. 205)

The Birding

Three sites near the town of Sutherlin provide quick birding stops, offering a respite from the tedium of driving the I–5 corridor. Ford's Pond is less than 2 miles off the interstate and can be checked in just a few minutes. Plat I and Cooper Creek Reservoirs are about 5 miles off the highway and allow longer birding rest stops.

Fords Pond

From I–5, take the exit for Oregon Route 138 west. In about 1.5 miles, turn left onto Church Road. Fords Pond will be on your right. A small cattail marsh will be on your left. This area is all private property, but there are several spots where you can pull off to the side of the road to view the water. Search the marshy edges for rails, Pied-billed Grebes, and Green Herons. Tricolored Blackbirds have nested in the cattails at the north end of Church Road. Flocks of waterfowl use the pond during migration and winter.

Plat I Reservoir

Retrace your route back to Sutherlin, continuing east on Central Avenue. At the east edge of town, Central Avenue becomes Nonpareil Road. A little more than 4 miles from the interstate, turn south onto Plat I Road, then turn left at the sign for the reservoir to reach the boat launch area at the dam. This is the only public access to Plat I Reservoir, but from this site you can see the whole lake. Scan the flocks of waterfowl during migration and winter. It is also possible to sight transient gulls. In summer look for Purple Martins, Ospreys, and Pied-billed Grebes. As with any reservoir, check the shores during low-water periods for migrant shorebirds. The county road completely circles the lake if you want to do a little birding from the car. The surrounding farmland and brushy habitats can be good for songbirds.

Cooper Creek Reservoir County Park

Return west on Nonpareil Road, turning south at the sign for Cooper Creek Reservoir. Enter the park and turn into the first boat launch area, located near the dam and restrooms. From this site you can scan the reservoir for waterfowl and the brushy riparian area below the dam for songbirds. Cooper Creek Road generally follows the north shore of the lake with several pullouts along the way. The area around the lake is wooded, attracting such species as Rufous Hummingbird, Steller's and Western Scrub-Jays, Chestnut-backed and Black-capped Chickadees, and Pileated Woodpeckers. Follow the road to the end of the lake, where you will find another boat launch area, restrooms, a swimming beach, and a cattail marsh.

28 Grants Pass Area

Habitats: Wet forest, meadow, chaparral, riparian

Elevation: 860 feet–2000 feet

What to see: Forest species, chaparral specialties, migrant songbirds

Specialty birds: Mountain Quail; Oak Titmouse; Blue-gray Gnatcatcher; California Towhee; Wrentit; Lesser Goldfinch; Black Phoebe; Red-shouldered Hawk

Best months: All year; songbirds most abundant May–October

Directions: Grants Pass is located along Interstate 5, about 30 miles north of the California border. (atlas, p. 205)

The Birding

Habitats around Grants Pass include the mature woodlands of Siskiyou National Forest, dry chaparral, and the riparian corridor along the scenic Rogue River.

Manzanita Rest Area

The Manzanita Rest Area is located on northbound I–5, just north of the Merlin exit. If you are in the northbound lane, you can simply pull into the rest area. If you are southbound or want to explore the area more thoroughly, leave the interstate at exit 61 (the Merlin exit), go east to Highland Avenue, and take Highland north toward Sportsman's Park. Highland parallels the interstate, so follow it north until you see the rest area on your left. You can park near the rest area or continue north and park at a wide spot in the road at the entrance to Sportsman's Park. If you reached the site from I–5, walk through the back of the rest area to reach Highland Avenue.

This site is famous among Oregon birders as a quick stop to find Oak Titmice, California Towhees, and Blue-gray Gnatcatchers. Search the brushy habitat along Highland for these three species. The wooded hillside east of the road is private property, but birding is good from the road. The rest area itself is good for Western Bluebirds, Lesser Goldfinches, and mixed winter sparrow flocks.

Forest Service Road 25

This road, also known as Briggs Valley Road and Taylor Creek Road, provides easy access into Siskiyou National Forest. The road is paved for about 15 miles, turns to gravel, then is paved again as it approaches U.S. Highway 199 southwest of Grants Pass, a total distance of 30 miles. Many side roads and trails connect to FS 25. These are worth exploring on foot if you have the time. To reach FS 25 take I–5 north from Grants Pass to the Merlin exit, travel west on Galice Road about 8.4 miles (stopping to enjoy stunning views of the Rogue River along the way), and turn left onto FS 25.

FS 25 climbs for about 10.6 miles before starting its decent into Briggs Valley. Watch for Mountain Quail crossing the road from mile 8 on. Family groups of these birds can be quite common in late summer.

Big Pine Campground is located about 12 miles up FS 25. Park in the day-use area and explore the easy loop trails along the creek and through mature pine forest.

At mile 13.3 you will see a sign for a horse camp on your right. Turn *left* here and park in the wide spot on the right side of the gravel road. Walk a little way down this road and past the locked gate to the Horse Creek Wildlife Area. The wet coniferous forest soon gives way to a meadow. Continue along the road. As you climb the length of the valley, the habitat along the edge of the meadow changes from pine forest to mixed hardwoods to ceanothus brush fields. The bird life changes accordingly, starting with forest species, such as Band-tailed Pigeons and Wild Turkeys, and progressing to MacGillivray's Warblers, Western Tanagers, Say's Phoebes, Wrentits, and Lazuli Buntings.

Return to FS 25. From here you can continue south toward US 199, stopping occasionally to look and listen for forest species, or retrace your route north to Galice Road.

Whitehorse County Park

This little park along the Rogue River, with its grasslands, brushy thickets, sloughs and ponds, and groves of large cottonwoods, has attracted 170 species of birds. From Grants Pass travel west on G Street, which becomes Upper River Road. Whitehorse County Park will be on your left in about 7.6 miles.

If you are starting from Merlin, drive south on Azalea Drive to Upper River Road and turn right. Enter the park and drive past the camping area to the parking lot at the day-use area by the river.

Paths lead both upstream and down from the parking area. Yellow-breasted Chats and Wrentits are common in the blackberry thickets. In winter, these same thickets attract a good variety of sparrows. The river attracts five species of swallows, Ospreys, waterfowl, and occasional shorebirds. The wooded areas attract flycatchers, vireos, woodpeckers, Red-shouldered Hawks, and a host of migrants. Be aware that low-lying areas close to the river are prone to flooding.

29 Medford Area

Habitats: Lake, grassland, oak savannah, mixed forest, chaparral, riparian, rimrock

Elevation: 1,000 feet–3,600 feet

What to see: Migrant and nesting songbirds, waterfowl, shorebirds

Specialty birds: Green Heron; Osprey; Common Poorwill; Acorn Woodpecker; Ash-throated Flycatcher; Oak Titmouse; White-breasted Nuthatch; Blue-gray Gnatcatcher; Western Bluebird; Wrentit; Yellow-breasted Chat; Spotted and California Towhees; Lark Sparrow; Western Meadowlark; Lesser Goldfinch

Best months: All year

Directions: Medford is located along Interstate 5, about 22 miles north of the California border. (atlas, p. 205)

The Birding

Several good birding sites lie close to Medford. Changes in habitats, ranging from lush riparian corridor to oak and mixed woodlands to chaparral and rimrock, are determined by changes in elevation.

Prescott Park

From I–5 in Medford take exit 27 and drive east on Barnett Road. After 2 miles turn north onto Phoenix Road, then turn east onto Hillcrest Road and follow it for 2 miles to the sign for Prescott Park. Turn left onto Roxy Ann Road. After 0.5 mile you will come to a gate, which is usually open during daylight hours. In another mile you will reach another gate, which is usually either locked or posted AUTHORIZED VEHICLES ONLY. Park here and continue walking up the road. It is approximately 2.5 miles from the second gate to the top of the butte.

Prescott Park encompasses most of Roxy Ann Peak. The sides of the peak are covered with grasses and shrubs at the lower elevations, changing to oak woodlands and eventually to mixed conifer-hardwood forest near the peak. The bird species change accordingly, with Lazuli Buntings, Blue-gray Gnatcatchers, Oak Titmice, Acorn Woodpeckers, and California Quail inhabiting the lower levels, and Mountain Quail, Mountain Chickadees, and Red-breasted Nuthatches appearing near the summit. Winter residents include Ruby-crowned Kinglets, Yellow-rumped Warblers, and Golden-crowned Sparrows.

As housing development increases around the base of Roxy Ann Peak, the protected areas of Prescott Park become increasingly important to migrant and nesting species alike.

Agate Lake

From Medford take Oregon Route 62 north for 5.5 miles, turn east onto Oregon Route 140 for 3.5 miles, and then turn right onto East Antelope Road. After 0.7 mile make a sharp right turn at the sign for Agate Lake.

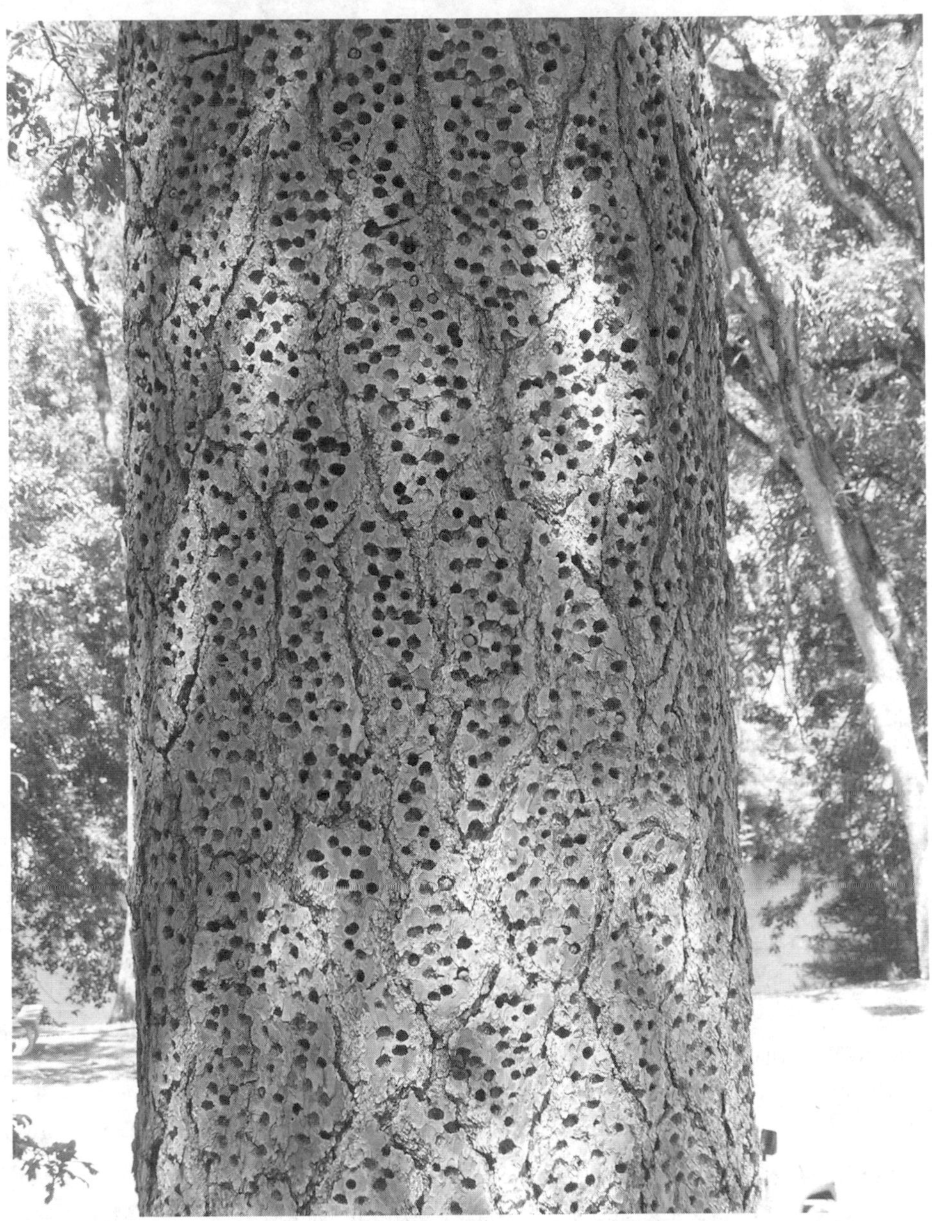

This large pine at Tou Velle State Park serves as a larder for the local Acorn Woodpeckers.

The entrance road to Agate Lake passes through grassland, blackberry thickets, and oak savannah before reaching the western shore of the lake. Lark Sparrows and Western Meadowlarks are found in the grassy areas. Tricolored Blackbirds have nested in the thickets along the entrance road. The typical oak-associated species become more obvious as you get closer to the lakeshore.

In August and September lower water levels expose mudflats, making this site one of the better spots in the Rogue Valley for migrant shorebirds. The eastern shore of the lake often has better shorebird habitat. To reach the east shore, return to East Antelope Road, continue past the sign for Agate Lake, and turn right onto Dry Creek Road. Turn right onto the gravel Old Dry Creek Road, then turn right again onto a dirt road that leads to the shore.

The lake itself attracts migrant and wintering gulls and waterbirds, including Western Grebes, American White Pelicans, Great Egrets, Wood Ducks, Ring-necked Ducks, and Common Mergansers.

Tou Velle State Park/Denman Wildlife Area

From I–5 take exit 33 and drive east on Biddle Road. In less than 1 mile, turn north onto Table Rock Road and proceed about 4 miles to the Tou Velle State Park entrance on your right *(fee)*. Drive through the park to the last parking area near the restrooms.

Despite its rather manicured parklike atmosphere, Tou Velle State Park provides easy access to good riparian and marsh habitats. The oaks in the picnic areas are home to Acorn Woodpeckers (note the large pine that serves as a granary, located near the restrooms at the last parking area), Oak Titmice, White-breasted Nuthatches, and Black-capped Chickadees.

From the parking lot follow the trail along the river. Yellow-breasted Chats nest here, along with Western Wood-Pewees, Black-headed Grosbeaks, and Lesser Goldfinches. Watch the river for Spotted Sandpipers, Common Mergansers, and Ospreys.

The trail leads out of the state park and into the Denman Wildlife Area. The extensive cattail marshes here are flooded in winter, and then they dry out by late summer. This area is open to hunting in the fall and winter. Follow the path until it intersects a dirt road leading to the right. Take this road toward a small pond, where a trail leads off to the right through marsh, oaks, and meadow back to the park, completing a 2-mile loop. Watch the marshes for Marsh Wrens, Soras, and Virginia Rails, and watch the upland grassy areas for Western Meadowlarks, Northern Harriers, and White-tailed Kites.

Returning to Table Rock Road, check out the boat launch area on the left side of the road just north of the park entrance. There is additional riparian habitat here.

Upper Table Rock/Lower Table Rock

These two mesas each rise about 1,000 feet above the valley floor. Their slopes contain grasslands, oak savannah, mixed woodland, and chaparral leading up to rimrock and meadows at the top. The typical birds of brush and oak woodland dominate the lower levels, replaced by woodland birds such as Bewick's and Winter Wrens, Cassin's and Hutton's Vireos, and Hermit Thrushes at higher levels. Check the rimrock areas for Canyon and Rock Wrens and Common Poorwills.

Both mesas harbor unique plant communities and are protected by the Nature Conservancy and the Bureau of Land Management (BLM). Stay on established

The Rogue River runs through Tou Velle State Park.

trails to protect the vegetation. Both sites have similar bird species. Since Lower Table Rock is a little more popular with hikers, Upper Table Rock might be a better bet for busy summer weekends.

To reach Upper Table Rock, continue north on Table Rock Road past the entrance for Tou Velle State Park. Take the right fork onto Modoc Road for 1.4 miles to the parking lot on your left. For Lower Table Rock, stay on Table Rock Road past Modoc Road, turn left onto Wheeler Road, then turn left again into the parking lot for the Lower Table Rock Trail.

Kirtland Road Sewage Ponds

From Table Rock Road, just south of Tou Velle State Park, turn west onto Kirtland Road. You will see the Vernon Thorpe Regional Water Reclamation Facility in about 1 mile on the right. This facility is fenced off, but you can ask at the office for permission to bird the ponds. East of the buildings are shallow ponds, which, if they aren't completely dry, attract migrant shorebirds. West of the buildings is a larger body of water, which can be good for waterfowl and gulls in winter. This pond can be scanned from Kirtland Road if you pull off at the locked gate.

30 Ashland Area

Habitats: Alpine meadows, dry forest, chaparral, lake, riparian, oak woodland

Elevation: 1,900 feet–6,700 feet

What to see: Migrant and nesting songbirds, mountain specialties, waterfowl

Specialty birds: Sooty Grouse; Mountain Quail; Acorn and Pileated Woodpeckers; Gray Jay; Oak Titmouse; Townsend's Solitaire; Western Bluebird; Wrentit; Green-tailed, Spotted, and California Towhees; Grasshopper, Lincoln's, and Fox Sparrows; Purple and Cassin's Finches

Best months: May–October for Mount Ashland, Howard Prairie and Hyatt Lakes, and Forest Service Road 37; all year for Bear Creek Greenway and Emigrant Lake

Directions: Ashland is located along Interstate 5, 15 miles from the California border. (atlas, p. 205)

Oak Titmice and Acorn Woodpeckers are common in the oak woodlands around Emigrant Lake.

The Birding

The habitats near Ashland include lower-elevation lakes and riparian habitats close to town, as well as higher-elevation lakes, meadows and woodlands to the south and east.

Bear Creek Greenway

From downtown Ashland drive north on Oak Street to Nevada Street. Turn left onto Nevada, then turn right onto a one-lane paved road opposite Helman Street. This road ends at a dog park with nice restrooms. Follow the path past the restrooms, past the sewage treatment plant, and across the bridge to join the bike path that runs along Bear Creek. This path continues for several miles through the towns of Talent and Central Point.

Bear Creek Greenway is an easy walk through riparian habitats of cottonwoods, willows, and blackberry thickets. The site is most productive during spring migration. Typical resident species include California Quail, Western Scrub-Jay, Wrentit, Spotted Towhee, and Lesser Goldfinch. Less common birds include Ash-throated Flycatchers, Anna's Hummingbirds, and Black Phoebes.

Mount Ashland

From I–5, take exit 6 to Old 99 south for about 0.8 mile, then turn right onto Mount Ashland Road. Follow this paved road about 8.5 miles to the ski area. If you continue past the ski area, the road turns to gravel and you soon come to a small campground, which provides another place to park. Be advised that a Sno-Park pass is required from November 15 to April 30, but birding is not as productive at this high-elevation site at that time of year.

From the parking lot, walk on the gravel road to explore meadows and stands of coniferous forest. Typical birds include Rufous Hummingbirds, Green-tailed Towhees, Olive-sided Flycatchers, Steller's Jays, and Mountain Chickadees. Sooty Grouse and Mountain Quail are both found here. The meadows are home to Lincoln's Sparrows and Lazuli Buntings, while the large spruces attract Hermit Warblers, Townsend's Solitaires, and Cassin's Finches. White-headed Woodpeckers are uncommon residents in the area.

If you walk the gravel road for 2 miles, take the left fork toward the Grouse Gap Shelter. The Pacific Crest Trail intersects this road. Take the trail back to the ski area, passing through wet meadows and woods along the way.

Emigrant Lake

From I–5 Exit 14 near Ashland, take Oregon Route 66 east about 3.5 miles to the turnoff for Emigrant Lake Park *(fee)*. The day-use area provides several small parking areas with picnic tables. The habitat is oak woodland surrounding the lakeshore. Acorn Woodpeckers, Oak Titmice, Red-breasted Sapsuckers, and Western Scrub-Jays use the oaks. Over the lake watch for Ospreys, Bald Eagles, and migrant waterfowl in season.

If summer weekend crowds reduce the bird activity in the picnic areas, try any of several access points around the reservoir. Stay on OR 66 past the main park entrance road. In 1.8 miles, just across from the Old Siskiyou Highway, there is a wide spot on the left where you can park. Walk down an old paved road about 0.5 mile to the lakeshore. If water levels are down, the muddy edges attract shorebirds, such as Least Sandpiper, yellowlegs, and Long-billed Dowitchers. The shrubby habitat on the way to the lake is home to California Quail and Lesser Goldfinches. Greensprings Spur is 2.7 miles past the entrance road. Check the oaks just after turning onto this road and then continue to the lake. Several trails run along the lakeshore and through grassland and oak habitat. The last access point to Emigrant Lake is Songer Wayside, 3 miles past the park entrance road.

Hyatt Lake/Howard Prairie Lake

From Ashland take OR 66 east past Emigrant Lake to Hyatt Prairie Road, just past milepost 17. Turn north onto Hyatt Prairie Road, which follows the shoreline of Hyatt Lake and continues on to Howard Prairie Lake. The resort areas around both lakes can be crowded and, therefore, not too birdy. But the less-traveled side roads and small campgrounds can be quite productive.

The Bureau of Land Management (BLM) maintains a wildlife viewing area on the west shore of Hyatt Lake. This small site provides good views of the water and can be quite good for land birds as well. Ospreys and Double-crested Cormorants nest in standing dead trees close to shore.

You'll find some of the best birding in the area by taking the side roads around Howard Prairie Lake. Buck Prairie Road (left from Hyatt Prairie Road) is a hard-surface road that will take you into good wooded habitat and along mountain meadows. Buck Prairie Road ends at a parking area along Dead Indian Road (Sno-Park pass required in winter). From here you can turn east toward the lake or west toward Ashland.

Just east of the intersection of Dead Indian Road and Buck Prairie Road, a left turn onto Conde Creek Canal Road leads to good wooded and meadow habitats along an irrigation ditch. If you go east on Dead Indian Road past the lake, turn right onto Keno Road to explore the area east of Howard Prairie Lake. Follow this road about 4.5 miles to the turnoff to the right that takes you around the south end of the lake before rejoining Hyatt Prairie Road.

Pay special attention to the meadows around both Hyatt and Howard Prairie Lakes. Great Gray Owls are occasionally seen in the area and Grasshopper Sparrows nest here.

Forest Service Road 37

From Dead Indian Road, east of Howard Prairie Lake, turn north onto FS 37 (Sno-Park pass required in winter). This paved road passes several small campgrounds and side roads that provide easy access to forest and riparian birds.

Buck Prairie Road provides access to woodlands and meadows west of Howard Prairie Lake.

Near the southern end of FS 37, Beaver Dam Campground contains the trailhead for the Beaver Dam Trail (2.1 miles), which passes the nearby Daly Creek Campground. Farther north North Fork Campground accesses the Fish Lake Trail, which leads toward the dam at Fish Lake in 0.6 miles.

After 8 miles FS 37 intersects Oregon Route 140, where you can turn left to reach the Medford area or turn right toward Upper Klamath Lake.

31 Upper Klamath Basin

Habitats: Marsh, wet meadow, lake, riparian, dry forest, wet forest

Elevation: 4,000 feet–5,000+ feet

What to see: Waterfowl, marsh species, forest species

Specialty birds: Tundra Swan; Red-necked, Western, and Clark's Grebes; American White Pelican; Least Bittern; Bald Eagle; Rough-legged Hawk; Yellow Rail; Black Tern; Flammulated and Great Gray Owls; White-headed Woodpecker; Gray Jay; Clark's Nutcracker; Pygmy, Red-breasted, and White-breasted Nuthatches; Tricolored Blackbird; Gray-crowned Rosy-Finch

Best months: May–early July for nesting species; October–April for waterfowl and raptors

Directions: The Klamath Basin extends north about 60 miles from the California border along U.S. Highway 97. (atlas, p. 206)

The Birding

The sites described in this section include those north of the city of Klamath Falls. Habitats range from the high-elevation forests of Crater Lake National Park to the wet meadows around Fort Klamath to the open waters of Agency and Upper Klamath Lakes. Several species that are hard to find elsewhere in Oregon regularly occur in this area. Klamath Falls contains many hotels and restaurants, but the tiny town of Fort Klamath is much closer to the sites described below.

Klamath Marsh National Wildlife Refuge

From US 97, about 45 miles north of Klamath Falls, turn east onto Silver Lake Road. Follow this road into Klamath Marsh National Wildlife Refuge. Silver Lake Road cuts through an expanse of tule and cattail marsh with canals on both sides of the road. Visibility is limited, and there is little opportunity to pull off the road, but waterfowl and raptors can be seen here, and Yellow Rails are heard after dark in the spring.

The only open-water viewing is in Wocus Bay, at the southeast corner of the refuge. *Unfortunately, the last few miles of road leading to Wocus Bay may not be passable in a normal passenger car.* To reach this area, continue east on Silver Lake Road. At 10.1 miles from US 97, bear right onto Forest Service Road 43 for 7.5 miles, then turn right onto Forest Service Road 4357 for about 2 miles to the west shore of Wocus Bay. This last road is unmaintained dirt, so proceed with extreme caution.

From Silver Lake Road continue east to Military Crossing Road (about 15 miles from US 97) and turn left. Military Crossing is a well-maintained gravel road, but may be dusty or muddy, depending on the weather. This section of Military Crossing Road runs through an impressive mature pine forest along the border of the refuge and Winema National Forest. Stop periodically to look for the typical forest birds. Pay special attention to areas where the forest meets meadow habitat, as these are the areas most likely to attract Great Gray Owls.

Follow Military Crossing Road west back into the marsh until the road crosses the Williamson River. Park here and scan the marsh for waterfowl, waders, rails, swallows, and Common Nighthawks. This is the most easily accessible viewing area for wetland species on the refuge and should be your first priority if time is limited. Continue west on Military Crossing Road to return to US 97 in about 8 miles.

Crater Lake National Park

Oregon's only national park so far, Crater Lake is home to a good variety of forest birds in the summer months. The south entrance to the park, accessible from Oregon Route 62, is open year-round. The famous Rim Drive, which encircles the lake, and the north entrance are closed in winter. The southern and eastern sections of the park are dominated by ponderosa pine forest, with typical birds including White-headed Woodpeckers, Pygmy Nuthatches, and Green-tailed Towhees. Lodgepole pine and mixed pine/hemlock forests cover the rest of the park. Watch for American Three-toed and Black-backed Woodpeckers, Steller's and Gray Jays, Clark's Nutcrackers, and Townsend's Solitaires in this habitat.

Just past the south entrance station, turn right into Mazama Campground and park near the amphitheater. The Annie Creek Canyon Trail is an easy 1.7-mile loop through riparian habitat. Watch for American Dippers, Swainson's Thrushes, and Wilson's, Yellow, and MacGillivray's Warblers.

From the park headquarters, about 3.6 miles from the south entrance station, walk the Castle Crest Wildflower Trail. This 1.1-mile loop runs through forest and meadow habitats. Rufous Hummingbirds are common and are sometimes joined by Calliope and Black-chinned Hummingbirds. Varied Thrushes, Golden-crowned Kinglets, Western Tanagers, and Winter Wrens nest here. Gray Jays and Clark's Nutcrackers can be found at the headquarters, Rim Village, and anywhere else there are people and food.

Many birders visiting the park are hoping to spot Gray-crowned Rosy-Finches. This species favors the highest elevations. Scan rocky slopes, meadows, and the edges of snowfields to find these birds. The Cloudcap overlook is the highest point in the park to which you can drive and makes a good spot to search for the finches. If you are up for a strenuous hike, the trails up to Mount Scott (8,929 feet) and The Watchman (8,013 feet) offer good Rosy-Finch habitat.

Fort Klamath

The tiny village of Fort Klamath is located along OR 62, about 30 miles north of Klamath Falls. The bird feeders at the post office and at the Aspen Inn are always good for a few Pine Siskins.

Park at the small cemetery just east of town, along OR 62, and explore the woods in the cemetery and around the adjacent dump. You will find Mountain

Military Crossing Road runs through the heart of Klamath Marsh National Wildlife Refuge.

Chickadee, Western Wood-Pewee, Pygmy Nuthatch, and other birds typical of the ponderosa pine forest. This site's claim to fame is the occasional Great Gray Owl.

A historical marker is just east of the cemetery along OR 62. Park here in the evening and listen for Yellow Rails in the wet sedge meadow behind the marker. For an auto loop tour of some excellent Yellow Rail habitat in this area, continue south on OR 62 and turn west onto Weed Road. This road goes west for about 2 miles, then it turns north. Continue on Weed Road to Loosley Road. You can drive east on Loosley to rejoin OR 62 or continue north on Weed to return to Fort Klamath. There are wet meadows and pastures throughout this area. Watch for raptors in these meadows in winter.

Sevenmile Guard Station

Sevenmile Guard Station sits at the very edge of Winema National Forest, providing a transition zone between forest and meadow/farmland habitats. From Fort

Klamath, drive 4 miles west on Nicholson Road. Continue straight onto Forest Service Road 3334 and immediately pull off into the gravel driveway just south of the guard station. Please note that Forest Service personnel may be living at the guard station in the summer, so birders should take care not to get too close to the building.

The combination of cottonwoods and aspen along the creek and the mixed conifer forest beyond make Sevenmile Guard Station an excellent site for woodland birds. Watch for Ruffed Grouse, warblers, and flycatchers along the creek, and American Dippers in the creek itself. Nesting species in the conifers include Flammulated, Northern Saw-whet, and Northern Pygmy-Owls; Mountain and Chestnut-backed Chickadees; and Pileated Woodpeckers.

Wood River Day-use Area

From OR 62, just east of Fort Klamath, drive north on Sun River Road (County Road 623) for 1 mile. Turn left onto the paved Forest Service Road 960 for 0.6 mile to the parking lot at Wood River Day-use Area. This grove of aspens and cottonwoods along the Wood River is attractive to sapsuckers, Warbling Vireos, Black-headed Grosbeaks, and a host of migrants. This is the best site in the Klamath area to spot Black-capped Chickadees among the common Mountain Chickadees. Watch for wetland species along the river. Black-billed Magpies and raptors utilize the open pastures beyond the river.

Take time to explore the wooded corridor along the entrance road to this site. The large pines attract all three species of nuthatches, woodpeckers, Cassin's Vireos, and Western Tanagers. Great Horned, Great Gray, and Northern Pygmy-Owls are all possible here.

Jackson F. Kimball State Park

From the Wood River Day-use Area, continue north on Sun Valley Road for another 1.8 miles to the entrance to Jackson F. Kimball State Park on the left. Drive to the campground and park. The woods here and the riparian habitat along the source of the Wood River are good for migrant and nesting songbirds in spring and early summer.

Agency Lake

From Fort Klamath drive south on OR 62 for about 7 miles and take the right fork onto Modoc Point Road. In 2 miles turn right into the Petric Park Boat Launch. This small county park is basically a parking lot and restroom, but it does provide views of the upper end of Agency Lake near the mouth of the Wood River. Make a quick check for waterfowl and marsh species.

Continue south on Modoc Point Road for another 0.5 mile to Wood River Wetlands. From the parking lot, walk past the gate to a series of trails that lead through marsh and riparian habitats. The wet areas are home to Black Terns, Wilson's Phalaropes, and American White Pelicans. Trees in the riparian areas support nesting Bullock's Orioles and Willow Flycatchers. This site is one of the more reliable nesting areas for Tricolored Blackbirds.

The last site along Agency Lake is Henzel County Park. This is another parking lot/restroom/boat launch park, but it provides excellent views of open water. Western and Clark's Grebes are common, along with a host of migrant waterfowl in spring and autumn. Continue south on Modoc Point Road to its intersection with US 97, 17 miles north of Klamath Falls.

West Side Road

The northwestern corner of Upper Klamath Lake contains the Upper Klamath National Wildlife Refuge, most of which is accessible only by boat. Several sites along West Side Road provide good birding in this transition zone between marsh and forest as well as access to the refuge's canoe trail. Yellow Rails and Least Bitterns are among the main attractions of this area. From Fort Klamath drive south on Weed Road, then drive west on Sevenmile Road until that road turns to the south and becomes West Side Road. If you are starting from Klamath Falls, drive west on Oregon Route 140 about 26 miles and turn north onto West Side Road.

Crystalwood Lodge is a private bed-and-breakfast located 9.6 miles north of the intersection of West Side Road and OR 140. Check with the office before birding this area of meadows and cottonwood/aspen groves. Yellow Rails have been found at the lodge's boat launch.

Malone Springs is located about 3.5 miles south of Crystalwood Lodge. Turn east at the sign for Malone Springs and continue 0.4 mile to the parking area and boat launch. You can bird along the abandoned road that leads north from the parking lot.

Rocky Point Resort is about 3 miles north of the OR 140/West Side Road intersection. Park at the boat launch (there are restrooms here) and walk out onto the floating pier. The pier provides a good vantage point from which to find Red-necked Grebes among the more common marsh species.

From the southern end of West Side Road, travel east on OR 140 about 3.5 miles to Forest Service Road 3639. Turn left onto this road, continue 1 mile to Odessa Creek Campground, and park in the day-use area. The pine forest here is good for White-headed and Pileated Woodpeckers and various songbirds. The brushy sloughs attract marsh species.

32 Lower Klamath Basin

Habitats: Lake, marsh, farmland, dry forest

Elevation: 4,100 feet

What to see: Migrant waterfowl and shorebirds, winter raptors

Specialty birds: Greater White-fronted, Snow, and Ross's Geese; Tundra Swan; Western, Clark's, and Eared Grebes; American White Pelican; American Bittern; Snowy Egret; White-faced Ibis; Bald Eagle; Rough-legged Hawk; Sandhill Crane; Bonaparte's, Ring-billed, and California Gulls; Forster's and Black Terns; Lewis's Woodpecker; Lapland Longspur; Snow Bunting; Tricolored and Yellow-headed Blackbirds

Best months: October–December and February–April for waterfowl; April–July for migrant and nesting shorebirds, marsh species, and songbirds; winter for raptors

Directions: These sites are close to the city of Klamath Falls, located on U.S. Highway 97 about 15 miles north of the California border. (atlas, p. 206)

The Birding

The Klamath Basin, which straddles the Oregon/California border, is one of the most important staging areas in North America for migrant waterfowl. These birds, in turn, attract large numbers of wintering Bald Eagles and other raptors. The flooded fields and shallow marshes harbor migrant shorebirds in the spring, with typical high-desert species staying to nest. The parks in the city of Klamath Falls, adjacent to Upper Klamath Lake, are great places to see migrant and nesting forest species, as well as gulls and waterfowl.

Howard Bay

Howard Bay is a large shallow bay at the southwest corner of Upper Klamath Lake. From Klamath Falls drive west on Lakeshore Drive to intersect Oregon Route 140. Continue west another 4 miles to the bridge over the Wocus Drainage Canal. Cross the bridge and immediately pull off to the wide gravel area on the left, being careful not to block the gate. Check the bridge for nesting swallows before walking along the dirt road by the canal. This is a good site for migrant songbirds in the spring. This is private property (Timber Resource Services), but birders are welcome to walk the road up into the forest.

Return to your car and continue west on OR 140 along the water's edge for 2 miles, where you will see a parking area on the right. Pull off here to watch for waterfowl, grebes, and Forster's and Black Terns. From here you can return to Klamath Falls or continue west on OR 140 to Odessa Creek Campground and West Side Road in Upper Klamath Basin.

Putnam's Point Park/Link River Trail

From US 97 in Klamath Falls, take the exit for Oregon Avenue and drive west on Nevada Street, which becomes Lakeshore Drive. Immediately after crossing the

Link River Bridge, turn right into Putnam's Point Park. This little park is a great site for Clark's and Western Grebes, gulls, and Black-crowned Night-Herons. Check the trees for migrant songbirds and the bushes for California Quail.

The northern terminus of the Link River Trail is just across the street from Putnam's Point. You can walk on this gravel path for 1.5 miles along the Link River to Lake Ewauna. This route serves as a migration corridor for migrants and for resident birds moving between Upper Klamath Lake and the Klamath River.

Moore Park

From Putnam's Point continue west on Lakeshore Drive another 0.5 mile to Moore Park. The parking area around the boat launch and restrooms provides good views of Upper Klamath Lake and its waterfowl. Walk any of the roads or trails uphill from here. The habitat changes from grassy parkland to juniper/sage steppe to pine forest. Lesser Goldfinches, White-breasted Nuthatches, Lewis's

White-faced Ibises and Ring-billed Gulls

Woodpeckers, Oak Titmice, Gray Flycatchers, Townsend's Solitaires, and Red Crossbills are just a few of the species that can be found here.

Lake Ewauna

Park at Veterans Memorial Park (not well marked) to access Lake Ewauna at the north end of the Klamath River. The park is located where US 97 passes over the Link River, at the southern end of downtown Klamath Falls. From southbound US 97 take the downtown exit, go east on Main Street across the river, and then take an immediate right to reach the park. From northbound US 97 take the same downtown exit, which leads you to Klamath Avenue (one-way). Turn left at your first opportunity, then turn left again onto Main Street. Turn left into the park just before Main crosses the river.

The boat launch at Veterans Memorial Park is a good vantage point from which to watch waterfowl, gulls, and terns on Lake Ewauna. Common gulls include Bonaparte's, California, and Ring-billed, but other species are possible.

The Lake Ewauna Nature Trail runs along the west shore of the lake and provides access to several small ponds and marshy areas. From Veterans Memorial Park, walk across the Main Street bridge then south along the Link River and the western shore of Lake Ewauna.

Klamath Wildlife Area (Miller Island Unit)

From Klamath Falls drive south on US 97 about 2.5 miles past the bridge over the Klamath River, turn west onto Miller Island Road, and follow the road to the entrance of the Klamath Wildlife Area. A parking area with a restroom and an information kiosk is near the entrance. Just beyond that is the entrance to a trail that leads along a canal and past some shallow ponds. These ponds are good for waterfowl and shorebirds, depending on water levels.

Continuing west, you will pass the state wildlife office on the left. This is a good stop for information and to spot California Quail. When the road makes a sharp turn to the left, pull into the little parking area to scan for Ross's and Greater White-fronted Geese in the fields and American Bitterns in the cattails.

The first 2 miles of Miller Island Road are paved, but then the road becomes a narrow, rough gravel lane. If you continue 1 mile to the end, you will find a parking area with a restroom and boat ramp at the Klamath River. Check any trees along the way for Bald Eagles and other raptors in winter and for Great Horned Owls any time. In spring watch for Tricolored Blackbirds in the cattails.

Lower Klamath National Wildlife Refuge

While most of Lower Klamath National Wildlife Refuge lies in California, parts do extend into Oregon. The area along the state line offers some excellent birding for the Oregon birder. In winter large flocks of ducks, geese, and swans are found in the fields and marshes. Check flocks of Horned Larks for the occasional Lapland Longspur and Snow Bunting. In spring the alkali lakes and flooded fields attract migrant shorebirds, with Black-necked Stilts, American Avocets, Long-billed Curlews, and the occasional Snowy Plover staying to nest.

From US 97 just south of the California/Oregon border, turn east onto California Route 161, also known as Stateline Road. From here to Oregon Route 39, a distance of 19 miles, Stateline Road passes through marshes, alkali lakes, and dry upland habitats. Strict Oregon state–listers should be aware that the first 9 miles of this road are in California. Thereafter, the road straddles the border.

Stateline Road is a very popular birding area, and with good reason. *Please be aware that this is a state highway with a speed limit of 65 mph.* If you stop to bird, pull completely off the highway. Always be aware of traffic approaching from behind you.

There is a wildlife viewing area on the south side of the road about 9 miles east of US 97. The open water here is good for waterfowl. Continue east a few more miles until the road crosses White Lake. This shallow alkali lake is one of the best sites in the area for shorebirds in the spring, but it is usually dry by late summer.

Another road worth exploring is Township Road, along the north edge of the refuge. From US 97, just south of Worden, turn east onto Township Road. This road passes agricultural fields, which flood in late winter and early spring, attracting waterfowl and raptors. Watch for longspurs and Snow Buntings in winter and shorebirds in spring.

Township Road crosses the Klamath Strait Drain 3.8 miles east of US 97. A gravel road runs along the east side of this canal, providing good views of the surrounding fields before intersecting State Line Road.

The eastern end of Township Road intersects Lower Klamath Lake Road. Turn right onto Lower Klamath Lake and follow it southeast and east for about 6 miles. You can then turn south on Merrill Pit Road or on Merrill Road in 1 mile. Both of these roads intersect State Line near White Lake.

If you turn north on Merrill Road, you will cross the tiny Lost River in about 1 mile. Check for Tricolored Blackbirds and other marsh species here before turning left onto OR 39 to return to Klamath Falls.

Pacific Coast and Coast Range

The waters of the Pacific Ocean, rocky headlands, sand beaches, and coastal and mountain forests combine to make the Oregon Coast and Coast Range an extremely productive birding destination at any time of year. The beaches in Oregon are public property, so access points are common all along the coast. Much of the land in the Coast Range is private property, so access is more limited.

The weather along the coast is strongly influenced by the ocean. Annual precipitation averages between 60 and 80 inches along the coast and can reach 200 inches in some of the higher elevations. Most of this falls from October through May, with summers being fairly dry. Along the coast winter temperatures are typically in the 40- to 50-degree range, while summers remain cool in the 60s. Inland sites experience a broader range of temperatures.

Birders should strongly consider getting out on the water to see the truly pelagic species, either on an organized birding trip or on a sightseeing or whale-watching boat. While shearwaters, jaegers, and alcids are visible from some coastal sites, you really need to go offshore to experience many of the seabirds off the Oregon Coast. Black-footed Albatrosses are common, but seldom venture closer than 10 miles from shore. Laysan Albatrosses are reported every year, and both Short-tailed and Shy Albatrosses occur on occasion.

Sooty, Short-tailed, Pink-footed, and Buller's Shearwaters are common sights in season. Manx and Flesh-footed Shearwaters require a little more luck. South Polar Skuas, all three jaegers, Sabine's Gulls, and Artic Terns are commonly reported from boat trips in late summer and early autumn.

All islands and reefs off the Oregon coast are part of the Oregon Islands National Wildlife Refuge. These rocks host immense seabird colonies. Nesting species include Common Murre, Pigeon Guillemot, Cassin's Auklet, Rhinoceros Auklet, Tufted Puffin, Brandt's and Pelagic Cormorants, Fork-tailed and Leach's Storm Petrels, and Western Gull.

Winter brings other species to the coastal waters, including Common, Red-throated, and Pacific Loons, Ancient Murrelets, Harlequin and Long-tailed Ducks, and both Red and Red-necked Phalaropes.

Gull aficionados will be kept very busy along the coast. Western Gulls are common year-round residents. These are joined by Heermann's Gulls, which follow the Brown Pelicans north in summer, and by Mew, California, Herring, Thayer's, and Glaucous-winged Gulls in winter. Western X Glaucous-winged hybrids are common. Glaucous Gulls occur in small numbers each winter. Gulls are found along jetties, in boat basins, at river mouths, and in coastal meadows.

While Oregon does not see the huge shorebird congregations found at Grey's Harbor, Washington, or Humboldt Bay, California, good numbers of shorebirds are found here, with Asian vagrants reported every year. Spring migration occurs in April, while "autumn" migration is spread out from July through October. Some shorebirds spend the winter on the Oregon coast. Black Oystercatchers nest on rocky shores and Snowy Plovers nest on sand beaches along the central and southern coast.

Many birders visiting the Oregon Coast hope to find Northwestern Crows. This hope is fueled by the fact that the coastal race of American Crow is noticeably smaller than inland races. But despite the range maps in some guides, there is no physical evidence that Northwestern Crows have ever occurred in Oregon.

Estuaries support large flocks of wintering waterfowl. Brant, Canada and Cackling Geese, all three scoters, American and Eurasian Wigeons, Northern Pintails, Greater and Lesser Scaups, mergansers, and Tundra Swans are just some of the species you can expect.

The vegetation along the coast begins with a mixture of shrubs and small conifers, which quickly gives way to forests of Sitka spruce, western hemlock, and western red cedar. Any patch of woods along the coast can be productive for migrant songbirds, and a few vagrants show up every year. Small numbers of Palm Warblers winter along the Oregon coast. A few Tropical Kingbirds are reported each autumn.

Farther inland, Douglas fir replaces the Sitka spruce and noble fir dominates at higher elevations. The forests in the Coast Range have been extensively logged, creating many areas of clear-cuts and young replanted forest, interspersed with small patches of mature forest.

Typical forest species in this region include Sooty Grouse; Band-tailed Pigeon; Hairy Woodpecker; Hammond's and Pacific-slope Flycatchers; Hutton's Vireo; Gray and Steller's Jays; Common Raven; Chestnut-backed Chickadee; Red-breasted Nuthatch; Winter Wren; Golden-crowned Kinglet; Swainson's and Varied Thrushes; Yellow-rumped, Hermit and Wilson's Warblers; Western Tanager; Dark-eyed Junco; and Purple Finch.

In brushy areas and mixed forests, watch for Mountain Quail; Anna's, Rufous, and Allen's Hummingbirds; Olive-sided and Willow Flycatchers; Bewick's Wren; Wrentit; Orange-crowned and MacGillivray's Warblers; Spotted Towhee; White-crowned Sparrow; Black-headed Grosbeak; and American Goldfinch.

33 Fort Stevens State Park

Habitats: Ocean, rocky shores, sand beach, wet forest, lake

What to see: Seabirds, shorebirds, waterfowl, songbirds

Specialty birds: Red-throated, Pacific and Common Loons; Sooty and Short-tailed Shearwaters; Black-bellied, American Golden, and Pacific Golden Plovers; Baird's Sandpiper; Black-legged Kittiwake; Caspian Tern; Willow and Pacific-slope Flycatchers; Savannah Sparrow; Lapland Longspur

Best months: August–May

Directions: From U.S. Highway 101, 9 miles north of Seaside or 7 miles south of Astoria, turn west onto Ridge Road and follow the signs to Fort Stevens State Park. Pass by the first turnoff to the park, which leads to the main camping area. Continue to the second turnoff for the South Jetty. Entrance to the park is free, but a parking permit is required at Coffenbury Lake. (atlas, p. 192)

The Birding

While the main attraction for birders when visiting Fort Stevens State Park is the south jetty of the Columbia River, the park offers access to forest, brush, and a freshwater lake as well. There is an excellent network of trails throughout the park.

South Jetty of the Columbia

From the park entrance follow the main road to Parking Lot C, where there is a vault toilet and an observation platform. From the platform watch for a variety of seabirds ranging from Common Murres and Pigeon Guillemots in the summer to Short-tailed Shearwaters and Northern Fulmars after autumn storms. A good variety of loons, grebes, gulls, and waterfowl can be expected here. Check the rocks of the jetty for Wandering Tattler and other rockpipers.

A series of tidal ponds is across the parking lot from the platform. While changes in vegetation in recent years have diminished the productivity of this spot, these ponds still attract shorebirds during high tides. In late summer and early autumn, be especially alert for the possibility of Buff-breasted Sandpipers and Pacific Golden Plovers. In winter these ponds occasionally attract Lapland Longspurs and Snow Buntings.

During high tides a tidal stream blocks the path along the jetty. But if the tide is low, walk west along the jetty to the beach at the mouth of the Columbia River. This beach is good for Black-bellied Plovers. If you are up for a hike (4.5 miles), you can walk along the beach all the way around the end of Clatsop Spit to Parking Lot D, then along the road through shrubby habitat back to Parking Lot C.

If your time or energy is limited, return to the main road and drive to Parking Lot D, where you'll find another vault toilet and an observation blind. Check the

Wrentit

small pines in this area for migrant songbirds. The blind itself does not offer great views of the estuary, but you can walk past it and along the shore to see waterfowl and/or shorebirds, depending on the tide. Snowy Owls and Gyrfalcons are possible here during winter.

Coffenbury Lake

To explore inland habitats, return to the main road and take the turnoff to Coffenbury Lake *(fee for parking)*. A trail leads all the way around the lake (about 2.4 miles) through forest on the west side and more open habitat on the east. This is a good area for migrant songbirds and for Wrentits all year. The lake hosts Pied-billed Grebes, Green Herons, Wood Ducks, and Hooded Mergansers. During late summer the lake level lowers to reveal mudflats on the south end. Watch for shorebirds here, especially during high tides.

On the way back to the main road, bear west toward the Wreck of the Peter Iredale. This parking lot provides more beach access and a restroom.

34 Seaside/Gearhart

Habitats: Ocean, rocky shores, sand beach
What to see: Waterfowl, seabirds, shorebirds
Specialty birds: Surf Scoter; Western Grebe; Sooty Shearwater; Heermann's Gull; Caspian Tern; Black Turnstone; Sanderling

Best months: All year
Directions: On U.S. Highway 101, about 15 miles south of Astoria. From Portland take U.S. Highway 26 west to US 101, then drive north on US 101 about 3 miles to Seaside. (atlas, p. 192)

The Birding

The town of Seaside is best known for factory outlet malls and arcades, but sites on the north and south ends of town provide exceptional birding.

The Cove

From US 101 at the south end of town, turn west onto U Avenue then left onto Edgewood Drive. Edgewood will become Sunset Boulevard. Park across from Seltzer Park, which offers restrooms and an observation deck. This area of rocky beach is known as "The Cove." The shore often hosts flocks of gulls and terns, and Black Turnstones are to be expected from autumn through spring. The water in the cove, a favorite among local surfers, is also very popular with scoters, grebes, and loons. Late summer brings large flocks of Sooty Shearwaters close to shore. Scan the flocks for other seabird species.

Necanicum Estuary Park

Return to US 101 and drive north to 12th Avenue. Turn west onto 12th, then right onto Holladay Drive. Continue north on Holladay for about 5 blocks. A small parking lot is on the left side of the road, across from the high school. This is Necanicum Estuary Park, where you can get a good view of the south shore of the estuary. Large flocks of gulls, Brown Pelicans, and waterfowl rest and bathe in the river and on the sand flats. Continue north on Holladay Drive, which will merge with 24th Avenue and lead you back to US 101.

South Shore of the Necanicum

If the tourists are not too thick, you might want to walk the beach to the south shore of the estuary. From US 101 turn west onto 12th Avenue. Continue past Holladay, cross the bridge, and park at Goodman Park. Walk west on 12th to the beach. To your left is the Seaside Promenade, a wide, paved walkway that runs the length of town along the beach. If you cross the dunes and turn right, you can walk about 1.5 miles along the beach to the shore of the Necanicum River.

North Shore of the Necanicum

Continue north on US 101 to the little town of Gearhart. Turn west onto G Street. Bear right and then left onto F Street, and then turn left onto Wellington Avenue. There is a small parking area on your right just before the dead end. This is the access to the north shore of the Necanicum River estuary. Follow the gravel path down toward the water. You can walk straight to the water's edge or turn right on a wide path to walk along the top of the bluff. It looks like you are walking into someone's backyard, but just stay on the main path and you will be fine. When the tide is out, this area provides extensive mudflats for migrating shorebirds. Walk along the water's edge at the base of the bluff for the best views. Follow the shoreline to the river's mouth and onto the sand beach. This beach is far less crowded than the one just across the river in Seaside. The brushy areas along the bluff host mixed flocks of sparrows in winter and a variety of songbirds in migration.

Stanley Lake

If high tides chase migrating shorebirds out of the estuary, many of the birds will fly to Stanley Lake. From US 101 on the north edge of Seaside, turn east at the sign for Lewis and Clark Road, then turn immediately south, and then turn left into the parking lot for the North Coast Family Fellowship. Stanley Lake is a tidal pond behind the church. Please note that this is private property. The church has been very gracious in allowing birders access to the shoreline.

35 Cannon Beach Area

Habitats: Ocean, sand beach, rocky shores, offshore rocks, wet forest, brush, lake
What to see: Seabirds, forest species
Specialty birds: Harlequin Duck; Tufted Puffin
Best months: All year
Directions: Cannon Beach is located along U.S. Highway 101, about 21 miles south of Astoria. (atlas, p. 192)

The Birding

The town of Cannon Beach is a very popular tourist town. As a result the city itself should probably be avoided on summer weekends. But a couple of sites in this area are definitely worth some birding time, especially in winter.

Ecola State Park *(fee)*

From the north end of Cannon Beach, or from the northernmost Cannon Beach exit on US 101, follow the signs to Ecola State Park. The entrance road leading to the park is about 2 miles long and winds through second-growth forest. Look for the giant stumps to get an idea of what this forest used to look like. The first parking lot you will come to is at Eagle Point.

The Banana Slug, the unofficial state "bird" of western Oregon, is found in wet forests of the Cascades and Coast Range.

Ecola State Park offers both an easily accessible seawatch site, and extensive hiking trails through mature coastal forest. The main parking lot at Eagle Point is the former. Walk across the big lawn, which may be inhabited by a mixed flock of gulls or a herd of Elk, to the rocky headland. From the overlooks here, watch for all the typical loons, cormorants, grebes, sea ducks, and shearwaters in migration. This is also a popular lookout for Gray Whales.

From the parking lot you can either hike south on the rather strenuous trail to Crescent Beach or north toward Indian Beach. Both paths lead you through lush woodland with the occasional ocean overlook. Look for Varied and Hermit Thrushes, Wrentits, Chestnut-backed Chickadees, and other forest species. If you would rather not walk the 2 miles to Indian Beach, you can drive to the parking lot there. From this lot the hiking trail continues north for another 6 miles across Tillamook Head.

Haystack Rock

Haystack Rock is a large rock formation right on the beach at the south end of Cannon Beach. You can park in town and walk to the beach, but it is much easier to continue south on US 101 and take the exit for Tolovana Beach State Wayside. Park in the lot and walk north along the beach about 1 mile to Haystack Rock.

Haystack Rock hosts large numbers of nesting birds in the summer. But unlike most seabird nest sites, it is close enough to shore to afford good views of the birds. In spring and summer this is one of the easiest places in Oregon to see Tufted Puffins. Most puffin nest burrows are on the seaward side of the rock, but the birds are easily seen flying by or sitting on the water. In winter the base of Haystack Rock is a very reliable site for Harlequin Ducks. The beach here is busy enough to keep bird diversity to a minimum, but many consider it worth a stop for either of these two species.

Cannon Beach Sewage Ponds

The Cannon Beach Sewage Ponds can be very productive, especially after winter storms. From downtown Cannon Beach drive east on Second Street to the large parking area at the sewage ponds. There is an observation deck to help you see over the fence.

Not only do these ponds attract freshwater ducks, such as Wood Ducks, Cinnamon Teal, Ring-necked Ducks, and American Wigeon, but when seas are rough, Greater and Lesser Scaups, Red-necked and Red Phalaropes, and a variety of gulls can be found here. Check the wet brushy area just across the road from the ponds for winter sparrow flocks and migrants.

36 Tillamook Bay Area

Habitats: Ocean, rocky shores, sand beach, wet forest, brush, meadow

What to see: Large concentrations of waterfowl in winter, nesting seabirds, migrant shorebirds and songbirds.

Specialty birds: Brant; Harlequin Duck; White-tailed Kite; Surfbird; Rock Sandpiper; Common Murre; Tufted Puffin; Purple Martin; Wrentit

Best months: All year

Directions: The city of Tillamook makes a good base of operations for exploring this section of the coast. Tillamook is located on U.S. Highway 101, about 65 miles south of Astoria. From Portland take U.S. Highway 26 west to Oregon Route 6 west to Tillamook (73 miles). (atlas, p. 192)

The Birding

The tour outlined below starts at Nehalem, about 10 miles north of Tillamook Bay, then jumps down to Barview Park, works south through the towns of Garibaldi, Bay City, and Tillamook, and then west to Bayocean Spit and Cape Meares State Park and National Wildlife Refuge. The key birding sites in this area can be checked in less than a day, but a birder could easily spend a couple of days exploring this area.

Nehalem Sewage Ponds

From US 101 south of the Nehalem River bridge, turn west toward the boat launch onto Tideland Road and follow this road a short distance to the Nehalem sewage ponds. Birders are welcome here, but check with the staff before entering the fenced area around the ponds. This area is good for shorebirds during high tides and for waterfowl and gulls in autumn and winter. White-tailed Kites are common in the meadows in this area. In winter it is often productive to drive on Tideland Road, which loops around for a few miles before intersecting Oregon Route 53. Turn right onto OR 53 to return to US 101. Watch the meadows for raptors and herons and the brushy areas for winter sparrow flocks.

Barview Park

From US 101 in the town of Barview, turn west on Cedar Avenue (there is a sign for Barview Park) and follow the road to the park entrance. Check in at the booth. There is a fee for camping in the park, but not for day use. Follow the main road through the park, always bearing left at intersections, to the parking area at the jetty.

Barview Jetty offers excellent views of the mouth of Tillamook Bay. Look for Double-crested, Brandt's, and Pelagic Cormorants all year. During the warmer months Common Murres and Pigeon Guillemots are common. Watch for Rhinoceros Auklets and other alcids, especially in winter. From autumn to spring the rocks

Bayocean Spit sits with Tillamook Bay on the right and Cape Meares Lake in the foreground.

of the jetty host large numbers of Black Turnstones and are a reliable site for Surfbirds. Rock Sandpipers are found here in the winter with some regularity. Scan the gull flocks on the rocks and the various loons and ducks flying by. Walking on the jetty is fairly easy near the parking area, but it becomes increasingly perilous as you walk farther out. The sand beach just north of the jetty occasionally hosts shorebirds when there are no people or dogs around.

On the way out of the park, stop and explore the campgrounds on foot. This brushy wooded habitat is home to Wrentits year-round and hosts a good variety of songbirds in winter and migration.

Another gravel parking lot overlooking a low area at the base of the jetty is just outside the park. During high tides check the tidal ponds for herons, shorebirds, and waterfowl. The brushy areas attract sparrows.

Three Graces Tidal Area

From Barview Park return to US 101 and head south. On the west side of the highway, just across from Harbourview Drive, pull into the gravel parking lot for the Three Graces Tidal Area. Follow the walking path along and then across the railroad tracks to view a series of offshore rocks. From autumn through spring, check the rocks and the shoreline for rockpipers, as well as cormorants, waterfowl, and gulls. During the winter this is a good site for Harlequin Ducks. The best time to visit the Three Graces is between high and low tides. If the tide is too high, much of the rocks will be inundated. If the tide is out, people may be out walking on the rocks.

Town of Garibaldi

Continue on US 101 south to the town of Garibaldi and turn right onto South 12th Street. When the road ends in a T, turn right along a narrow paved road to a gravel parking area at the public dock. Walk out on the dock to observe scoters, Common Goldeneyes, grebes, and gulls.

Continue south on US 101 and turn right onto Third Street. You will see a large smokestack from a former lumber mill. Follow Third past the Lions Club booth and turn left on American Avenue, then turn left on Jerry Creasy Drive and drive to the public parking area along the docks. This parking area may be closed in the winter. If so, just park where the road is blocked. Walk along the shoreline to explore the waters of Miami Cove. The area by the big smoke stack belongs to the Old Mill RV Park. Birders cannot drive onto the property, but they are welcome to walk along the shoreline to the boat launch area to explore the cove. Look for shorebirds during low tide and waterfowl when the tide is higher.

Bay City

The Pacific Oyster plant and restaurant is near the north end of Bay City on the west side of US 101. Park in the lot and walk out onto the little peninsula. This provides a good view of the bay and its abundant waterfowl. The pilings at the end of the peninsula provide roosts for cormorants and nest boxes for Purple Martins. The rocky shores of this site are the winter home of many Black Turnstones and host other shorebirds in migration. Large piles of oyster shells from the plant can be found near the highway. These piles provide food for gulls and turnstones.

From US 101 near the south end of Bay City, exit west onto Warren Street. From Warren turn right onto Spruce Street. Spruce jogs to the right, becomes gravel, and ends at the Bay City sewage ponds. Park, being careful not to block the gate. If the gate is open, you can walk through to explore the two ponds and the brushy areas around them. The ponds attract freshwater species such as Ring-necked Ducks, Lesser Scaups, teal, and Mallards. Brushy areas should be checked for migrant songbirds and wintering sparrows. Scan the bayshore just west of the ponds for shorebirds and waterfowl.

Kilchis Park

Continue south on US 101. If you want to leave the coastal plain to try for more upland species, a 6-mile detour from US 101 will take you to Kilchis Park. From the highway turn left onto Alderbrook Loop Road, then bear left at the sign for Kilchis Park *(entrance fee in summer)*. Check the Kilchis River for American Dippers and the brushy shores for migrating warblers, Winter Wrens, and thrushes.

City of Tillamook

The city of Tillamook is surrounded by coastal meadows. During the winter months these fields may hold large mixed-species flocks of gulls, waterfowl, and Great Egrets. Cattle Egrets are a possibility. During migration high tides may force flocks of shorebirds into the meadows. Unfortunately, there is no public access to these fields. Driving on county roads in the area may produce some good birding, but take great care not to block narrow roads or trespass on private property.

Bayocean Spit

From US 101 in Tillamook, turn west on 3rd Street and follow the signs for the Three Capes Scenic Route (Oregon Route 131, Netarts Highway). Just west of town, turn north onto Fenk Road. The wet meadows along this short road often host shorebirds and waterfowl, especially during high tides. Return to OR 131 and continue west.

After crossing the Tillamook River, turn right onto Bayocean Road (there is a sign for Cape Meares). This route passes through meadows and along the edge of Tillamook Bay. While the habitat looks very promising, there are few places where you can safely pull over. At milepost 5, turn right onto Bayocean Spit (not well marked). The entrance road provides good views of the bayshore and patches of shrubby vegetation. Keep watch for Northern Harriers and White-tailed Kites. Park in the lot at the end of the entrance road and take one of the paths east of the parking lot to the edge of the bay. These mudflats are very productive for shorebirds just before high tide.

To truly appreciate the variety of habitats and birds on the spit, consider taking the 8-mile hike lovingly referred to as The Tillamook Death March. Starting in the parking lot, walk north along the bayshore on the gravel road. This path provides good views of the bay and access to woods and salal thickets. Wrentits are regular on this route, as are Fox Sparrows and Red Crossbills. Spring and autumn migrations bring a good variety of songbirds. At the north end of the spit, check the jetty and the mouth of the bay for rockpipers and alcids. Return south along the ocean side of the spit. Species diversity is usually not as good here as on the bay side, but the sandy beach often hosts good numbers of Least Sandpipers, Sanderlings, and Semipalmated Plovers. Be alert for the possibility of Snowy Plovers. The coastal breeding population of this species has experienced a sharp decline in recent years, but Bayocean Spit was once a reliable site. There are several marked trails that cut across the spit back to the east side and the parking lot. The shrub-covered dunes host Savannah, Song, White-crowned, and Golden-crowned Sparrows, among other songbirds. The exit road from the spit is higher than the entrance road, providing good views of Cape Meares Lake, a freshwater lake at the base of the spit. Scan the lake for Ring-necked Ducks, Lesser Scaups, Canvasbacks, Redheads, and Pied-billed Grebes.

Cape Meares State Park and National Wildlife Refuge

From Bayocean Spit turn right onto Bayocean Road, then turn left at the sign for Cape Meares State Park. Drive a little more than 1 mile to the park entrance on your right. The entrance road cuts through a small patch of old-growth spruce forest before reaching the parking area. At the right of the parking area is the first of several overlooks. Scan the water for alcids and the rocks for Black Oystercatchers. In recent years a pair of Peregrine Falcons has nested on the cliffs. Walk the trail down to the lighthouse, taking advantage of the overlooks along the way. The woods here are home to Chestnut-backed Chickadees, Bushtits, Brown Creepers, both kinglets, Varied Thrushes, and Wrentits. The overlook at the end of the trail provides views of large flocks of Common Murres on the water. This is also a good spot to see breeding Tufted Puffins. In migration watch for shearwaters, terns, jaegers, and gulls. The waters below the headland often hold Western Grebes, scoters, and Marbled Murrelets. Follow the trail around to return to the parking area, watching for both seabirds and songbirds. A trail to the restrooms and to the "Octopus Tree," a large multitrunked spruce, is across the parking lot. The trail continues past the big tree for another 0.5 mile through woods and thickets.

A small parking area is back at the entrance to Cape Meares State Park. This lot provides access to two trails, one leading through mature forest to a huge spruce, the other through shrubby habitat to the beach.

37 Siletz Bay Area

Habitats: Sandy beach, mudflats, rocky shores, ocean

What to see: Gulls, shorebirds, seabirds

Specialty birds: Scoters; loons; Northern Fulmar; Pink-footed, Sooty, and Short-tailed Shearwaters; Black-bellied Plover; Black Oystercatcher; Whimbrel; Red and Red-necked Phalaropes; Bonaparte's and Thayer's Gulls; Marbled and Ancient Murrelets

Best months: September–May

Directions: Siletz Bay lies south of Lincoln City, which is just south of the intersection of U.S. Highway 101 and Oregon Route 18. (atlas, p. 192)

The Birding

While not one of the major birding destinations along the coast, the area around the sprawling tourist town of Lincoln City offers a few good sites that can be checked fairly quickly. Boiler Bay State Wayside is just a few miles to the south. This nondescript little roadside rest stop is one of the most important birding sites on the entire Oregon coast.

D River State Wayside

From US 101 in Lincoln City, turn into the D River State Wayside. This beach-access site offers a parking lot and restrooms where the short D River flows onto the beach. In the winter large flocks of gulls come here to roost and bathe in the fresh water. Western, Glaucous-winged (and their hybrids), and California Gulls are most common, but watch for Thayer's and Herring Gulls as well.

Mouth of Siletz Bay

Near the south end of Lincoln City, turn west onto 51st Street and follow it to the parking lot at its end. There is a public dock behind Mo's Restaurant from which you can view the mouth of the bay. Loons, grebes, cormorants, various ducks, and Harbor Seals can be expected here. Watch for congregations of gulls and terns on the south spit, just across the narrow bay mouth.

Return to US 101 and head south across the bridge over Schooner Creek. Just south of the bridge, pull off into the little parking area on the west side of the road to check the small offshore rocks for rockpipers.

Josephine Young Memorial Park

Continue south on US 101 and turn right onto SW 62nd Street in Cutler City. In a few blocks 62nd bears left and becomes SW Fleet Avenue. Turn right onto SW 65th at the sign for Josephine Young Memorial Park. This little park provides a restroom, one parking space, some picnic tables, and access to the shores of Siletz Bay. This area can be very good for shorebirds on the incoming tide. The bay tends

Thayer's Gull

to fill completely at high tide, driving the shorebirds off the mudflats. You can walk either direction on the beach. The mouth of Drift Creek is about 1 mile to the south.

Cutler City Wetlands Park

From US 101 turn west onto SW 63rd Street and drive to the parking lot for Cutler City Wetlands Park. A 1-mile hiking trail winds through conifer forest and freshwater marsh.

Continuing south on US 101, the highway passes marsh and mudflat habitats. Watch for Ospreys, Bald Eagles, White-tailed Kites, herons, and shorebirds as you go, although there is little opportunity to pull off the road.

South End of Siletz Bay

Where US 101 reaches the south end of the bay, turn into the Shops at Salishan shopping center and park at the north end of the parking lot. Walk west toward the golf course to a trail on the right, which leads along a channel to the south shore of the bay. Depending on the tide level, this area has mudflats for shorebirds or shallow water for gulls and waterfowl.

Boiler Bay State Wayside

Boiler Bay State Wayside is about 5 miles south of Siletz Bay. This is one of the best sites in Oregon for seeing pelagic species from shore and for viewing migration along the coast. Expected species include Common Murre, Marbled Murrelet, Pigeon Guillemot, scoters, cormorants, and Black Oystercatchers. Bird movements are often heaviest in the early mornings.

Pacific Loons fly past by the hundreds in migration. Autumn brings large flocks of Sooty Shearwaters, which are replaced by smaller numbers of Short-tailed Shearwaters in winter. Buller's, Pink-footed, Black-vented, and Manx Shearwaters have all been reported from this site. Winter brings small numbers of Ancient Murrelets, Rhinoceros Auklets, and Cassin's Auklets. Anything might turn up after winter storms.

38 Newport Area

Habitats: Offshore rocks, rocky shores, sand beach, mudflats, brush

What to see: Seabirds, shorebirds, songbirds

Specialty birds: Brant; three scoters; three loons; Red-necked Grebe; Whimbrel; Surfbird; Rock Sandpiper; Heermann's, Mew and California Gulls; Caspian Tern; Marbled Murrelet; Rhinoceros Auklet; Tufted Puffin; Tropical Kingbird; Palm Warbler

Best months: All year

Directions: This area surrounds the town of Newport, at the intersection of U.S. Highway 101 and U.S. Highway 20. (atlas, p. 198)

Yaquina Bay, at Newport, hosts gulls, waterfowl, and seabirds.

The Birding

Yaquina Bay is one of the more productive estuaries for birding on the Oregon coast, due in part to easy access to offshore rocks, rocky jetties, and estuarine mudflats. The city of Newport has hotels and restaurants in abundance, but, like many coastal communities, conditions can be quite crowded on summer weekends.

Yaquina Head Natural Area *(fee)*

From US 101, about 2.5 miles north of Newport, turn west on the well-marked road to Yaquina Head Natural Area and Lighthouse. Follow the road to the parking area near the lighthouse. The overlooks here provide excellent views of the seabird nesting colonies just offshore. Common Murres, Pigeon Guillemots, Pelagic and Brandt's Cormorants, Tufted Puffins, and Western Gulls are the more common nesters. Watch for Rhinoceros Auklets, Marbled Murrelets, and all three scoters in the water.

During migration Sooty Shearwaters and other seabirds may be seen flying by the headlands. Winter storms bring Short-tailed Shearwaters, Northern Fulmars, and Red Phalaropes close to shore. Watch for migrant songbirds in the brushy patches in spring and autumn and for Snow Buntings and Lapland Longspurs in open areas in winter. The walkways through the tide pools are not particularly birdy, but are fascinating nonetheless.

Yaquina Bay State Recreation Area

From US 101 in Newport, turn west at the sign for Yaquina Bay State Recreation Area. The stand of lodgepole pines near the parking area is home to Wrentits, White-crowned Sparrows, and a variety of migrants. Follow the path down to the beach and the north jetty. The sandy beach can be good for mixed flocks of gulls and the occasional shorebird, while the rocky jetty attracts rockpipers. Walk upstream along the bayshore toward the bridge watching for loons, grebes, and ducks in the bay. Gulls often rest on the shore beneath the bridge.

South Jetty

From the south end of the Yaquina Bay Bridge on US 101, exit at the sign for the Marine Science Center. The road will loop around under the bridge. Turn west onto SW 26th Street, which becomes Jetty Way. The south jetty offers another excellent view of the bay. (The light may be better from this side than from the north.) Watch for ducks, grebes, loons, and alcids from the bridge all the way west to the jetty. Stop at the pullouts along the rocky shore to scan the bay for water birds and the rocks for shorebirds. As you continue west you will find several tidal ponds between the road and the bay. Check these for American Pipits, shorebirds, and longspurs. Park at the lot at the base of the jetty and scan both the river and the open ocean.

Mark O. Hatfield Marine Science Center

From the south end of the Yaquina Bay Bridge, follow the signs to the Mark O. Hatfield Marine Science Center (not to be confused with the Oregon Coast Aquarium, which is also nearby). The area around the Marine Science Center is usually the best site in the area for shorebirds, gulls and terns, and vagrant songbirds. The little cove and docks by the parking lot offer close views of ducks and gulls. From the parking lot follow the nature path along the bayshore, checking the brushy patches for songbirds. This is a fairly consistent site for Tropical Kingbirds and Palm Warblers in late autumn. The mudflats along the bay are a favorite resting area for gulls and terns, and they are a feeding area for shorebirds.

Seal Rock State Wayside

Seal Rock State Wayside is 10 miles south of Newport on US 101. The rocky tide pools are good for rockpipers in migration and winter. This is one of the more reliable sites for wintering Rock Sandpipers. Watch for them among the large flocks of Black Turnstones and Surfbirds.

39 Florence Area

Habitats: Brush, ocean, sand beach, rocky shores

What to see: Seabirds, waterfowl, migrant shorebirds, songbirds

Specialty birds: Tundra Swan; Harlequin Duck; scoters; Osprey; White-tailed Kite; Rough-legged Hawk; Peregrine Falcon; Black-bellied and Snowy Plovers; Marbled and Ancient Murrelets; American Pipit

Best months: All year

Directions: Florence is located at the intersection of U.S. Highway 101 and Oregon Route 126, about 60 miles west of Eugene. (atlas, p. 198)

Some sections of beach are closed to public access during the summer to protect the rare Snowy Plovers.

The Birding

The mouth of the Siuslaw River marks the northern end of the Oregon Dunes National Recreation Area. Although much of the naturally shifting sand in this area has been hobbled by introduced European Beach Grass, the huge dunes and broad sand beaches offer an interesting contrast to the rocky headlands to the north and south. This part of the Oregon coast is one of the last strongholds for the declining coastal population of Snowy Plovers. These sandy expanses also attract large numbers of off-highway vehicles, but the sites described below are generally protected from such activity.

North Jetty of the Siuslaw

From the intersection of US 101 and OR 126, go west on 9th Street for 0.8 mile, turn north onto Rhododendron Drive for 3 miles, and then turn west onto Jetty Road North. If approaching Florence from the north on US 101, turn west onto Heceta Beach Road for 1.9 miles, then turn south onto Rhododendron to Jetty Road North.

Harbor Vista Campground is about 0.10 mile down Jetty Road on your left. The park has clean restrooms and access to trees and brush that attract songbirds. Continue on Jetty Road another 0.10 mile to a gravel pullout on your right. This overlooks a tidal mudflat, which is good for shorebirds, gulls, and terns. Just beyond this pullout on your left, there is a paved road leading to a day-use area overlooking the same mudflat from the west. Lighting may be better from here late in the day.

Continue another 0.8 mile to the parking area at the end of Jetty Road. From here you can access the beach or the base of the jetty to scan the river and ocean for alcids and pelagic species.

South Jetty of the Siuslaw

From Florence drive south on US 101 for about 1.5 miles before turning right onto South Jetty Road *(fee)*. After about 2 miles, Jetty Road turns to the north and parallels the large foredune along the beach. From this turn to the end of Jetty Road, there are five parking lots on the west side of the road. Each has a restroom and a path leading to the beach. If the beach is not too crowded, make quick stops at these parking lots to scan for shorebirds and seabirds from the foredune.

Park at the third parking lot and walk south along the road a short distance to a path leading east along a dike. This path takes you out onto the deflation plain, a patchwork of brush and meadow. When water levels are low, this area can be extremely good for shorebirds. Also watch for American Pipits, Horned Larks, and Lapland Longspurs in autumn. In winter the area floods and attracts flocks of Tundra Swans and other waterfowl, along with a variety of raptors.

There is a gravel pullout overlooking a good mudflat for shorebirds and terns about 5.3 miles from US 101. This same mudflat can be viewed from the crab dock/fishing pier located another 0.2 mile north on Jetty Road. The pier also provides good views of the river. Look here for loons, grebes, and ducks.

Just past the parking area for the crab dock, there is another lot, at which the pavement ends. Continue west on a gravel road leading to the base of the south jetty. From the jetty scan the ocean and river for alcids, gulls, and other seabirds.

Siltcoos Recreation Area

About 7.5 miles south of Florence, turn west onto Siltcoos Access Road at the sign for the Siltcoos Recreation Area *(fee)*. There are several stops along this road on the way to the mouth of the river.

You will soon come to the Lodgepole Picnic Area on your right. This is worth a quick check for songbirds in the trees and waterfowl on the river. Next, pass the Lagoon Campground on your right and continue on to the bridge to the Waxmyrtle Campground on your left. If you cross the bridge, there is room for one or two vehicles to park near the entrance to the campground. There is also a small parking area a little farther down Siltcoos Access Road at the Stagecoach Trailhead. Just across the road from the bridge to Waxmyrtle Campground is the start of the Lagoon Trail, which runs along an oxbow lake behind the Lagoon Campground. This trail can be good for sighting herons, rails, and other wetland species.

The Waxmyrtle Trail begins near the entrance to Waxmyrtle Campground. This trail follows the river through a pine forest, branching into the Estuary Trail, and ends up at the beach near the south shore of the river mouth. The mudflats near the river's mouth can be very good for shorebirds. Be advised that much of the estuary may be closed to public access from March 15 to September 15 to protect nesting Snowy Plovers.

Continue west on Siltcoos Access Road to the parking area at its end. From here you can walk to the beach, then walk south to the river's mouth. Again, watch for signs designating protected nesting areas.

40 Reedsport Area

Habitats: Wet forest, lake, sand beach, meadow, mudflats, rocky shores

What to see: Forest species, migrant shorebirds, raptors, waterfowl

Specialty birds: Tundra Swan; all three teal; Western, Horned, and Red-necked Grebes; Osprey; White-tailed Kite; Chestnut-backed Chickadee; Western Tanager

Best months: March–May; September–December

Directions: Reedsport is located at the intersection of U.S. Highway 101 and Oregon Route 38, about halfway between Florence and Coos Bay. (atlas, p. 198)

Roosevelt Elk are often seen lounging in the meadows at the Dean Creek Elk Viewing Area. These meadows also attract White-tailed Kites and waterfowl.

The Birding

While Reedsport is usually not as productive as some other coastal areas, there are several good sites that can be birded quickly.

Tahkenitch Campground

About 7 miles north of Reedsport on US 101, turn into Tahkenitch Campground and park at the trailhead at the south end. The trail soon branches into two, each a couple of miles long. One leads south toward Threemile Lake and the other leads west toward the dunes and the beach. The pines near the campground and along both trails house typical forest species, such as Winter Wren, Western Tanager, Varied Thrush, and Chestnut-backed Chickadee.

Stables Road Wetlands

From US 101, just north of Reedsport, turn east onto Smith River Road. In less than 0.5 mile, just past the weigh station, turn left onto Stables Road. At low tide check the mudflats along the south side of the road for shorebirds. Waterfowl will be found in the wetlands on the north side of the road. Watch for migrant and wintering songbirds in the brushy areas.

Dean Creek Elk Viewing Area

From Reedsport drive east on OR 38 for about 3 miles to the Dean Creek Elk Viewing Area on the south side of the highway. The most obvious attraction of this site is the herds of Roosevelt Elk, which often lounge in the wet meadows here. But this is also a good spot for finding White-tailed Kite and other raptors. Puddle ducks use the wet meadows, while divers can be found on the Umpqua River on the north side of the highway.

Winchester Bay

The little town of Winchester Bay is about 5 miles south of Reedsport on US 101. Turn west onto Salmon Harbor Drive for 0.2 mile, and then turn north onto Ork Rock Road. Follow this road along the boat basin to Ork Rock Park at the end of the spit. Check the river and the mouth of the boat basin for loons and grebes. There is often a flock of gulls hanging out in the parking lot.

41 Coos Bay Area

Habitats: Ocean, sand beach, rocky shores, mudflat, wet forest

What to see: Shorebirds, waterfowl, seabirds, songbirds, raptors

Specialty birds: Brant; Harlequin Duck; Long-tailed Duck; Virginia Rail; American and Pacific Golden Plovers; Snowy Plover; Red Knot; Buff-breasted Sandpiper; Marbled and Ancient Murrelets; Black Phoebe; Palm Warbler

Best months: All year

Directions: Coos Bay is located along U.S. Highway 101, about 25 miles south of Reedsport. (atlas, p. 204)

The Birding

Coos Bay is the largest estuary in Oregon, providing extensive mudflats for migrant shorebirds and waterfowl. The surrounding freshwater marshes, woodlands, and coastal headlands add to the species diversity, making this area one of the most productive birding areas in the state.

North Spit

From US 101, north of the town of North Bend, turn west at the sign for Horsfall Beach, onto the Trans-Pacific Parkway. Continue for just over 1 mile to where the road forks. The right fork leads to Horsfall Beach. The woods and brushy areas along Horsfall Beach Road can be good for migrant songbirds. Two miles down this road is the trailhead for the Bluebill Trail, a 1.2-mile loop around a seasonal lake. Horsfall Beach Campground at the end of Horsfall Beach Road provides access to the beach, but this is a popular off-highway vehicle (OHV) area in the summer. Walking south along the beach will eventually take you out of the OHV area. It is 10 miles from the campground to the end of the spit. Return to the beginning of Horsfall Beach Road and turn right onto the Trans-Pacific Parkway.

The parkway leads west and then south down the North Spit. Continue south to the North Spit Boat Launch on your left. This is an easy spot from which to scan the bay for waterfowl before retracing your route back to US 101. Check out any brushy areas and ponds along the roadside for migrant songbirds and shorebirds.

Pony Slough

From US 101 in the town of North Bend, turn west on Virginia Avenue at the signs for Charleston. Turn north onto Marion Street, across from the Pony Village Mall, and park in the rough gravel lot next to the locked airport gate. A small inlet of Coos Bay, Pony Slough was once an exceptional birding site when the western shore was open to the public. Due to current airport restrictions, only the south shore of the slough is accessible. But this site is still worth a visit to look for shorebirds at low tide and for wintering waterfowl when the slough is flooded. A variety of herons and raptors can also be expected in winter.

Empire/Charleston

From Pony Slough continue west on Virginia Avenue, following the signs for Charleston. You will turn south onto Broadway and then west onto Newmark. In the town of Empire, Newmark turns south and becomes Empire Boulevard. Continue for 0.5 mile, turn west onto Fulton Avenue, and park by the sewage treatment plant. There is a picnic table here. (Only birders would picnic by a smelly sewage treatment plant!) Walk along the outside of the fence to explore the shoreline. Snowy Egrets are known to winter here.

Continue south on Empire Boulevard another 2.2 miles. An unmarked parking area next to a small water treatment building is on the west side of the road. This is a popular wintering area for grebes and waterfowl, which are attracted to the rocky bottom in this part of the bay.

In another 1.6 miles you will cross the Charleston Bridge. At the west end turn right onto Boat Basin Drive, continue for 0.5 mile, and park across the street from the Oregon Department of Fish and Wildlife Office. Walk along the dike road toward the fish-packing plant. The sandy cove on your left and the boat basin on your right attract loons, grebes, and ducks. A gravel road leads up the hill behind the Fish and Wildlife Office. The woods here can be good for migrants, as well as nesting thrushes, warblers, Western Tanagers, and Wrentits.

Cape Arago Highway

Continuing west from the Charleston Bridge, you will find several sites along the Cape Arago Highway that offer good birding for both seabirds and forest species.

Just west of Charleston turn right onto Coos Head Road and drive 1 mile to the large parking area at the south jetty of the Coos River. The base of the jetty is paved for easy walking. Look for seabirds on the ocean and in the river mouth. Cormorants and Pigeon Guillemots nest on the cliffs here. Check the brushy areas for songbirds, such as Wrentit and Black Phoebes.

Leaving the jetty parking lot on Coos Head Road, turn right at your first opportunity. This road runs along Bastendorff Beach before rejoining Cape Arago Highway. A pullout on your right, 0.7 mile from Coos Head Road, affords a good view of the beach, with its gulls and shorebirds.

Continue on to Cape Arago Highway and turn right. In 1.5 miles you will reach Sunset Bay State Park. Park in the day-use area and explore the woods and brush for migrant songbirds.

The next park on this road is Shore Acres State Park *(fee)*. The sea cliffs here overlook stunning rock formations. Look for sea ducks, alcids, and rockpipers. Trails lead through stands of pine and spruce, home to migrant and resident forest

Shore Acres State Park contains sea cliffs, patches of woodland, and an extensive flower garden.

species. The park's manicured flower garden should be checked for Rufous and Anna's Hummingbirds in the spring and summer.

The pullout for Simpson Reef is 1 mile past Shore Acres. This overlook is worth a stop just for the marine mammals that sun themselves on the rocks, but check for sea ducks and rockpipers while you are here.

Cape Arago Highway ends at Cape Arago State Park. The sea cliffs offer good views of migrating loons, grebes, and gulls. Several trails lead through woods and brush down to the shore. Retrace your route back toward Charleston.

South Slough National Estuarine Research Reserve

From Cape Arago Highway in Charleston, turn south onto Seven Devils Road, follow the signs about 4 miles to the South Slough National Estuarine Research Reserve, and park at the Interpretive Center. The Reserve is a 4,500-acre property dedicated to education and research. Several trails and boardwalks provide access to fresh- and saltwater marshes, as well as extensive upland areas. Detailed trail guides e available at the Interpretive Center, open every day during the summer (except holidays) and Monday to Friday between Labor Day and Memorial Day.

Millicoma Marsh

From the city of Coos Bay, drive south on US 101. Take the left fork at the sign for Allegany to reach Coos River Road. After 1.1 mile turn left onto D Street, turn right onto 4th Avenue, then turn right down the gravel driveway to the athletic field. The small parking lot here has a sign with a map and information about Millicoma Marsh.

This is an easily accessible site with both fresh- and saltwater marshes. The right fork of the main trail leads to a cattail marsh and an observation deck overlooking a sedge meadow. A nearby sewage pond is fenced off, but it should still be scanned for waterfowl. The left fork of the main trail makes a loop past extensive mudflats along the bay and back through a grove of alder and blackberry thickets.

The freshwater habitats are home to Virginia Rails, Yellow Warblers, Common Yellowthroats, and Marsh Wrens. Blackberry thickets attract mixed sparrow flocks in winter. The mudflats along the bay are good for shorebirds, and the trail along the dike provides excellent viewing, but a scope is usually necessary. Don't neglect to scan the alder thickets for songbirds and any open water for waterfowl. Millicoma Marsh can be very good for raptors, especially in winter.

42 Bandon

Habitats: Mudflats, rocky shores, brush, sand beach, ocean

What to see: Shorebirds, seabirds, songbirds

Specialty birds: Pelagic and Brandt's Cormorants; American and Pacific Golden Plovers; Wandering Tattler; Marbled Godwit; Ruddy Turnstone; Red Knot; Common Murre; Pigeon Guillemot; Tufted Puffin

Best months: March–October

Directions: Bandon is located about 18 miles south of Coos Bay on U.S. Highway 101 along the Coquille River. (atlas, p. 204)

The Birding

The Bandon area is one of the best in the state for migrant shorebirds. All of the regularly occurring species can be found here, along with an impressive list of vagrants. Large offshore rocks in the area support colonies of nesting seabirds. As with any coastal site, check the forests and brushy areas for migrant and wintering songbirds.

Bullards Beach

From US 101, just north of the Coquille River Bridge, turn west into Bullards Beach State Park. Check the day-use areas for the typical songbirds, Wrentits, Spotted Towhees, warblers, and sparrows.

From the state park, continue west and then south toward the lighthouse. The road parallels the beach behind the large foredune. Check the deflation plane along the east side of the road, as this area attracts shorebirds during high tides when the mudflats are flooded. Near the south end of the spit, a gravel road forks to the left, providing access to the west shore of the bay.

The main road ends at the lighthouse and the north jetty of the Coquille River. Much of the jetty is paved, allowing easy walking. Look for seabirds in the river and ocean; rockpipers on the jetty; and gulls, terns, and shorebirds on the beach.

Bandon Marsh National Wildlife Refuge

From US 101, just south of the Coquille River, bear west onto Riverside Drive. In just under 1 mile, there is a parking area at the large sign for Bandon Marsh National Wildlife Refuge. A short path leads to an observation deck. If the tide is out, take the stairs down to explore the extensive mudflats. This site is consistently one of the best shorebird spots on the coast. Try to plan your visit between mid- to high tide for best viewing.

South Jetty of the Coquille River

Continue south on Riverside Drive to First Street in the town of Bandon. Turn right and immediately pull off to the right side of the road. There is a small mud-

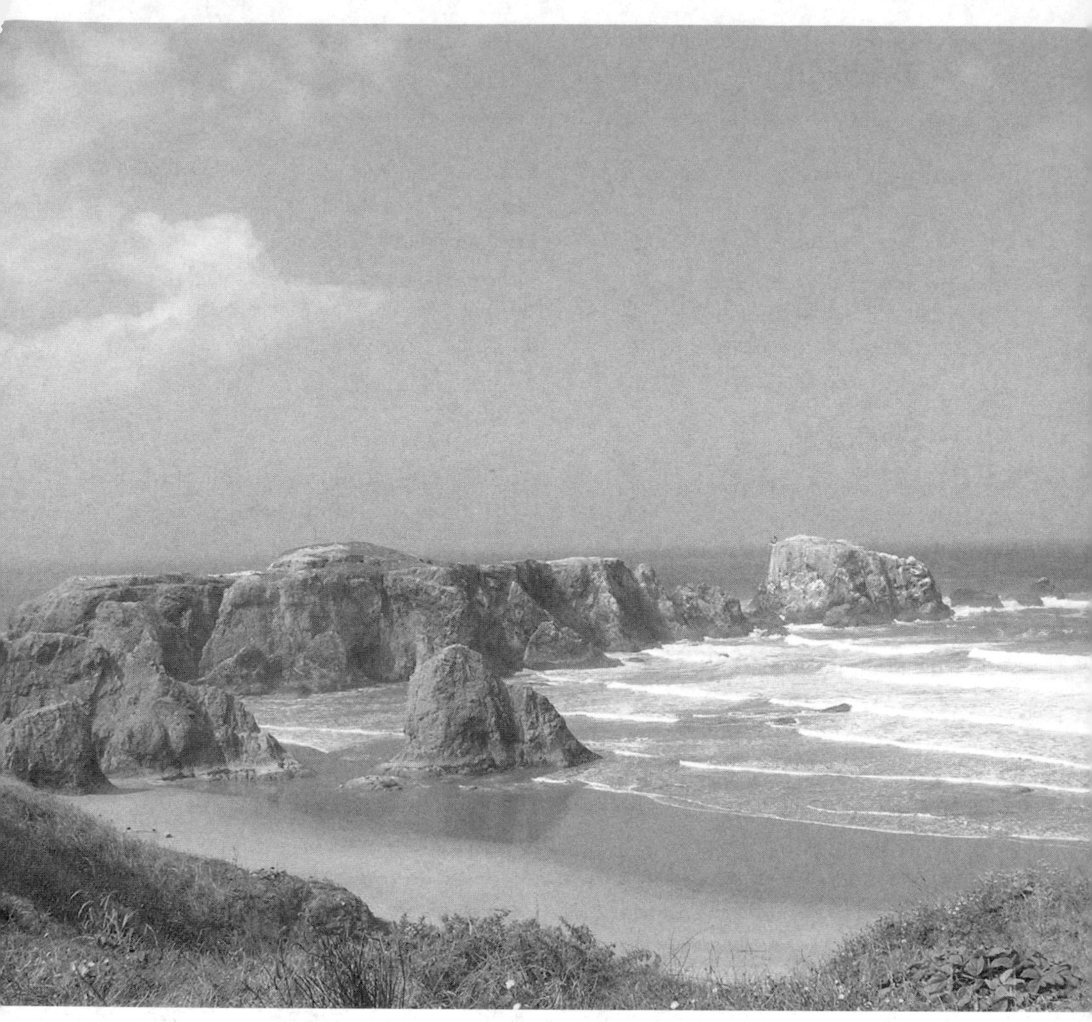

The rocks at Coquille Point host large colonies of nesting seabirds.

flat with pilings and rocky edges here. In addition to the mud-loving species seen at the refuge, check for Ruddy and Black Turnstones, Surfbirds, and Wandering Tattlers. On the west edge of this little bay is a public dock, which is worth a look if it is not too crowded.

Continue west on First Street, which becomes Edison, and turn right onto Jetty Road. On your way to the south jetty, it may be worthwhile to pull over occasionally and scan the rocky shoreline for rockpipers (you will need to climb the dike for a good view). Once you reach the south jetty, scan the river and ocean for seabirds and the rocks for shorebirds.

Coquille Point

From the south jetty return to the intersection of Jetty Road and Edison and turn right. Turn west onto Fourth Street and follow the bends of this road as it becomes Ocean Drive, Seventh Street, and finally Beach Loop Road as it turns south. Turn west onto Eleventh Street to reach the parking lot at Coquille Point.

Coquille Point is part of the Oregon Islands National Wildlife Refuge. Paved trails lead to interpretive signs and great views of the large offshore rocks. From April through July or early August, these rocks are home to large seabird nesting colonies. Common Murres, Tufted Puffins, Pelagic and Brandt's Cormorants, Western Gulls, and Black Oystercatchers can be expected here. The rocks are also home to both Fork-tailed and Leach's Storm Petrels, but these birds' nocturnal habits make them very hard to see.

A stairway leads down to the beach, where you can get a better view of grebes and waterfowl in the surf. It is only about 1 mile north along the beach to the south jetty.

43 Cape Blanco/Port Orford

Habitats: Brush, riparian, wetland, ocean, sand beach, rocky shores, wet forest

What to see: Waterfowl, gulls, seabirds, songbirds, raptors

Specialty birds: Harlequin and Long-tailed Ducks; White-tailed Kite; Red-shouldered Hawk; Marbled and Ancient Murrelets; Allen's Hummingbird; Marsh Wren; American Pipit

Best months: All year

Directions: From U.S. Highway 101, about 22 miles south of Bandon, turn west onto Cape Blanco Highway. (atlas, p. 204)

The Birding

Cape Blanco is the westernmost point in Oregon. In addition to the beaches and headlands, habitats here include freshwater wetlands and brushy meadows in the Sixes River Valley. The nearby town of Port Orford offers a productive state park and boat basin.

The first 3 miles of Cape Blanco Highway go through private property, but watch the roadsides as you go. The wetlands, pastures, brushy fencerows, and wooded patches attract raptors, Northern Shrikes in winter, and flocks of sparrows and finches. Allen's Hummingbirds are present in spring and summer. Stop at the entrance to Cape Blanco State Park to check the wetland there for raptors, waterfowl, and rails.

Sixes River Valley

Continue west to the turnoff for the Hughs House. Follow this road down to the day-use area along the Sixes River. A path leads from the parking area to the beach (0.5 mile). The marshy meadow along the river is good for Marsh Wrens, sparrows, and American Goldfinches. Watch for waterfowl on the river and raptors perched in the larger trees. If any sandbars are exposed in the river, check them for American Pipits, Lapland Longspurs, and resting waterfowl and gulls.

Horse Camp Road

After returning to Cape Blanco Highway, continue west for 1 mile, and then turn left at the sign for the horse camp. There are several trails along this road that lead through brushy and wooded habitats. Follow Horse Camp Road to the parking area at its end. There is a great view of a sandy beach just beyond the parking area. A good variety of seabirds can be seen from this viewpoint during migration.

Cape Blanco

Return to Cape Blanco Highway and continue west for another 0.7 mile to several gravel pullouts. Trails from these parking areas lead through woods and brush, with views of the ocean. Be especially alert for vagrant songbirds in autumn and late spring.

The lighthouse is at the end of Cape Blanco Highway. The land around the lighthouse is closed to public entry unless you are taking the lighthouse tour, so it is usually more profitable to park in the aforementioned pullouts.

Port Orford Heads State Park

From Cape Blanco return to US 101 and continue south about 4 miles to the town of Port Orford. Turn west onto Ninth Street and follow the state park signs to Port Orford Heads State Park. This is a wonderful little park with stands of pines and extensive areas of brush. Several short trails lead to ocean overlooks. Watch for Allen's Hummingbirds, along with Rufous and Anna's, when the manzanita blooms in spring.

Port of Port Orford

Return to US 101 and drive south for another 2 blocks. Turn west at the sign for the Port of Port Orford. This is a busy working dock, but there is a parking area

The view from Port Orford Heads includes Humbug Mountain on the right.

for cars. This little bay can be very productive for waterfowl and alcids, especially in winter. Scan the rocks for Black Oystercatchers and other rockpipers.

Battle Rock Historic Wayside is just south of Port Orford, on US 101. This is an easy spot at which to pull off and check for birds. The sandy beach occasionally hosts shorebirds. Scope the ocean and the large offshore rocks for seabirds.

Humbug Mountain State Park

Located about 6 miles south of Port Orford on US 101, Humbug Mountain State Park provides easy access to mature coastal forest. Park in the trailhead parking lot, 0.25 mile south of where the highway crosses Brush Creek. The trail leads south into the forest for 1 mile and then forks. Both forks lead to the summit (1,756 feet) and join the other to form a loop. The hike to the summit is about 4.5 miles round-trip. Typical forest birds include Varied Thrushes, Winter Wrens, Hermit Warblers, Red-breasted Nuthatches, and Chestnut-backed Chickadees. Continue south on US 101 to reach the park's day-use area along the creek, where you can check for riparian and forest species.

44 Brookings Area

Habitats: Sand beach, rocky shores, offshore rocks, ocean, wet forest, brush

What to see: Seabirds, waterfowl, shorebirds, songbirds

Specialty birds: Red-shouldered Hawk; Elegant Tern; Tufted Puffin; Allen's Hummingbird

Best months: All year

Directions: Brookings lies along U.S. Highway 101, about 6 miles north of the California border. (atlas, p. 204)

The Birding

The southernmost 25 miles or so of Oregon's coastline have several productive birding sites, most of which can be checked fairly quickly. Be especially alert for Elegant Terns and Allen's Hummingbirds in summer and Tropical Kingbirds in autumn, as these species become less likely as you travel farther north.

Pistol River State Park

About 11 miles south of the town of Gold Beach, US 101 crosses the Pistol River at Pistol River State Park. Large ponds lie among the sand dunes at both ends of the bridge, creating havens for shorebirds and waterfowl. Park in the lot at the

Allen's, Anna's, and Rufous Hummingbird (above) can all be found along the southern coast in spring.

south end of the bridge and walk along the river to the sand beach, watching for Sanderlings, Whimbrels, and open-country songbirds. Check any offshore rocks for nesting Tufted Puffins and Pigeon Guillemots.

Samuel H. Boardman State Park

Lying about halfway between Pistol River and Brookings, Samuel H. Boardman State Park covers 12 miles of coastline along US 101. There are four separate park entrances from the highway. You can make quick stops at any of these or spend a day exploring the trails and viewpoints. The park includes stands of mature coastal forest, rocky headlands and offshore rocks, open meadows, and sand beaches.

Harris Beach State Park

Located on the north edge of Brookings, along US 101, Harris Beach State Park provides another access point to the sand beaches and rocky headlands typical of the south coast. Just offshore is Goat Island (also known as Bird Island), the largest island off the Oregon coast and, as one would expect, a major seabird nesting site.

Chetco Point Park

From US 101 in the center of Brookings, turn south onto Wharf Street and follow it to its end at Chetco Point Park. This little park provides good viewpoints for watching seabirds and marine mammals.

Azalea Park

From US 101 near the east end of Brookings, turn north onto Constitution Way and follow the signs to Azalea Park. The flower gardens and trees in this 33-acre city park attract a nice variety of migrant and resident songbirds, but the main target of most birders is Allen's Hummingbirds. This species is most easily found in spring and early summer. Rufous and Anna's Hummingbirds are also common here.

South Jetty of the Chetco River

Cross the bridge over the Chetco River and turn south onto Lower Harbor Road. At the end of this road, turn west onto Boat Basin Road and follow it to the parking area at the south jetty. From here you have excellent views of the river and both jetties. Watch for loons, grebes, and ducks in the river and alcids on the ocean. Good numbers of gulls and terns rest on the north jetty. Watch for Black-legged Kittiwakes in winter.

Checklist of Oregon Birds and Seasonal Abundance Chart

Below is a list of 505 species of birds known to have occurred in Oregon as of August 2006. Introduced species are marked with an (I). Extirpated species are marked with an (E).

Following each species name are indications of that species' seasonal abundance. For the purpose of this chart, winter includes the months of December to February; spring is March to May; summer is June to August; and autumn is September to November. Bear in mind that different species migrate at different times. Shorebirds that are common in summer are actually engaged in their "autumn" migration. Some insectivorous birds listed as common in spring may not actually arrive in Oregon until late May.

Abundance of each species is designated as follows:

C — Common, to be expected in proper range and habitat.
U — Uncommon, present in small numbers or in limited range.
R — Rare, present in very small numbers or in very limited range.
X — Accidental, a few scattered records. Not to be expected.

Abundance designations do not necessarily denote actual numbers of individuals. For example, both Red-tailed Hawk and European Starling are listed as common, but on any given day you may see only ten Red-tails and several hundred starlings. Irruptive species, such as Bohemian Waxwing or Pine Grosbeak, may be very numerous in some years and completely absent in others. Leach's Storm-Petrel is listed as common because this species nests in large numbers on offshore rocks along the coast. But since these birds spend the daylight hours 50 miles out to sea and come to their nests only under cover of darkness, birders seldom see them.

Species marked with an asterisk (*) are designated review species by the Oregon Bird Records Committee (OBRC). Sightings of these birds (or of any species not included on this list) should be reported to the OBRC, P.O. Box 10373, Eugene, OR 97440.

SPECIES	WINTER	SPRING	SUMMER	AUTUMN
❑ *Fulvous Whistling-Duck	X			
❑ Greater White-fronted Goose	U	C		C
❑ Emperor Goose	R	R		R
❑ Snow Goose	C	C		C
❑ Ross's Goose	R	C		C
❑ Brant	U	C	R	C
❑ Cackling Goose	C	C		C

SPECIES	WINTER	SPRING	SUMMER	AUTUMN
❑ Canada Goose	C	C	C	C
❑ Trumpeter Swan	U	U	U	U
❑ Tundra Swan	U	C		C
❑ ★Whooper Swan	X	X		X
❑ Wood Duck	U	C	C	C
❑ Gadwall	C	C	C	C
❑ ★Falcated Duck	X			
❑ Eurasian Wigeon	U	U		U
❑ American Wigeon	C	C	U	C
❑ ★American Black Duck	X	X	X	X
❑ Mallard	C	C	C	C
❑ Blue-winged Teal	R	U	R	U
❑ Cinnamon Teal	R	C	C	C
❑ Northern Shoveler	C	C	C	C
❑ Northern Pintail	C	C	C	C
❑ ★Garganey		X		X
❑ ★Baikal Teal	X			
❑ Common Teal	R	R		R
❑ Green-winged Teal	C	C	U	C
❑ Canvasback	C	C	C	C
❑ Redhead	U	C	C	C
❑ Ring-necked Duck	C	C	U	C
❑ Tufted Duck	R	R		R
❑ Greater Scaup	C	C	R	C
❑ Lesser Scaup	C	C	U	C
❑ ★Steller's Eider	X			
❑ ★King Eider	X	X		X
❑ Harlequin Duck	U	U	R	U
❑ Surf Scoter	C	C	U	C
❑ White-winged Scoter	C	C	U	C
❑ Black Scoter	U	U	R	U
❑ Long-tailed Duck	R	R		R
❑ Bufflehead	C	C	U	C
❑ Common Goldeneye	U	C		C
❑ Barrow's Goldeneye	U	U	U	U
❑ ★Smew	X			
❑ Hooded Merganser	U	U	U	U
❑ Common Merganser	C	C	C	C

SPECIES	WINTER	SPRING	SUMMER	AUTUMN
❑ Red-breasted Merganser	C	C		C
❑ Ruddy Duck	C	C	C	C
❑ Chukar (I)	C	C	C	C
❑ Gray Partridge (I)	U	U	U	U
❑ Ring-necked Pheasant (I)	C	C	C	C
❑ Ruffed Grouse	C	C	C	C
❑ Greater Sage-Grouse	U	U	U	U
❑ Spruce Grouse	U	U	U	U
❑ Dusky Grouse	C	C	C	C
❑ Sooty Grouse	C	C	C	C
❑ ★Sharp-tailed Grouse	R	R	R	R
❑ Wild Turkey (I)	U	U	U	U
❑ Mountain Quail	C	C	C	C
❑ California Quail	C	C	C	C
❑ Northern Bobwhite (I) (E)				
❑ Red-throated Loon	U	C	R	C
❑ ★Arctic Loon		X		
❑ Pacific Loon	U	C	U	C
❑ Common Loon	C	C	R	C
❑ Yellow-billed Loon	R	R	R	R
❑ Pied-billed Grebe	C	C	C	C
❑ Horned Grebe	U	C	U	C
❑ Red-necked Grebe	U	U	R	U
❑ Eared Grebe	U	C	C	C
❑ Western Grebe	C	C	C	C
❑ Clark's Grebe	R	U	C	U
❑ ★Shy Albatross			X	
❑ Laysan Albatross	U	R	R	R
❑ Black-footed Albatross	U	C	C	U
❑ ★Short-tailed Albatross	X	X	X	X
❑ Northern Fulmar	C	R	R	U
❑ ★Murphy's Petrel		X		X
❑ Mottled Petrel	X	X	X	R
❑ ★Juan Fernandez Petrel			X	
❑ ★Cook's Petrel				X
❑ ★Parkinson's Petrel				X
❑ ★Streaked Shearwater				X

SPECIES	WINTER	SPRING	SUMMER	AUTUMN
❑ Pink-footed Shearwater		U	C	C
❑ Flesh-footed Shearwater	R	R	R	U
❑ *Wedge-tailed Shearwater		X		X
❑ Buller's Shearwater	R		R	C
❑ Sooty Shearwater	R	C	C	C
❑ Short-tailed Shearwater	C	U		C
❑ *Manx Shearwater		R		R
❑ *Black-vented Shearwater			R	R
❑ *Wilson's Storm-Petrel		X	X	
❑ Fork-tailed Storm-Petrel	U	U	U	U
❑ Leach's Storm-Petrel	U	C	C	U
❑ *Black Storm-Petrel				X
❑ *Masked Booby			X	
❑ *Blue-footed Booby				X
❑ *Brown Booby				X
❑ American White Pelican		C	C	C
❑ Brown Pelican	U	C	C	C
❑ Brandt's Cormorant	C	C	C	C
❑ Double-crested Cormorant	C	C	C	C
❑ Pelagic Cormorant	C	C	C	C
❑ *Magnificent Frigatebird	X		X	
❑ American Bittern	R	U	U	R
❑ Least Bittern		R	R	
❑ Great Blue Heron	C	C	C	C
❑ Great Egret	C	C	C	C
❑ Snowy Egret	R	U	U	R
❑ *Little Blue Heron	X	X	X	
❑ *Tricolored Heron		X		X
❑ Cattle Egret	R	R	R	R
❑ Green Heron	R	U	U	R
❑ Black-crowned Night-Heron	U	C	C	U
❑ *White Ibis				X
❑ White-faced Ibis	R	C	C	U
❑ Turkey Vulture	R	C	C	C
❑ *California Condor (E)				
❑ Osprey	R	C	C	U
❑ White-tailed Kite	U	R	R	U

SPECIES	WINTER	SPRING	SUMMER	AUTUMN
❑ Bald Eagle	C	C	C	C
❑ Northern Harrier	C	C	C	C
❑ Sharp-shinned Hawk	U	U	U	C
❑ Cooper's Hawk	C	C	U	C
❑ Northern Goshawk	U	U	U	U
❑ Red-shouldered Hawk	U	U	U	U
❑ *Broad-winged Hawk		R		R
❑ Swainson's Hawk		C	C	U
❑ Red-tailed Hawk	C	C	C	C
❑ Ferruginous Hawk	R	U	U	U
❑ Rough-legged Hawk	U	R		U
❑ Golden Eagle	R	U	U	U
❑ *Crested Caracara	X		X	X
❑ American Kestrel	C	C	C	C
❑ Merlin	U	U	R	U
❑ Gyrfalcon	R	R		R
❑ Peregrine Falcon	U	U	U	U
❑ Prairie Falcon	U	U	U	U
❑ Yellow Rail		U	U	
❑ Virginia Rail	R	U	U	U
❑ Sora	R	U	U	U
❑ *Common Moorhen	X	X		
❑ American Coot	C	C	C	C
❑ Sandhill Crane	U	C	C	C
❑ Black-bellied Plover	U	C	U	C
❑ American Golden Plover		R	U	U
❑ Pacific Golden Plover	R	R	U	U
❑ *Lesser Sand-Plover			X	X
❑ Snowy Plover	R	U	U	U
❑ *Wilson's Plover				X
❑ Semipalmated Plover	R	C	C	C
❑ *Piping Plover				X
❑ Killdeer	C	C	C	C
❑ *Mountain Plover	X			X
❑ *Eurasian Dotterel				X
❑ Black Oystercatcher	U	U	U	U
❑ Black-necked Stilt		U	U	U

SPECIES	WINTER	SPRING	SUMMER	AUTUMN
❑ American Avocet	R	C	C	C
❑ Spotted Sandpiper	R	C	C	C
❑ Solitary Sandpiper		R	R	R
❑ Wandering Tattler	R	C	C	C
❑ *Spotted Redshank	X			
❑ Greater Yellowlegs	U	C	C	C
❑ Willet	R	C	C	U
❑ Lesser Yellowlegs	R	U	U	C
❑ Upland Sandpiper		R	R	R
❑ Whimbrel	R	C	C	C
❑ *Bristle-thighed Curlew		X		X
❑ Long-billed Curlew	R	C	C	U
❑ *Hudsonian Godwit		X		X
❑ *Bar-tailed Godwit		X	X	X
❑ Marbled Godwit	R	U	U	U
❑ Ruddy Turnstone	R	U	U	U
❑ Black Turnstone	C	C	U	C
❑ Surfbird	C	U	C	C
❑ *Great Knot			X	
❑ Red Knot	R	U	U	U
❑ Sanderling	C	C	U	C
❑ Semipalmated Sandpiper		R	U	R
❑ Western Sandpiper	U	C	C	C
❑ *Red-necked Stint			X	
❑ *Little Stint			X	X
❑ *Long-toed Stint			X	X
❑ Least Sandpiper	U	C	C	C
❑ *White-rumped Sandpiper			X	
❑ Baird's Sandpiper		R	U	U
❑ Pectoral Sandpiper		R	U	C
❑ Sharp-tailed Sandpiper				R
❑ Rock Sandpiper	U	R		R
❑ Dunlin	C	C	R	C
❑ *Curlew Sandpiper			X	X
❑ Stilt Sandpiper		R	R	R
❑ Buff-breasted Sandpiper		X	R	R
❑ Ruff		R	R	R
❑ Short-billed Dowitcher		C	C	C
❑ Long-billed Dowitcher	U	C	C	C
❑ Wilson's Snipe	U	C	C	U

SPECIES	WINTER	SPRING	SUMMER	AUTUMN
❑ Wilson's Phalarope		C	C	C
❑ Red-necked Phalarope		C	C	C
❑ Red Phalarope	U	C	U	C
❑ ★Laughing Gull		X	X	X
❑ Franklin's Gull	R	C	C	U
❑ ★Little Gull	X	X	X	X
❑ ★Black-headed Gull	X			X
❑ Bonaparte's Gull	R	C	U	C
❑ Heermann's Gull	R	U	C	C
❑ Mew Gull	C	U	R	C
❑ Ring-billed Gull	C	C	C	C
❑ California Gull	C	C	C	C
❑ Herring Gull	U	C	R	C
❑ Thayer's Gull	U	C		C
❑ ★Iceland Gull	X			
❑ ★Lesser Black-backed Gull		X		
❑ ★Slaty-backed Gull	X			
❑ Western Gull	C	C	C	C
❑ Glaucous-winged Gull	C	C	U	A
❑ Glaucous Gull	R	R		R
❑ Sabine's Gull	R	C	R	C
❑ Black-legged Kittiwake	U	C	U	C
❑ ★Red-legged Kittiwake	X	X	X	
❑ ★Ross's Gull		X		X
❑ ★Least Tern		X	X	
❑ Caspian Tern		C	C	C
❑ Black Tern		U	U	U
❑ Common Tern		C	U	C
❑ Arctic Tern		U	R	U
❑ Forster's Tern		U	U	U
❑ Elegant Tern			U	R
❑ South Polar Skua			R	U
❑ Pomarine Jaeger	R	U	C	C
❑ Parasitic Jaeger		R	U	U
❑ Long-tailed Jaeger		R	U	U

SPECIES	WINTER	SPRING	SUMMER	AUTUMN
❑ Common Murre	C	C	C	C
❑ ★Thick-billed Murre	X			X
❑ Pigeon Guillemot	R	C	C	C
❑ ★Long-billed Murrelet			X	X
❑ Marbled Murrelet	R	U	U	U
❑ ★Xantus's Murrelet			X	X
❑ Ancient Murrelet	U	R	R	U
❑ Cassin's Auklet	U	C	C	C
❑ ★Parakeet Auklet	X	X		X
❑ Rhinoceros Auklet	R	U	U	U
❑ Horned Puffin	R	U	R	R
❑ Tufted Puffin	R	C	C	U
❑ Rock Pigeon (I)	C	C	C	C
❑ Band-tailed Pigeon	U	C	C	C
❑ ★Eurasian Collared Dove (I)	X	X	X	X
❑ ★White-winged Dove		X		X
❑ Mourning Dove	U	C	C	C
❑ Common Ground Dove			X	
❑ ★Yellow-billed Cuckoo			R	
❑ Barn Owl	U	U	U	U
❑ Flammulated Owl			U	U
❑ Western Screech Owl	C	C	C	C
❑ Great Horned Owl	C	C	C	C
❑ Snowy Owl	R			
❑ ★Northern Hawk-Owl	X			X
❑ Northern Pygmy-Owl	U	U	U	U
❑ Burrowing Owl	R	U	U	R
❑ Spotted Owl	U	U	U	U
❑ Barred Owl	U	U	U	U
❑ Great Gray Owl	U	U	U	U
❑ Long-eared Owl	U	U	U	U
❑ Short-eared Owl	U	C	C	C
❑ ★Boreal Owl	R	R	R	R
❑ Northern Saw-whet Owl	C	C	C	C
❑ Common Nighthawk		R	C	U
❑ Common Poorwill		U	U	U

SPECIES	WINTER	SPRING	SUMMER	AUTUMN
❑ Black Swift		U	U	U
❑ Vaux's Swift		C	C	C
❑ White-throated Swift		C	C	C
❑ ★Broad-billed Hummingbird				X
❑ ★Ruby-throated Hummingbird				X
❑ Black-chinned Hummingbird		U	U	R
❑ Anna's Hummingbird	C	C	C	C
❑ Costa's Hummingbird	R	R	R	R
❑ Calliope Hummingbird		C	C	R
❑ Broad-tailed Hummingbird		U	U	
❑ Rufous Hummingbird	R	C	C	U
❑ Allen's Hummingbird		C	C	
❑ Belted Kingfisher	C	C	C	C
❑ Lewis's Woodpecker	U	U	U	U
❑ Acorn Woodpecker	U	U	U	U
❑ Williamson's Sapsucker	U	U	U	U
❑ ★Yellow-bellied Sapsucker	X		X	X
❑ Red-naped Sapsucker	R	C	C	C
❑ Red-breasted Sapsucker	U	U	U	U
❑ ★Nuttall's Woodpecker	X			X
❑ Downy Woodpecker	C	C	C	C
❑ Hairy Woodpecker	C	C	C	C
❑ White-headed Woodpecker	U	U	U	U
❑ American Three-toed Woodpecker	R	R	R	R
❑ Black-backed Woodpecker	U	U	U	U
❑ Northern Flicker	C	C	C	C
❑ Pileated Woodpecker	U	U	U	U
❑ Olive-sided Flycatcher		U	U	U
❑ Western Wood-Pewee		C	C	R
❑ ★Eastern Wood-Pewee		X		
❑ Willow Flycatcher		C	C	U
❑ Least Flycatcher	X	R	R	R
❑ Hammond's Flycatcher		C	C	U
❑ Gray Flycatcher		U	U	U
❑ Dusky Flycatcher		U	U	U
❑ Pacific-slope Flycatcher		C	C	C

SPECIES	WINTER	SPRING	SUMMER	AUTUMN
❑ Cordilleran Flycatcher		U	U	U
❑ Black Phoebe	C	C	C	C
❑ *Eastern Phoebe	X	X	X	X
❑ Say's Phoebe	R	C	C	U
❑ *Vermilion Flycatcher	X			X
❑ *Dusky-capped Flycatcher	X			
❑ Ash-throated Flycatcher		U	U	R
❑ Tropical Kingbird	X		X	R
❑ *Cassin's Kingbird			X	X
❑ Western Kingbird		C	C	R
❑ Eastern Kingbird		R	C	R
❑ *Scissor-tailed Flycatcher		X	X	X
❑ Loggerhead Shrike	R	U	U	U
❑ Northern Shrike	U	U		U
❑ *Bell's Vireo		X		
❑ *Yellow-throated Vireo			X	
❑ *Plumbeous Vireo		R	R	R
❑ Cassin's Vireo		U	U	U
❑ *Blue-headed Vireo		X		X
❑ Hutton's Vireo	U	U	U	U
❑ Warbling Vireo		C	C	C
❑ *Philadelphia Vireo		X		X
❑ Red-eyed Vireo		R	U	U
❑ Gray Jay	U	U	U	U
❑ Steller's Jay	C	C	C	C
❑ Blue Jay	R	R	X	R
❑ Western Scrub-Jay	C	C	C	C
❑ Pinyon Jay	U	U	U	U
❑ Clark's Nutcracker	U	U	U	U
❑ Black-billed Magpie	C	C	C	C
❑ American Crow	C	C	C	C
❑ Common Raven	C	C	C	C
❑ Horned Lark	C	C	C	C
❑ Purple Martin		U	U	
❑ Tree Swallow	R	C	C	U

SPECIES	WINTER	SPRING	SUMMER	AUTUMN
❑ Violet-green Swallow	R	C	C	U
❑ Northern Rough-winged Swallow		U	U	R
❑ Bank Swallow		U	U	R
❑ Cliff Swallow		C	C	U
❑ Barn Swallow	R	C	C	U
❑ Black-capped Chickadee	C	C	C	C
❑ Mountain Chickadee	C	C	C	C
❑ Chestnut-backed Chickadee	C	C	C	C
❑ Oak Titmouse	C	C	C	C
❑ Juniper Titmouse	U	U	U	U
❑ Bushtit	C	C	C	C
❑ Red-breasted Nuthatch	C	C	C	C
❑ White-breasted Nuthatch	U	U	U	U
❑ Pygmy Nuthatch	C	C	C	C
❑ Brown Creeper	C	C	C	C
❑ Rock Wren	R	C	C	U
❑ Canyon Wren	U	U	U	U
❑ Bewick's Wren	C	C	C	C
❑ House Wren		C	C	U
❑ Winter Wren	C	C	U	C
❑ *Sedge Wren		X	X	
❑ Marsh Wren	U	C	C	C
❑ American Dipper	U	U	U	U
❑ Golden-crowned Kinglet	C	C	C	C
❑ Ruby-crowned Kinglet	C	C	C	C
❑ Blue-gray Gnatcatcher	X	U	U	R
❑ *Northern Wheatear			X	X
❑ Western Bluebird	U	U	U	U
❑ Mountain Bluebird	U	C	C	C
❑ Townsend's Solitaire	C	U	U	C
❑ Veery			U	

SPECIES	WINTER	SPRING	SUMMER	AUTUMN
❑ ★Gray-cheeked Thrush				X
❑ Swainson's Thrush		C	C	C
❑ Hermit Thrush	U	U	U	U
❑ ★Wood Thrush		X		X
❑ American Robin	C	C	C	C
❑ Varied Thrush	U	U	U	U
❑ Wrentit	C	C	C	C
❑ Gray Catbird			U	R
❑ Northern Mockingbird	R	R	R	R
❑ Sage Thrasher	R	C	C	U
❑ ★Brown Thrasher	X	X	X	X
❑ ★California Thrasher	X	X	X	X
❑ European Starling (I)	C	C	C	C
❑ ★Eastern Yellow Wagtail			X	
❑ ★White Wagtail	X	X		X
❑ ★Red-throated Pipit				X
❑ American Pipit	U	C	U	C
❑ ★Sprague's Pipit				X
❑ Bohemian Waxwing	U	U		U
❑ Cedar Waxwing	U	C	C	C
❑ ★Phainopepla	X	X	X	
❑ ★Blue-winged Warbler		X	X	
❑ ★Golden-winged Warbler			X	
❑ Tennessee Warbler	X	X	X	X
❑ Orange-crowned Warbler	R	C	C	C
❑ Nashville Warbler	R	U	U	C
❑ ★Virginia's Warbler			X	X
❑ ★Lucy's Warbler	X			
❑ Northern Parula		X	X	X
❑ Yellow Warbler		C	C	U
❑ Chestnut-sided Warbler		X	X	X
❑ ★Magnolia Warbler		X	X	X
❑ ★Cape May Warbler	X	X	X	X
❑ Black-throated Blue Warbler	R	X	X	R

SPECIES	WINTER	SPRING	SUMMER	AUTUMN
❑ Yellow-rumped Warbler	U	C	C	C
❑ Black-throated Gray Warbler	R	C	C	C
❑ ★Black-throated Green Warbler	X	X	X	X
❑ Townsend's Warbler	U	C	C	C
❑ Hermit Warbler	R	C	C	C
❑ ★Blackburnian Warbler		X	X	X
❑ ★Yellow-throated Warbler	X	X	X	X
❑ ★Pine Warbler				X
❑ ★Prairie Warbler	X			X
❑ Palm Warbler	R	R		R
❑ ★Bay-breasted Warbler		X	X	X
❑ Blackpoll Warbler		X	X	X
❑ Black-and-white Warbler	X	X	X	X
❑ American Redstart	X	R	R	R
❑ ★Prothonotary Warbler		X	X	X
❑ ★Worm-eating Warbler			X	X
❑ Ovenbird		X	X	
❑ Northern Waterthrush	X		U	R
❑ ★Louisiana Waterthrush				X
❑ ★Kentucky Warbler			X	X
❑ ★Mourning Warbler			X	X
❑ MacGillivray's Warbler	X	C	C	U
❑ Common Yellowthroat	R	C	C	C
❑ ★Hooded Warbler		X	X	X
❑ Wilson's Warbler	X	C	C	C
❑ ★Canada Warbler			X	X
❑ Yellow-breasted Chat		U	U	R
❑ ★Summer Tanager	X	X	X	X
❑ ★Scarlet Tanager			X	X
❑ Western Tanager		C	C	U
❑ Green-tailed Towhee	X	U	U	U
❑ Spotted Towhee	C	C	C	C
❑ California Towhee	U	U	U	U
❑ American Tree Sparrow	U	U		U
❑ Chipping Sparrow	R	C	C	C
❑ Clay-colored Sparrow	R	R		R
❑ Brewer's Sparrow		C	C	U
❑ ★Black-chinned Sparrow			R	

SPECIES	WINTER	SPRING	SUMMER	AUTUMN
❑ Vesper Sparrow		U	U	U
❑ Lark Sparrow	U	U	U	U
❑ Black-throated Sparrow		U	U	
❑ Sage Sparrow	R	C	C	C
❑ *Lark Bunting	X	X	X	X
❑ Savannah Sparrow	U	C	C	C
❑ Grasshopper Sparrow	X	U	U	R
❑ *LeConte's Sparrow				X
❑ Fox Sparrow	C	C	U	C
❑ Song Sparrow	C	C	C	C
❑ Lincoln's Sparrow	U	C	U	C
❑ Swamp Sparrow	R	R		R
❑ White-throated Sparrow	R	R	X	R
❑ Harris's Sparrow	R	X		X
❑ White-crowned Sparrow	C	C	C	C
❑ Golden-crowned Sparrow	C	C		C
❑ Dark-eyed Junco	C	C	C	C
❑ *McCown's Longspur	X			X
❑ Lapland Longspur	R	R		U
❑ *Smith's Longspur	X			
❑ *Chestnut-collared Longspur		X		X
❑ *Rustic Bunting		X		X
❑ Snow Bunting	U	R		R
❑ *McKay's Bunting	X			
❑ Rose-breasted Grosbeak	X	X	X	X
❑ Black-headed Grosbeak	X	C	C	U
❑ *Blue Grosbeak	X		X	
❑ Lazuli Bunting		C	C	R
❑ *Indigo Bunting	X	X	X	X
❑ *Painted Bunting	X		X	X
❑ *Dickcissel	X	X	X	X
❑ Bobolink		U	U	R
❑ Red-winged Blackbird	C	C	C	C
❑ Tricolored Blackbird	U	U	U	U
❑ Western Meadowlark	U	C	C	C
❑ Yellow-headed Blackbird	R	C	C	C
❑ *Rusty Blackbird	X	X		X
❑ Brewer's Blackbird	C	C	C	C

SPECIES	WINTER	SPRING	SUMMER	AUTUMN
❑ ★Common Grackle	X	X	X	X
❑ ★Great-tailed Grackle	X	X	X	X
❑ Brown-headed Cowbird	R	C	C	C
❑ ★Orchard Oriole	X	X		X
❑ ★Hooded Oriole	X	X	X	
❑ ★Streak-backed Oriole				X
❑ Bullock's Oriole	X	C	C	U
❑ ★Baltimore Oriole	X	X	X	X
❑ ★Scott's Oriole			X	
❑ ★Brambling	X	X		X
❑ Gray-crowned Rosy-Finch	U	U	U	U
❑ Black Rosy-Finch	R	R	U	U
❑ Pine Grosbeak	U	U	U	U
❑ Purple Finch	U	U	U	U
❑ Cassin's Finch	C	C	C	C
❑ House Finch	C	C	C	C
❑ Red Crossbill	U	U	U	U
❑ White-winged Crossbill	R	R	R	R
❑ Common Redpoll	R	X		R
❑ ★Hoary Redpoll	X			
❑ Pine Siskin	C	C	C	C
❑ Lesser Goldfinch	C	C	C	C
❑ ★Lawrence's Goldfinch	X	X		
❑ American Goldfinch	C	C	C	C
❑ Evening Grosbeak	U	U	U	U
❑ House Sparrow (I)	C	C	C	C

Resources and Contact Information

USDA Forest Service

If you are planning to do any extensive hiking in a national forest or driving on secondary Forest Service roads, you should obtain an official map of that forest. The Web sites for each national forest provide excellent information on trails, campgrounds, and current conditions.

USDA Forest Service–Pacific Northwest Region
PO Box 3623, 333 SW First Avenue
Portland, Oregon 97208-3623
(503) 808–2468
www.fs.fed.us/r6/welcome.shtml

Columbia River Gorge National Scenic Area
902 Wasco Avenue, Suite 200
Hood River, OR 97031
(541) 348–1700
www.fs.fed.us/r6/columbia/forest

Deschutes National Forest
1001 SW Emkay Drive
Bend, OR 97702
(541) 383–5300
www.fs.fed.us/r6/centraloregon

Fremont–Winema National Forests
1301 South G Street
Lakeview, OR 97630
(541) 947–2151
www.fs.fed.us/r6/frewin

Malheur National Forest
PO Box 909
431 Patterson Bridge Road
John Day, OR 97845
(541) 575–3000
www.fs.fed.us/r6/malheur

Mount Hood National Forest
16400 Champion Way
Sandy, OR 97055
(503) 668–1700
www.fs.fed.us/r6/mthood

Ochoco National Forest
3160 NE Third Street
Prineville, OR 97754
(541) 416–6500
www.fs.fed.us/r6/centraloregon

Rogue River–Siskiyou National Forest
PO Box 520
333 West Eighth Street
Medford, OR 97501
(541) 858–2200
www.fs.fed.us/r6/rogue-siskiyou

Siuslaw National Forest
4077 SW Research Way
PO Box 1148
Corvallis, Oregon 97339
(541) 750–7000
www.fs.fed.us/r6/siuslaw

Umatilla National Forest
2517 SW Hailey Avenue
Pendleton, OR 97801
(541) 278–3716
www.fs.fed.us/r6/uma

Umpqua National Forest
2900 Stewart Parkway
Roseburg, OR 97470
(541) 672–6601
www.fs.fed.us/r6/umpqua

Wallowa–Whitman National Forest
PO Box 907
1550 Dewey Avenue
Baker City, OR 97814
(541) 523–6391
www.fs.fed.us/r6/w-w

Willamette National Forest
211 E. 7th Avenue
Eugene, OR 97401
(541) 225–6300
www.fs.fed.us/r6/willamette

Bureau of Land Management

The Bureau of Land Management oversees much of the sage-steppe habitat in eastern Oregon, as well as forests, canyonlands, and river corridors throughout the state.

Oregon/Washington State Office
333 SW First Avenue
Portland, OR 97208
(503) 808–6001
www.blm.gov/or/

Burns District
28910 Highway 20 West
Hines, OR 97738
(541) 573–4400
www.blm.gov/or/districts/burns

Coos Bay District
1300 Airport Lane
North Bend, OR 97459
(541) 756–0100
www.blm.gov/or/districts/coosbay

Eugene District
2890 Chad Drive
PO Box 10226
Eugene, OR 97440
(541) 683–6600
www.blm.gov/or/districts/eugene

Lakeview District
1301 South G Street
Lakeview, OR 97630
(541) 947–2177
www.blm.gov/or/districts/lakeview

Medford District
3040 Biddle Road
Medford, OR 97504
(541) 618–2200
www.blm.gov/or/districts/medford

Prineville District
3050 NE Third Street
Prineville, OR 97754
(541) 416–6700
www.blm.gov/or/districts/prineville

Roseburg District
777 NW Garden Valley Boulevard
Roseburg, OR 97470
(541) 440–4930
www.blm.gov/or/districts/roseburg

Salem District
1717 Fabry Road SE
Salem, OR 97306
(503) 375–5646
www.blm.gov/or/districts/salem

Vale District
100 Oregon Street
Vale, OR 97918
(541) 473–3144
www.blm.gov/or/districts/vale

Oregon State Parks and Wildlife Areas

The Oregon Parks and Recreation Department manages hundreds of state parks throughout the state, ranging from tiny roadside picnic areas to parks with large campgrounds and extensive tracts of wildlife habitat. The Web site below enables you to locate any of the state parks and provides photographs, brochures, and maps of many individual sites.

Oregon Parks and Recreation Department
State Parks
725 Summer Street NE, Suite C
Salem, OR 97301
(800) 551–6949
www.oregon.gov/OPRD/PARKS

The Oregon Department of Fish and Wildlife manages fourteen wildlife areas throughout the state. While these areas are open to hunting during certain seasons, they also provide birding opportunities. The Web site below lists these properties and provides directions. Please note that the roads leading to some of these sites are very primitive and should not be attempted in a passenger car.

Oregon Department of Fish and Wildlife
3406 Cherry Avenue NE
Salem, OR 97303-4924
(503) 947–6000
www.dfw.state.or.us

National Park Service

Crater Lake National Park
PO Box 7
Crater Lake, OR 97604
(541) 594–3100
www.nps.gov/crla

John Day Fossil Beds National Monument
32651 Highway 19
Kimberly, OR 97848-9701
(541) 987–2333
www.nps.gov/joda/

Oregon Caves National Monument
19000 Caves Highway
Cave Junction, OR 97523
(541) 592–2100
www.nps.gov/orca

National Wildlife Refuges

Klamath Basin National Wildlife Refuges
4009 Hill Road
Tulelake, CA 96134
(530) 667–2231
www.fws.gov/klamathbasinrefuges

Malheur National Wildlife Refuge
36391 Sodhouse Lane
Princeton, OR 97721
(541) 493–2612
www.fws.gov/malheur

Mid-Columbia River National Wildlife Refuges
PO Box 1447
Richland, WA 99352
(509) 371–9212
www.fws.gov/midcolumbiariver

Oregon Coast National Wildlife Refuge Complex
2127 SE Marine Science Drive
Newport, OR 97365
(541) 867–4550
www.fws.gov/oregoncoast

Sheldon-Hart Mountain National Antelope Refuge
PO Box 111, 18 South G
Lakeview, OR 97630
(541) 947–3315
www.fws.gov/sheldonhartmtn/Hart

Tualatin River National Wildlife Refuge
16507 Roy Rogers Road
Sherwood, OR 97140
(503) 590–5811
www.fws.gov/tualatinriver

Willamette Valley National Wildlife Refuge Complex
26208 Finley Refuge Road
Corvallis, OR 97333-9533
(541) 757–7236
www.fws.gov/willamettevalley

Oregon Birding and Conservation Organizations

Deschutes Basin Land Trust
760 NW Harriman, Suite 100
Bend, OR 97701
(541) 330–0017
www.deschuteslandtrust.org

East Cascades Bird Conservancy
16 NW Kansas Avenue
Bend, OR 97701
(541) 385–6908
www.ecbcbirds.org

Klamath Bird Observatory
PO Box 758
Ashland, OR 97520
(541) 201–0866
www.klamathbird.org

The Nature Conservancy in Oregon
821 SE 14th Avenue
Portland, OR 97214
(503) 802–8100
www.nature.org/wherewework/northamerica/states/oregon

Oregon Field Ornithologists
PO Box 10373
Eugene, OR 97440
www.oregonbirds.org

Audubon Societies

Audubon Society of Corvallis
PO Box 148
Corvallis, OR 97339
www.audubon.corvallis.or.us

Audubon Society of Portland
5151 Northwest Cornell Road
Portland, OR 97210
(503) 292–6855
www.audubonportland.org

Cape Arago Audubon Society
723 7th Terrace
Coos Bay, OR 97420

Central Oregon Audubon Society
PO Box 565
Bend, OR 97709
http://users.bendnet.com/coaudubon

Kalmiopsis Audubon Society
PO Box 1265
Port Orford, OR 97465
www.harborside.com/~pfandha/audubon

Klamath Basin Audubon Society
PO Box 354
Klamath Falls, OR 97601
www.klamathaudubon.org

Lane County Audubon Society
PO Box 5086
Eugene, OR 97405
(541) 485–2473
www.laneaudubon.org

Rogue Valley Audubon Society
PO Box 8597
Medford, OR 97504
(541) 734–2473
www.roguevalleyaudubon.org

Salem Audubon Society
189 Liberty Street NE, Suite 210
Salem, OR 97301-3682
(503) 588–7340
www.salem-audubon.org

Siskiyou Audubon Society
PO Box 2223
Grants Pass, OR 97528
www.siskiyouaudubon.org

Umpqua Valley Audubon Society
PO Box 381
Roseburg, OR 97470

Oregon Birding Trails

Oregon Birding Trails is an ongoing project, which will eventually describe birding sites along designated routes throughout Oregon. The Oregon Cascades Birding Trail and the Klamath Basin Birding Trail are the first two to be completed.

www.oregonbirdingtrails.org
www.oregonbirdingtrails.org/cascades.htm
www.klamathbirdingtrails.com

Oregon's Important Bird Areas

The Oregon's Important Bird Areas program works to identify areas of particular importance to breeding, foraging, or resting birds. The Web site includes a map showing the location of all the sites. Each site has its own Web page.

www.oregoniba.org

Checklists and Trip Reports for Specific Birding Sites

www.birdnotes.net

Road Conditions, Construction, Closures, Weather Updates

www.tripcheck.com

Birding Guides

While birding tour companies from around the country lead trips to Oregon, the two listed below are Oregon-based. The Bird Guide Inc. offers pelagic trips off the Oregon coast. Paradise Birding offers group tours as well as private guiding services across the state.

Greg Gilson
The Bird Guide, Inc.
345 NE Autumn Rose Way, #H
Hillsboro, OR 97124
(503) 640–4570
www.thebirdguide.com

Steve Shunk
Paradise Birding
69320 Sisters View Drive
Sisters, OR 97759
(541) 549–8826
www.paradisebirding.com

References

Adamus, P. R., et al. 2001. *Oregon Breeding Bird Atlas.* Eugene, Ore.: Oregon Field Ornithologists. CD-ROM.

American Birding Association. 1994. *Birdfinding in Forty National Forests and Grasslands.* Colorado Springs, Colo.: American Birding Association.

Brown, Stephen, et al. 1996. *Birding the Southern Oregon Coast.* Coos Bay, Ore.: Cape Arago Audubon Society.

Burrows, R., and J. Gilligan. 2003. *Birds of Oregon.* Auburn, Wash.: Lone Pine Publishing.

Evanich Jr., Joseph E. 1990. *The Birder's Guide to Oregon.* Portland, Ore.: Portland Audubon Society.

Fitchen, John. 2004. *Birding Portland and Multnomah County.* Portland, Ore.: Catalyst Publications.

Gilson, Greg. 2003. *Oregon Central Coast Self-Guided Birding Trail.* Hillsboro, Ore.: The Bird Guide, Inc.

Heinl, S., and M. Hunter. 1985. *Birds of Fern Ridge Reservoir.* Eugene, Ore.: Oregon Department of Fish and Wildlife.

Houck, M., and M. Cody, eds. 2000. *Wild in the City: A Guide to Portland's Natural Areas.* Portland, Ore.: Oregon Historical Society Press.

Janes, Stewart, et al. 2002. *Birds of Jackson County Oregon, Distribution and Abundance.* Medford, Ore.: Rogue Valley Audubon Society.

Kemper, John. 2002. *Southern Oregon's Bird Life.* Medford, Ore: Outdoor Press.

Marshall, D. B., M. G. Hunter, and A. L. Contreras, eds. 2003. *Birds of Oregon: A General Reference.* Corvallis, Ore.: Oregon State University Press.

Massey, B., and D. Vroman. 2003. *Guide to Birds of the Rogue Valley.* Eugene, Ore.: Oregon Field Ornithologists.

Nature Conservancy of Oregon, The. 2001. *Guide to Oregon Preserves.* Portland, Ore.: The Nature Conservancy of Oregon.

Peter, S., et al., eds. 2002. *Exploring the Tualatin River Basin.* Corvallis, Ore.: Oregon State University Press.

Pojar, J., and A. MacKinnon, eds. 1994. *Plants of the Pacific Northwest Coast.* Auburn, Wash.: Lone Pine Publishing.

Reid, Alan. 2004. Cabin Lake, Past and Present. *Oregon Birds,* 30 (4):169–70.

Riley, Laura, and William Riley. 1992. *Guide to the National Wildlife Refuges.* New York: Collier Books.

Shunk, Stephen. 2004. Woodpecker Wonderland. *Winging It,* 16 (3):1–5.

Storm, R., and W. Leonard, eds. 1995. *Reptiles of Washington and Oregon.* Seattle, Wash.: Seattle Audubon Society.

Strycker, Noah. 2003. *Birds of Fern Ridge Reservoir.* Lowell, Ore.: U.S. Army Corps of Engineers.

____. 2003. Birdfinding in Eugene, Oregon. *Birding,* 35 (2):146–54.

____. 2004. Malheur National Wildlife Refuge. *Bird Watcher's Digest,* 26 (3):104–13.

Sullivan, William. 2001. *100 Hikes in Northwest Oregon.* Eugene, Ore.: Navillus Press.

____. 2002. *100 Hike/Travel Guide: Oregon Coast and Coast Range.* Eugene, Ore.: Navillus Press.

____. 2005. *100 Hikes in the Central Oregon Cascades.* Eugene, Ore.: Navillus Press.

Vroman, Dennis. 2004. A 2003 Josephine County Big Year. *Oregon Birds,* 30 (1):22–25.

Index

Bird Species are in bold.

D

H

M

N

O

Y

About the Author

Before turning to birding full time, John Rakestraw took jobs as a music teacher, farm laborer, and hardware salesman to pay for his birding habit. He worked as a naturalist in Kansas and Ohio before finally settling in Oregon. Rakestraw writes articles for birding and nature publications, teaches classes, leads field trips, and works as a guide. An advocate of birding close to home, his current birding goal is to tally 400 species in Oregon. He lives in a cohousing community near Portland with his wife, Marsha, and their schizophrenic cat.

Overview

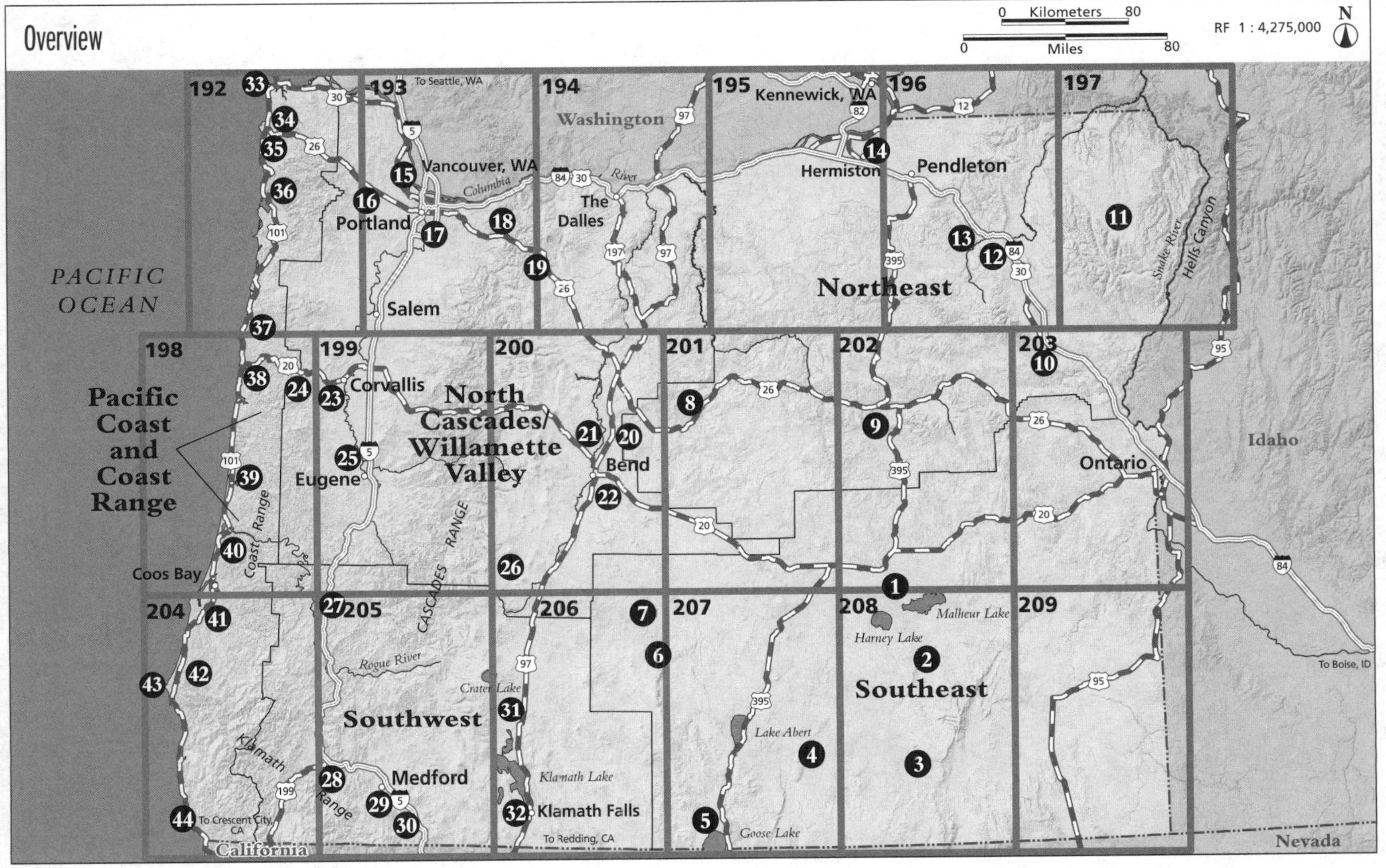

0 Kilometers 80
0 Miles 80
RF 1 : 4,275,000
N
PACIFIC OCEAN
Washington
Idaho
Nevada
California
Northeast
North Cascades/ Willamette Valley
Pacific Coast and Coast Range
Southwest
Southeast
Kennewick, WA
Hermiston
Pendleton
Vancouver, WA
Portland
Salem
The Dalles
Corvallis
Eugene
Bend
Ontario
Coos Bay
Medford
Klamath Falls
To Seattle, WA
To Boise, ID
To Redding, CA
To Crescent City, CA
Columbia River
Snake River
Hells Canyon
Coast Range
CASCADES RANGE
Klamath Range
Rogue River
Crater Lake
Klamath Lake
Lake Abert
Goose Lake
Harney Lake
Malheur Lake
192
193
194
195
196
197
198
199
200
201
202
203
204
205
206
207
208
209

0 5 10 Miles
0 5 10 Kilometers
RF 1 : 730,000 Lambert Projection NAD83 Datum
Washington
124°00'W
123°30'W
46°00'N
45°30'N
45°00'N
PACIFIC OCEAN
Ilwaco
Chinook
Cape Disappointment
Altoona
Skamokawa
Columbia River
Lewis & Clark N.W.R.
Cathlamet
Fort Stevens
Hammond
Astoria
Warrenton
Knappa
Bradley
Westport
Clatskanie
Clatsop
Clatsop State Forest
Del Rey Beach
Gearhart
Seaside
Tillamook Head
Saddle Mountain
Mist
Jewell
Ecola
Cannon Beach
Tolovana Beach
Arcadia Beach
Hug Point
Arch Cape
Oswald West
Elsie
Vernonia
Manzanita
Nehalem
Nehalem Bay
Wheeler
Timber
Tillamook State Forest
Manhattan Beach
Rockaway Beach
Barview
Kings Mtn. 3,226 ft.
Glenwood
Garibaldi
Tillamook Bay
Bay City
Cape Meares NWR
Washington
Hagg Lake
Oceanside
Oceanside Beach
Netarts
Tillamook
Cherry Grove
Netarts Bay
Tillamook
Cape Lookout
Munson Creek Falls
Yamhill
Clay Myers
Carlton
Beaver
Whalen Island
Cape Kiwanda
Hebo
Siuslaw National Forest
Yamhill
Pacific City
Cloverdale
McMinnville
Bob Straub
Grande Ronde Indian Reservation
Whiteson
Erratic Rock
Neskowin
Neskowin Beach
Van Duzer Forest
Sheridan
Amity
Cascade Head
Willamina
Grand Ronde
Roads End
Neotsu
Otis
Rose Lodge
Perrydale
D River State
Lincoln City
Devil's Lake
Brackett Slough NWR
Siuslaw National Forest
Polk
Gleneden Beach
Kernville
Dallas
Gleneden Beach
Lincoln Beach
Fogarty Creek
Black Rock
Boiler Bay
Falls City
Independence
Depoe Bay
Monmouth
Rocky Creek
Siletz River
Sarah Helmick
33
34
35
36
37
101
401
4
30
409
47
202
26
53
6
8
131
22
18
99W
223
51
229

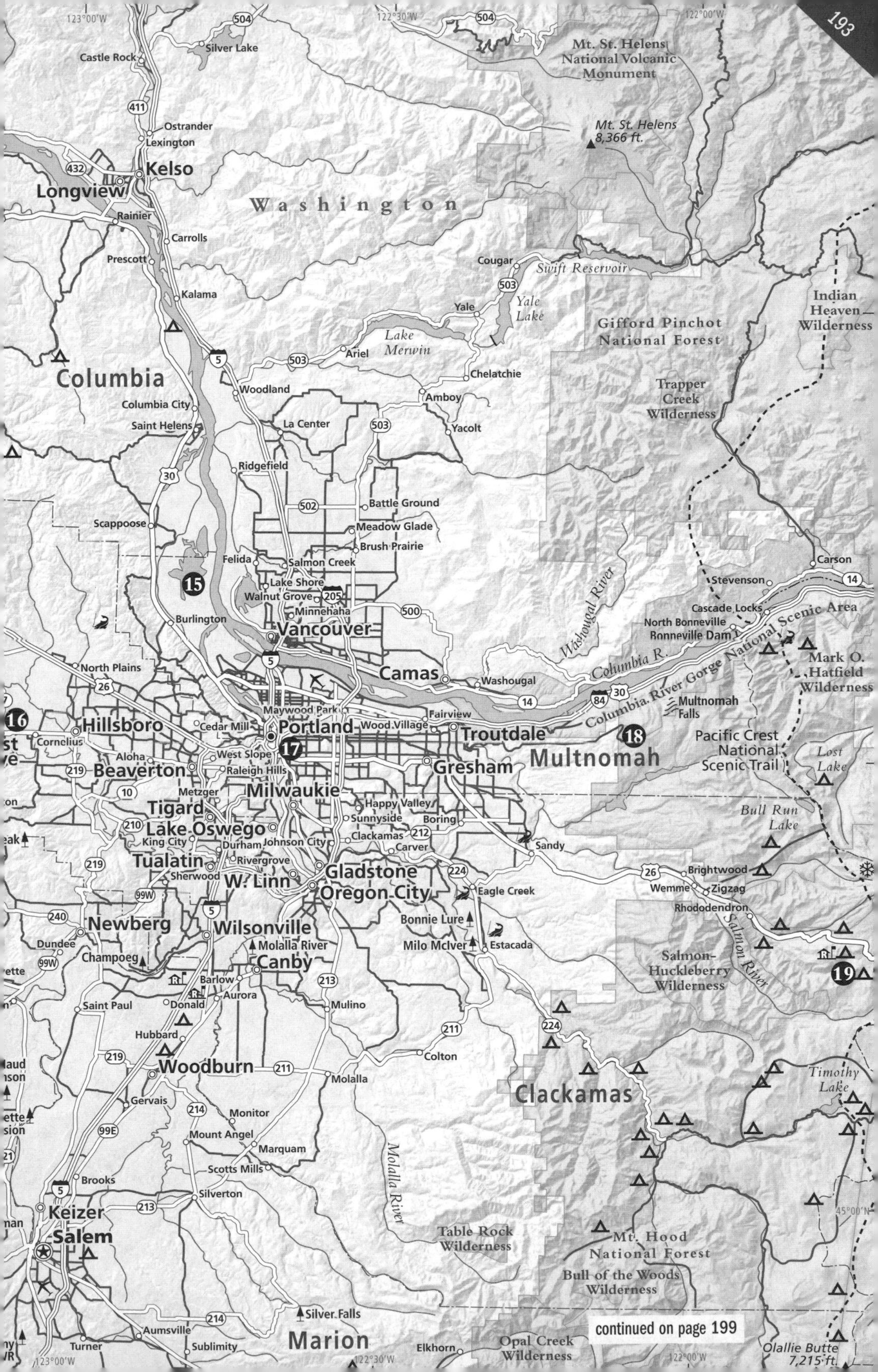

continued on page 199

121°30'W
121°00'W
120°30'W
0 5 10 Miles
0 5 10 Kilometers
RF 1 : 730,000 Lambert Projection NAD83 Datum
Mount Adams Wilderness
Mt. Adams 12,226 ft.
Gifford Pinchot National Forest
Indian Heaven Wilderness
Klickitat River
Washington
Glenwood
Trout Lake
Laurel
141
Wahkiacus
Klickitat
142
Blockhouse
Goldendale
Husum
Centerville
Carson
Hood
White Salmon
Bingen
14
Hood River
Lyle
Mosier
Rowena
84
30
Cliffs
John Day Dam
Maryhill
Wishram
Rufus
Biggs
97
Chenoweth
Dallesport
Heritage Landing
The Dalles Dam
The Dalles
206
Wasco
Odell
Mark O. Hatfield Wilderness
Dee
Parkdale
Lost Lake
Hood River
35
Moro
Dufur
Sherman
Deschutes River
Mt. Hood Wilderness
Mt. Hood 11,240 ft.
197
Grass Valley
John Day River
Tygh Ridge Summit 2,665 ft.
Badger Creek Wilderness
Bennett Pass 4,647 ft.
19
Government Camp
216
Tygh Valley
Wamic
White River Falls
Blue Box Summit 4,025 ft.
Mt. Hood National Forest
26
Maupin
Kent
Timothy Lake
Wapinitia
Wasco
Mt. Wilson 5,599 ft.
45°00'N
Mutton Mountains
Simnasho
Shaniko
218
Pacific Crest National Scenic Trail
Warm Springs Indian Reservation
Antelope
293
Olallie Butte 7,215 ft.

continued on page 201

119°00'W
118°30'W
0 5 10 Miles
0 5 10 Kilometers
RF 1 : 730,000 Lambert Projection NAD83 Datum
Eureka
Prescott
Dayton
Huntsville
Waitsburg
Pasco
Burbank
Finley
Washington
Dixie
Wallula
Garrett
Walla Walla
Touchet
College Place
Walla Walla River
46°00'N
Wenaha-Tucannon Wilderness
Umapine
Milton-Freewater
Holdman
Helix
Athena
Weston
Umatilla National Forest
Adams
North Fork Umatilla Wilderness
Gibbon
Pendleton
Rieth
Mission
Cayuse
Umatilla Indian Reservation
McKay Creek NWR
McKay Reservoir
Black Mtn. 5,445 ft.
Emigrant Springs
Blue Mountain Forest
Umatilla National Forest
Elgin
Meacham
Summerville
45°30'N
Pilot Rock
Nye
Imbler
Umatilla
Kamela
Mt. Emily 6,110 ft.
Alice
Hilgard
Island City
Hilgard Jct.
La Grande
Cove
Cape Horn Summit 3,748 ft.
Battle Mountain Forest
Battle Mtn. Summit 4,270 ft.
Red Bridge
BLUE MOUNTAINS
Union
Union
Grande Ronde River
Johnson Rock 5,714 ft.
Umatilla National Forest
Ukiah
Ukiah-Dale Forest
Tower Mtn. 6,850 ft.
Bridge Creek Wildlife Area
North Powder
Telocaset
Anthony Lake
Dale
North Fork John Day Wilderness
Meadow Brook Summit 4,127 ft.
Haines
Umatilla National Forest
Elkhorn Mountains
Rock Creek Butte 9,106 ft.
119°00'W
118°30'W
13
12
12
124
125
730
37
11
84
204
395
74
82
237
203
244
30

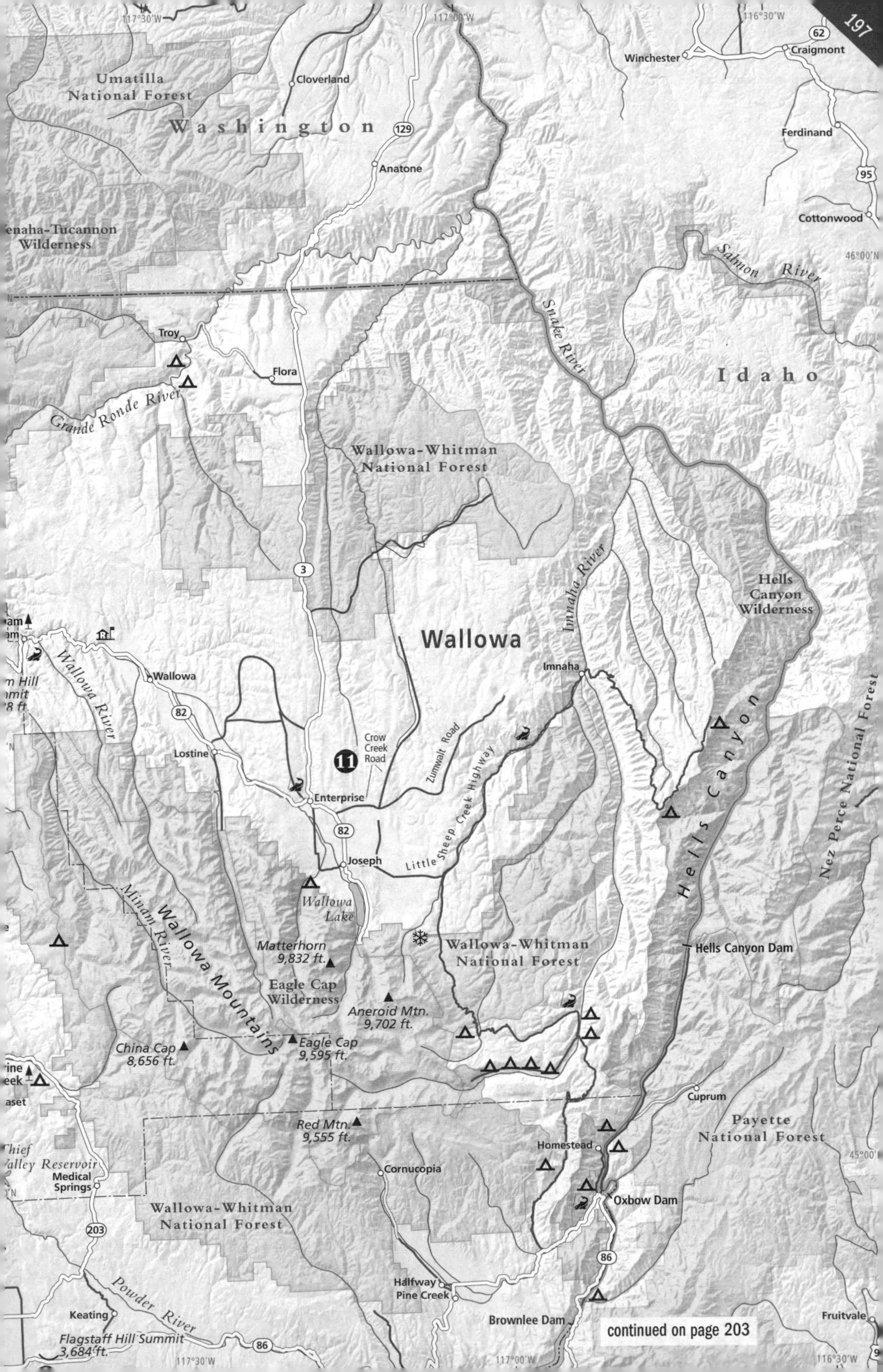

continued on page 203

continued on page 192

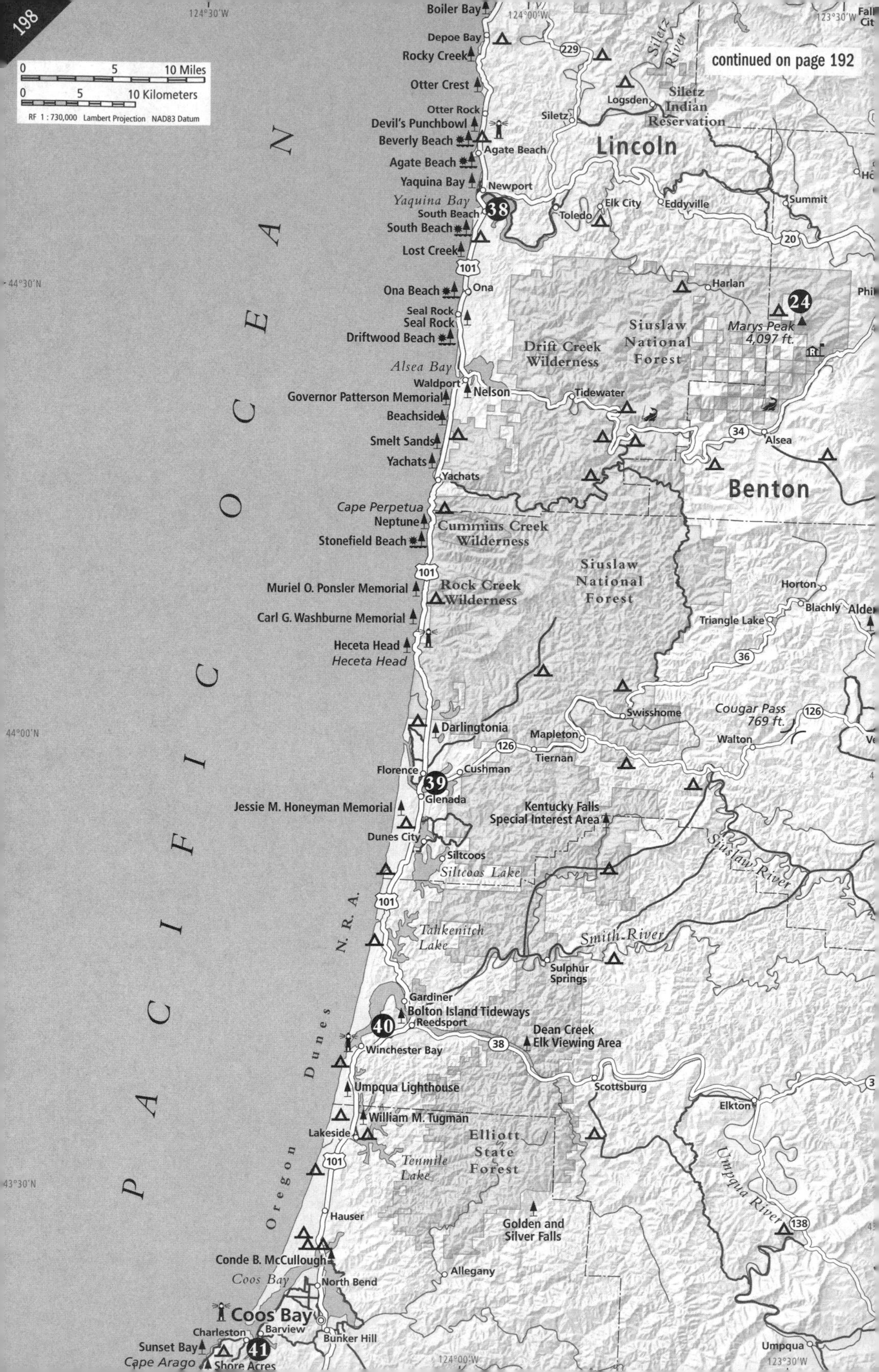

continued on page 205

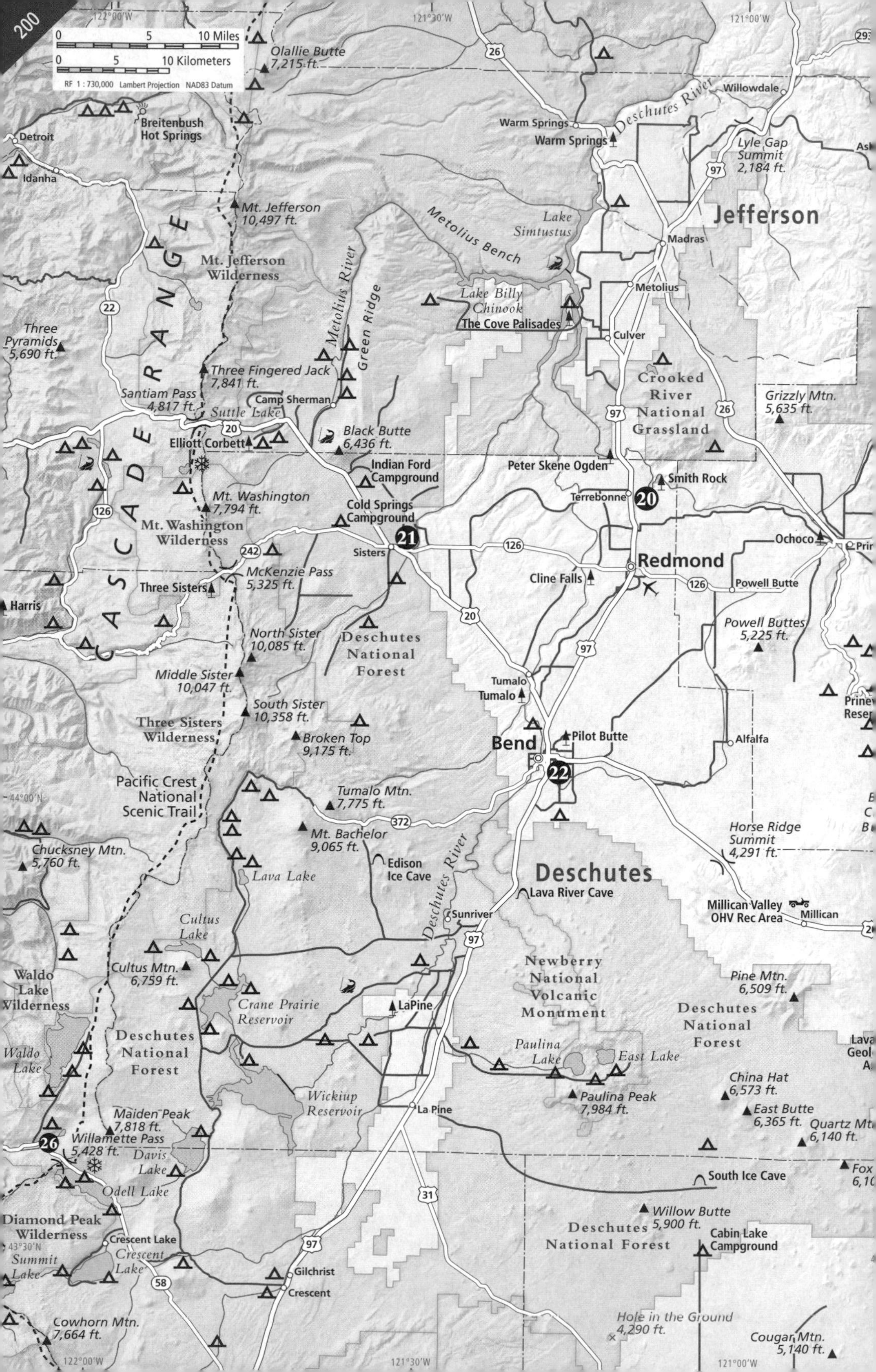
122°00'W
121°30'W
121°00'W
0 5 10 Miles
0 5 10 Kilometers
RF 1 : 730,000 Lambert Projection NAD83 Datum
Olallie Butte
7,215 ft.
26
293
Breitenbush
Hot Springs
Detroit
Idanha
Warm Springs
Warm Springs
Deschutes River
Willowdale
Lyle Gap
Summit
2,184 ft.
97
Mt. Jefferson
10,497 ft.
CASCADE RANGE
Mt. Jefferson
Wilderness
Metolius Bench
Lake
Simtustus
Jefferson
Madras
Metolius
Metolius River
Green Ridge
Lake Billy
Chinook
The Cove Palisades
Culver
22
Three
Pyramids
5,690 ft.
Three Fingered Jack
7,841 ft.
Crooked
River
National
Grassland
Grizzly Mtn.
5,635 ft.
Santiam Pass
4,817 ft.
Camp Sherman
Suttle Lake
20
Black Butte
6,436 ft.
Elliott Corbett
Indian Ford
Campground
Peter Skene Ogden
Smith Rock
Terrebonne
Mt. Washington
7,794 ft.
126
Mt. Washington
Wilderness
Cold Springs
Campground
21
Sisters
242
Ochoco
Redmond
McKenzie Pass
5,325 ft.
Three Sisters
Harris
Cline Falls
Powell Butte
North Sister
10,085 ft.
Deschutes
National
Forest
Powell Buttes
5,225 ft.
Middle Sister
10,047 ft.
Tumalo
Tumalo
South Sister
10,358 ft.
Three Sisters
Wilderness
Broken Top
9,175 ft.
Bend
Pilot Butte
Alfalfa
Pacific Crest
National
Scenic Trail
44°00'N
Tumalo Mtn.
7,775 ft.
372
Mt. Bachelor
9,065 ft.
Chucksney Mtn.
5,760 ft.
Edison
Ice Cave
Horse Ridge
Summit
4,291 ft.
Lava Lake
Deschutes
Lava River Cave
Millican Valley
OHV Rec Area
Millican
Cultus
Lake
Sunriver
Cultus Mtn.
6,759 ft.
Newberry
National
Volcanic
Monument
Waldo
Lake
Wilderness
Crane Prairie
Reservoir
LaPine
Pine Mtn.
6,509 ft.
Deschutes
National
Forest
Waldo
Lake
Deschutes
National
Forest
Paulina
Lake
East Lake
China Hat
6,573 ft.
Paulina Peak
7,984 ft.
Wickiup
Reservoir
La Pine
Maiden Peak
7,818 ft.
East Butte
6,365 ft.
Quartz Mt
6,140 ft.
26
Willamette Pass
5,428 ft.
Davis
Lake
South Ice Cave
Odell Lake
31
Willow Butte
5,900 ft.
Diamond Peak
Wilderness
Crescent Lake
43°30'N
Deschutes
National Forest
Cabin Lake
Campground
Summit
Lake
Crescent
Lake
97
Gilchrist
58
Crescent
Hole in the Ground
4,290 ft.
Cowhorn Mtn.
7,664 ft.
Cougar Mtn.
5,140 ft.

continued on page 195

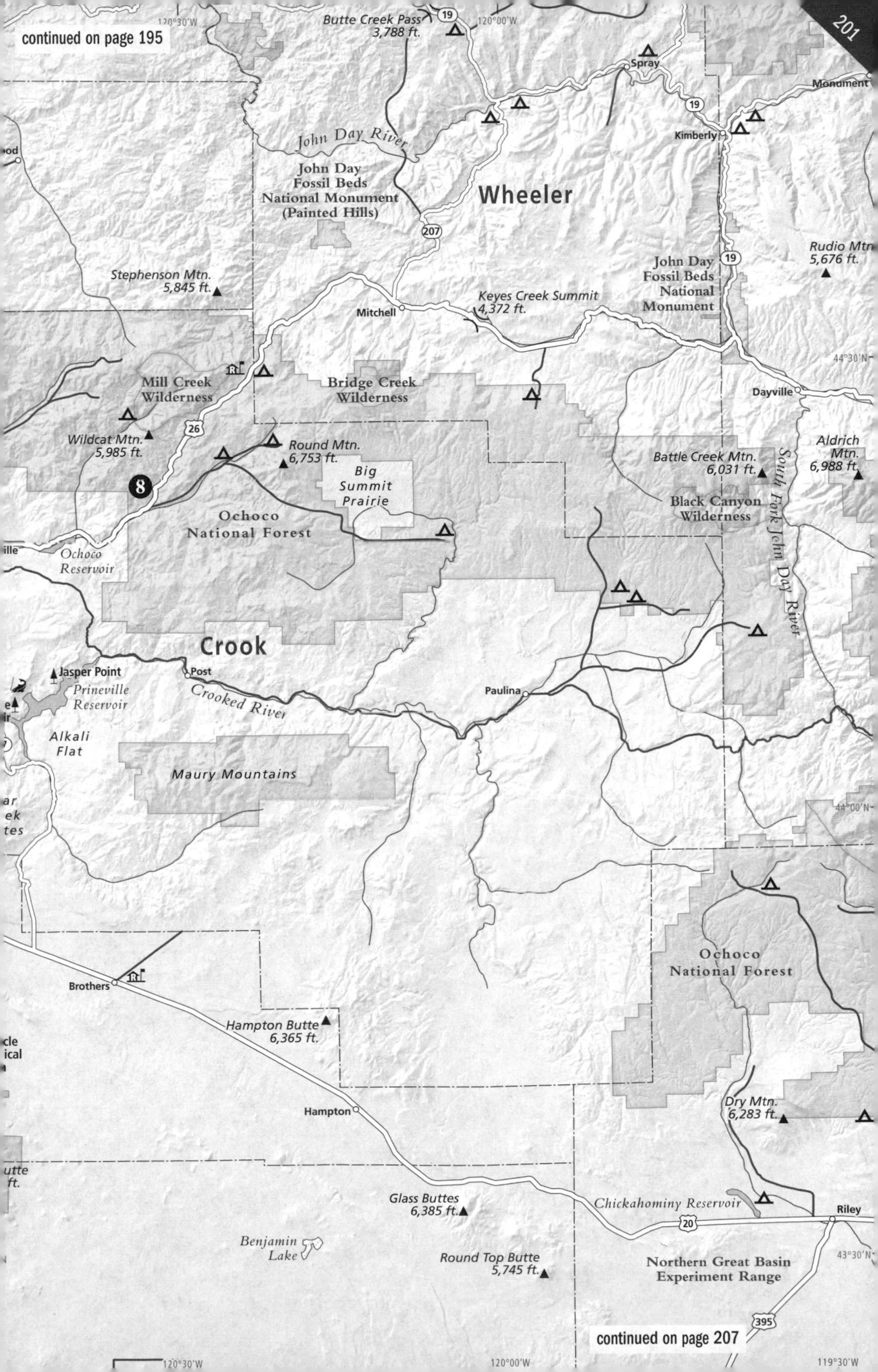

continued on page 207

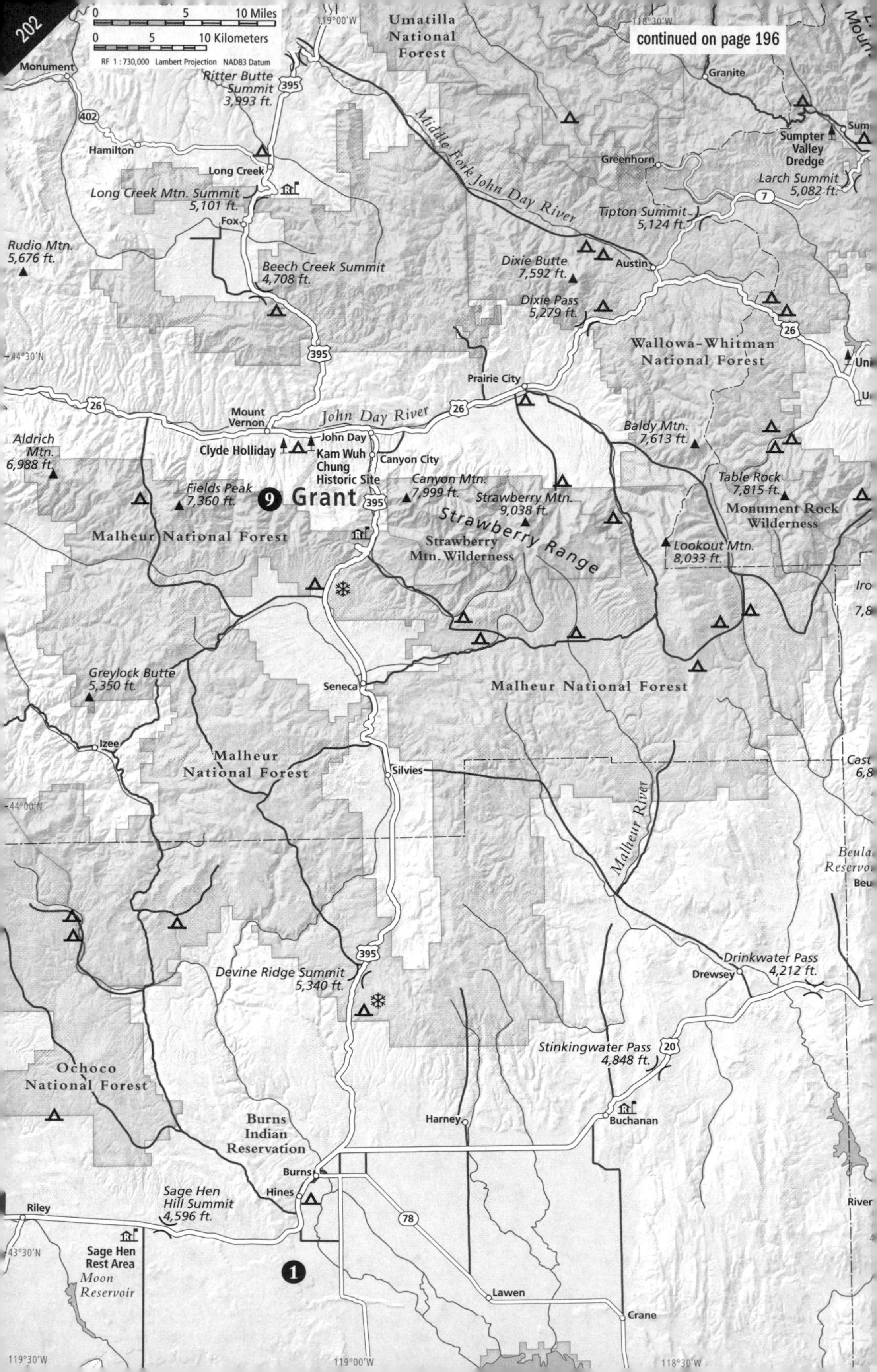
0 5 10 Miles
0 5 10 Kilometers
RF 1 : 730,000 Lambert Projection NAD83 Datum
continued on page 196
Umatilla National Forest
Monument
Ritter Butte Summit 3,993 ft.
Hamilton
Long Creek
Long Creek Mtn. Summit 5,101 ft.
Fox
Rudio Mtn. 5,676 ft.
Beech Creek Summit 4,708 ft.
Middle Fork John Day River
Granite
Sumpter Valley Dredge
Greenhorn
Larch Summit 5,082 ft.
Tipton Summit 5,124 ft.
Dixie Butte 7,592 ft.
Austin
Dixie Pass 5,279 ft.
Wallowa-Whitman National Forest
Prairie City
Mount Vernon
John Day River
John Day
Clyde Holliday
Kam Wuh Chung Historic Site
Canyon City
Aldrich Mtn. 6,988 ft.
Fields Peak 7,360 ft.
9 Grant
Canyon Mtn. 7,999 ft.
Strawberry Mtn. 9,038 ft.
Strawberry Range
Strawberry Mtn. Wilderness
Baldy Mtn. 7,613 ft.
Table Rock 7,815 ft.
Monument Rock Wilderness
Lookout Mtn. 8,033 ft.
Malheur National Forest
Greylock Butte 5,350 ft.
Seneca
Izee
Silvies
Malheur River
Drinkwater Pass 4,212 ft.
Drewsey
Devine Ridge Summit 5,340 ft.
Stinkingwater Pass 4,848 ft.
Ochoco National Forest
Burns Indian Reservation
Harney
Buchanan
Burns
Hines
Riley
Sage Hen Hill Summit 4,596 ft.
Sage Hen Rest Area
Moon Reservoir
1
Lawen
Crane
River
44°30'N
44°00'N
43°30'N
119°30'W
119°00'W
118°30'W
395
402
26
7
20
78

continued on page 209

continued on page 198

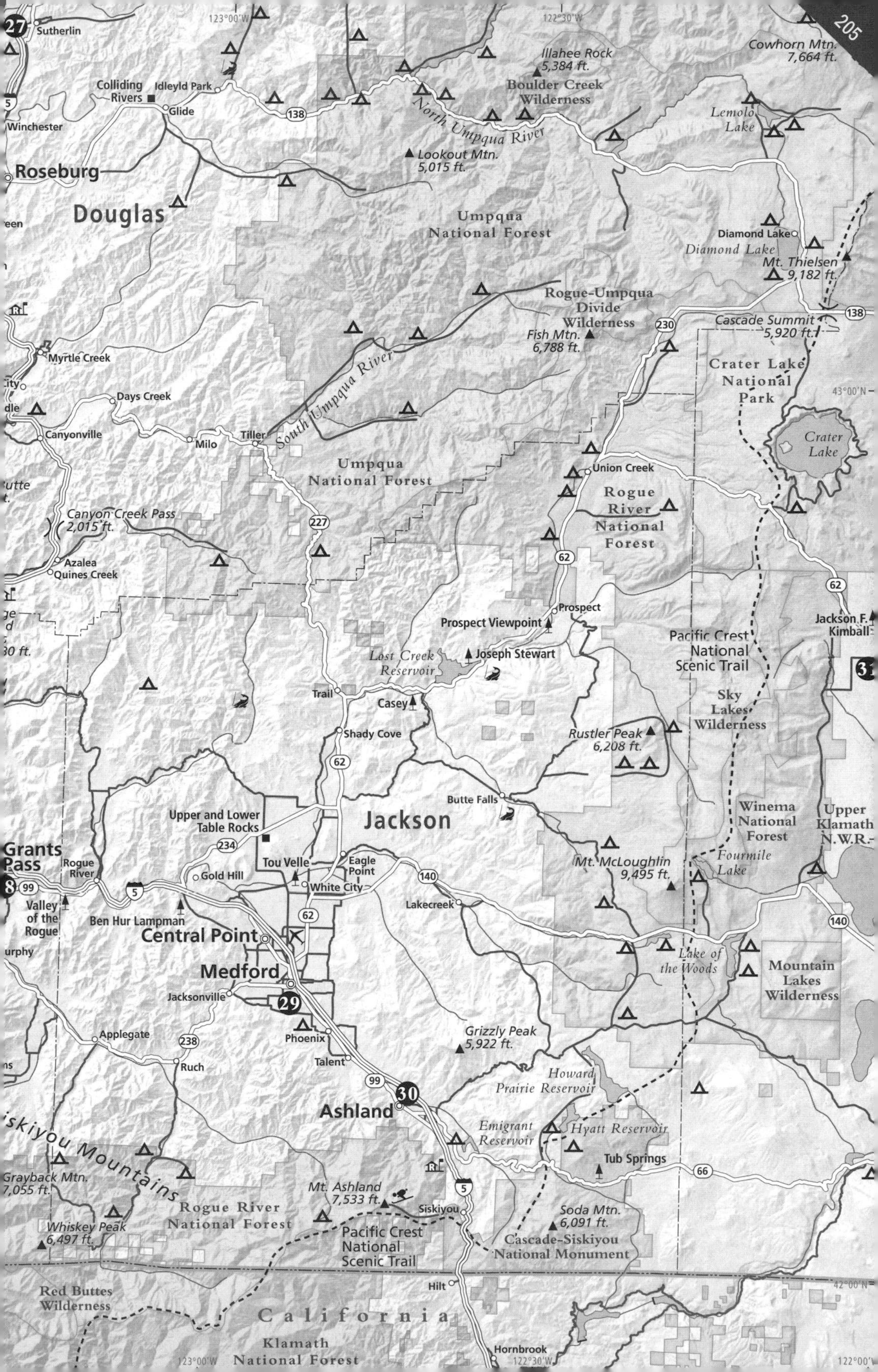
Sutherlin
Colliding Rivers
Idleyld Park
Glide
Winchester
Roseburg
Douglas
Illahee Rock 5,384 ft.
Boulder Creek Wilderness
North Umpqua River
Lookout Mtn. 5,015 ft.
Cowhorn Mtn. 7,664 ft.
Lemolo Lake
Umpqua National Forest
Diamond Lake
Mt. Thielsen 9,182 ft.
Rogue-Umpqua Divide Wilderness
Fish Mtn. 6,788 ft.
Cascade Summit 5,920 ft.
Crater Lake National Park
Crater Lake
Myrtle Creek
Days Creek
Canyonville
Milo
Tiller
South Umpqua River
Union Creek
Rogue River National Forest
Canyon Creek Pass 2,015 ft.
Azalea
Quines Creek
Prospect
Prospect Viewpoint
Lost Creek Reservoir
Joseph Stewart
Jackson F. Kimball
Pacific Crest National Scenic Trail
Sky Lakes Wilderness
Trail
Casey
Shady Cove
Rustler Peak 6,208 ft.
Butte Falls
Jackson
Upper and Lower Table Rocks
Winema National Forest
Upper Klamath N.W.R.
Grants Pass
Rogue River
Valley of the Rogue
Gold Hill
Tou Velle
Eagle Point
White City
Mt. McLoughlin 9,495 ft.
Fourmile Lake
Lakecreek
Ben Hur Lampman
Central Point
Medford
Jacksonville
Lake of the Woods
Mountain Lakes Wilderness
Applegate
Phoenix
Talent
Ruch
Grizzly Peak 5,922 ft.
Howard Prairie Reservoir
Ashland
Siskiyou Mountains
Emigrant Reservoir
Hyatt Reservoir
Tub Springs
Grayback Mtn. 7,055 ft.
Mt. Ashland 7,533 ft.
Siskiyou
Soda Mtn. 6,091 ft.
Whiskey Peak 6,497 ft.
Rogue River National Forest
Pacific Crest National Scenic Trail
Cascade-Siskiyou National Monument
Hilt
Red Buttes Wilderness
California
Klamath National Forest
Hornbrook
123°00'W
122°30'W
122°00'W
43°00'N
42°00'N

0 5 10 Miles
0 5 10 Kilometers
RF 1 : 730,000 Lambert Projection NAD83 Datum
121°30'W
121°00'W
Hole in the Ground 4,290 ft.
Cougar Mtn. 5,140 ft.
Cowhorn Mountain 7,664 ft.
Pacific Crest National Scenic Trail
58
Deschutes National Forest
Fort Rock
Fort Rock
7
Fremont National Forest
31
Miller Lake
Mt. Thielsen Wilderness
Chemult
Winema National Forest
97
Mt. Thielsen 9,182 ft.
Beaver Marsh
Paulina Marsh
Cascade Summit 5,920 ft.
Silver Lake
138
Diamond Lake Junction
Silver Lake
43°00'N
Picture Rock Pass 4,830 ft.
Hager Mtn. 7,185 ft.
Klamath Marsh NWR
Crater Lake
Dead Indian Mtn. 7,066 ft.
Thompson Reservoir
Klamath Marsh
Fremont National Forest
Winter Ridge
Sycan Marsh
Winema National Forest
62
97
Jackson F. Kimball
Kirk
Williamson River
Sun Pass State Forest
Applegate Butte 6,074 ft.
Fort Klamath
31
Collier Memorial
Fuego Mtn. 6,810 ft.
Fremont National Forest
OC&E State Trail
Klamath Agency
Chiloquin
62
Agency Lake
Upper Klamath N.W.R.
Saddle Mtn. 6,841 ft.
Gearhart Mtn. Wilderness
Klamath
Gearhart Mtn. 8,364 ft.
Winema National Forest
Sprague River
Sprague River
Beatty
140
Bly
Upper Klamath Lake
OC&E State Trail
Mountain Lakes Wilderness
Bly Mtn. Pass 5,087 ft.
140
Quartz Mtn. Pass 5,504 ft.
Swan Lake
Fremont National Forest
Aspen Lake
Klamath Falls
Dairy
32
Altamont
70
Fishhole Lake
140
Gerber Reservoir
Bonanza
Lost River
Olene
140
Barnes Rim
Keno
Midland
Bear Valley N.W.R.
97
39
Worden
Lower Klamath N.W.R.
Merrill
42°00'N
Malin
Langell Valley
161
Dorris
Tulelake
California
Modoc National Forest
Lower Klamath Lake
122°00'W
121°30'W
121°00'W

continued on page 201

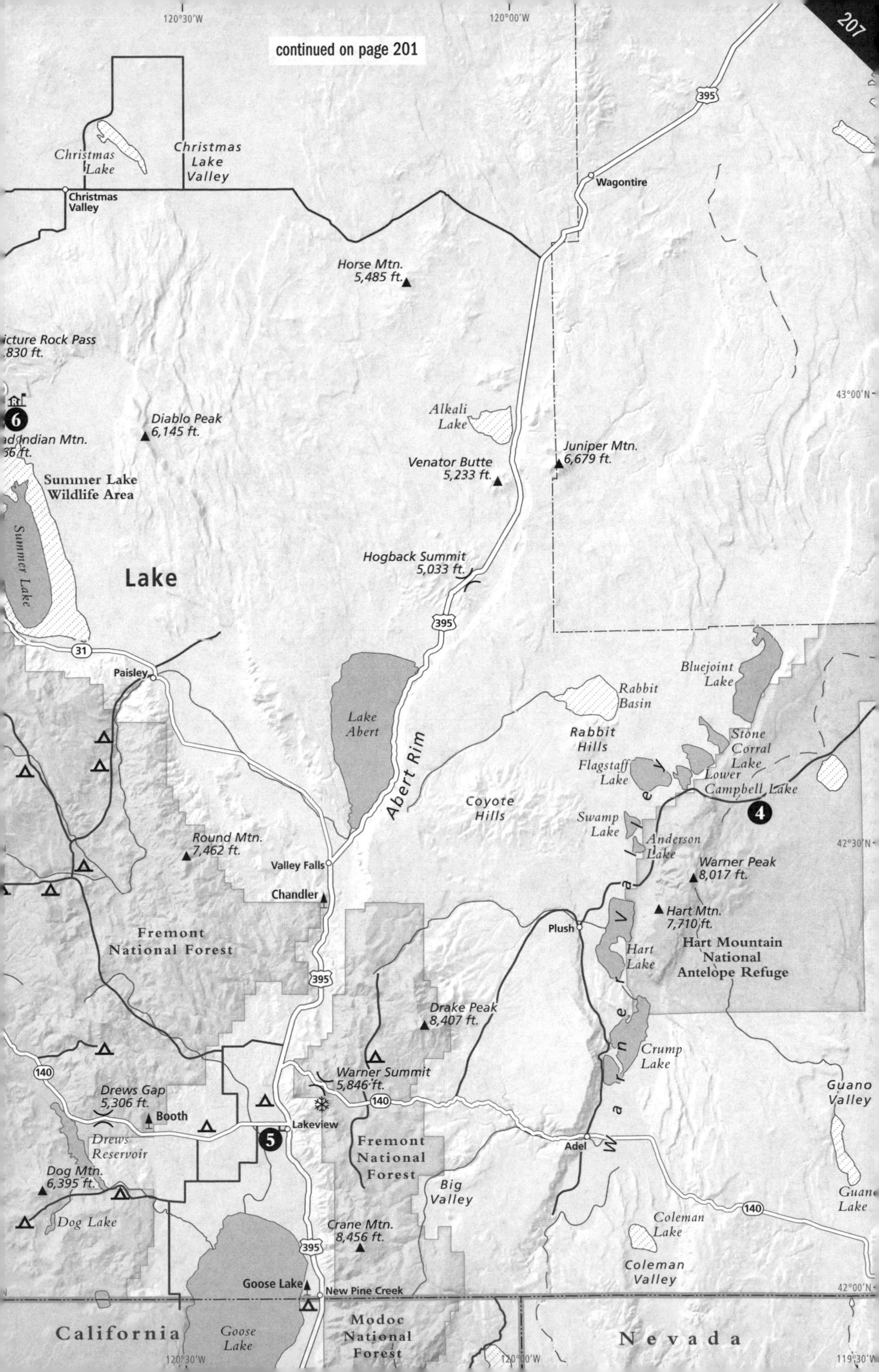

120°30'W
120°00'W
395
Christmas Lake
Christmas Lake Valley
Christmas Valley
Wagontire
Horse Mtn. 5,485 ft.
Picture Rock Pass 4,830 ft.
6
Diablo Peak 6,145 ft.
Bad Indian Mtn.
Alkali Lake
Juniper Mtn. 6,679 ft.
Venator Butte 5,233 ft.
Summer Lake Wildlife Area
Summer Lake
Lake
Hogback Summit 5,033 ft.
43°00'N
31
Paisley
Lake Abert
Abert Rim
Bluejoint Lake
Rabbit Basin
Rabbit Hills
Stone Corral Lake
Flagstaff Lake
Lower Campbell Lake
Coyote Hills
4
Swamp Lake
Anderson Lake
Round Mtn. 7,462 ft.
Valley Falls
Chandler
Warner Peak 8,017 ft.
42°30'N
Hart Mtn. 7,710 ft.
Plush
Fremont National Forest
Hart Lake
Hart Mountain National Antelope Refuge
Drake Peak 8,407 ft.
Warner Valley
Crump Lake
Warner Summit 5,846 ft.
140
Drews Gap 5,306 ft.
Booth
Lakeview
5
Guano Valley
Adel
Drews Reservoir
Fremont National Forest
Dog Mtn. 6,395 ft.
Big Valley
Guano Lake
Dog Lake
Coleman Lake
Crane Mtn. 8,456 ft.
Coleman Valley
Goose Lake
New Pine Creek
42°00'N
California
Goose Lake
Modoc National Forest
Nevada
120°30'W
120°00'W
119°30'W

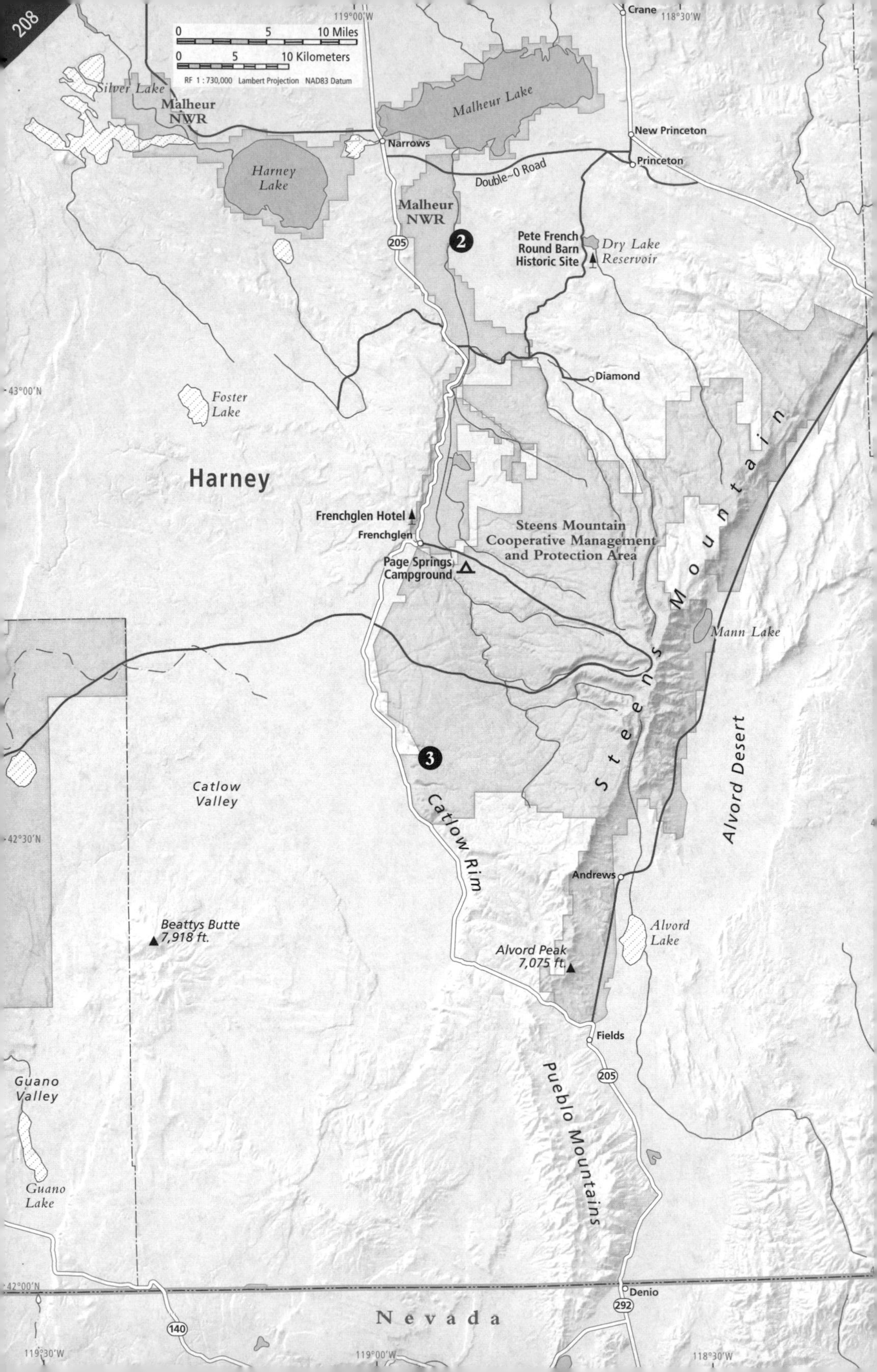

0 5 10 Miles
0 5 10 Kilometers
RF 1 : 730,000 Lambert Projection NAD83 Datum
119°00'W
Crane
118°30'W
Silver Lake
Malheur NWR
Malheur Lake
Narrows
New Princeton
Princeton
Harney Lake
Double~O Road
Malheur NWR
205
2
Pete French Round Barn Historic Site
Dry Lake Reservoir
Diamond
43°00'N
Foster Lake
Harney
Frenchglen Hotel
Frenchglen
Steens Mountain Cooperative Management and Protection Area
Page Springs Campground
Steens Mountain
Mann Lake
3
Catlow Valley
Catlow Rim
Alvord Desert
42°30'N
Andrews
Beattys Butte 7,918 ft.
Alvord Lake
Alvord Peak 7,075 ft.
Fields
205
Pueblo Mountains
Guano Valley
Guano Lake
42°00'N
Denio
292
Nevada
140
119°30'W
119°00'W
118°30'W